PLUMBING

edited by Nadir Lahiji and D.S. Friedman

with a preface by Ignasi de Solà-Morales

Sounding Modern Architecture

D1496501

PRINCETON ARCHITECTURAL PRESS · NEW YORK

In memory of
Mary Louise Melia Friedman

PUBLISHED BY
Princeton ArchitecturalPress
37 East 7th Street
New York, NY 10003
212.995.9620

For a free catalog of books published by
Princeton Architectural Press, call 800.722.6657
Visit us on the World Wide Web at www.papress.com

On the cover: detail from Margaret Morgan, "Portrait of Modern
Art As Sanitary System," 1992–93

Book design and production editing: Therese Kelly
Special thanks to Eugenia Bell, Caroline Green, Clare Jacobson,
Mark Lamster, Annie Nitschke, and Sara Stemen of
Princeton Architectural Press—Kevin C. Lippert, Publisher.

LIBRARY OF CONGRESS CATALOGING-IN-PUBLICATION DATA
Plumbing: sounding modern architecture / edited by
 Nadir Lahiji and D.S. Friedman.
  p. cm.
 Includes bibliographical references and index.
 ISBN 1-56898-107-4 (alk. paper)
 1. Architecture—Environmental aspects. 2. Architecture,
Modern—20th. 3. Plumbing—Influence. 4. Modernism (Art) I.
Lahiji, Nadir, 1948-   . II. Friedman, Daniel S., 1951-   .
NA2542.35.P58 1997   97-10075
720' .47—dc21   CIP

contents

Acknowledgments

Among other teachers, we owe the topic and title of this book to Adolf Loos, essay master, who long before us studied plumbing in Philadelphia. Loos in Philadelphia is the site of speculation from which we set out seven years ago, tacking through Chestnut Street not far from the house of Loos's uncle, where the young Viennese pioneer doubtless encountered a bit of American hygiene. Pioneering work is always freighted with the old world's equipment, which in the course of clearing and cleaning new ground leaves its imprint on worlds to follow. We posed the paradoxical question of Loos's imprint on the modern condition to a lively if unlikely mix of perspicacious surveyors, to whom we owe this book's contours. First to them we direct our thanks

We wish to thank the Graham Foundation for Advanced Studies in the Fine Arts for its grant, also Professors Joseph Rykwert and John Hancock for their advocacy at the beginning. We owe thanks to many friends and colleagues—Jay Chatterjee, Gordon Simmons, Anton Harfmann, Elie Haddad, Susan Baehr, Celeste Elick, Kiel Moe, and Michael Young. At Princeton Architectural Press we are especially grateful to Therese Kelly; she lightened our task with editorial guidance and insight, patient questioning, and optimistic wit.

In particular we wish to thank our level-headed compatriot Xavier Costa, a fellow traveler whose decisive navigation greatly improved the journey; and Victor Burgin, for permission to include "The City in Pieces" in this volume.

For endless accommodation and encouragement we fear one debt is too great to satisfy with thanks: however fragmented its body or incomplete its heart, we dedicate the whole of our part in this book to Nayere Zaeri and Ann Marie Borys.

Morton Schamberg, *God*, 1918.
Milter box and plumbing trap; assisted in
construction by Elsa von Freytag Loringhoven.
Courtesy Philadelphia Museum of Art: The
Louise and Walter Arensberg Collection.

INCORPORATIONS

Ignasi de Solà-Morales

THE VERY IDEA OF POSTMODERNISM IS DEEPLY AMBIGUOUS. FOR some it involves, in the main, a reactionary attack on the fundamental project of emancipation of both the individual and society, squandering the rational and critical inheritance of the Enlightenment in a belated phase of capitalist perversion of values (Habermas, Jameson). For others, however, the postmodern condition evokes a discourse born of hard times and the need, in the wake of the crisis of humanism, to construct partial and provisional discourses that can act like ephemeral plateaus, lending support to a ceaseless work of interpretation (Foucault, Deleuze, Lyotard).

In architecture, the dismantling of the building of modern architecture, of the stability of its progressivist foundations and the effectiveness of abstract-constructivist methods, left the door open to procedures of a different kind. These are all marked by the solipsism of an experimentation endlessly trapped in the limits of a self-reflexive discourse that has been transformed into a veritable gilded cage.

Since the end of the 1960s, and up to the early 1990s, architecture has dived into the complex depths of its own identity, turning its own crisis into an exercise in self-analysis, either from the side of its figurative condition, or from that of its structural dispositions. The years of the postmodern crisis have generated a concern with images and the linguistic phenomena associated with these. The rhetoric of technical images, the

perpetuation of tradition, and the pseudo-democratic appropriation of popular idioms, are some of the main lines of experimentation in design and
theory. In the face of its populism, and its evident success, the analysts of
deep structures immersed themselves in the identification of more sophis-
ticated notions. Typology, geometry, "patterns," generative grammar, were
some of the theoretical tools of equally immanent discourses caught in the
net of the internal logic of architectural production.

In the 1990s a new phenomenological opening seems to favor
what Hal Foster has recently termed as 'The Return of the Real.' This
refers clearly to a mediatized reality, at times expressionist and irrational,
providing a space for heeding the materiality of objects, the interaction
between these and the body, and the necessary reinvention of the subject
as the ultimate reference to legitimize architectural schemes. Yet this is
also a return of the real as something problematic, plural, in a permanent
process of appearance and disappearance, of fiction and reality.

Sensations, events, experiences that are instantaneous, localized
and practical, prove themselves to be the sole referents from which to construct architectural discourse. The prothetic, distorted, or dismembered
organic-mechanical body constitutes the only material referent and vehicle
for a more desired than wholly-reached reality.

In the philosophical field, the corporeal-perceptual coagulates in a
nomadic dispersion (Deleuze-Guattari) whereas the physical condition of
sensations tends to shape the corporeal materiality of subjects permeated
by experiences of pleasure, of excess, of death (Onfray, Ferry, Bataille).

The kind of book Nadir Lahiji and Daniel S. Friedman have put
together sheds light on this emerging *episteme*. More than exploring the
architecture of the house or the impact of technology on housing, what
finds them sharing a common sensibility is the re-reading of Loos or
Ozenfant-Jeanneret, not as prophets of modernization but rather as analysts of the relationship between body and architecture, via a quasi-tactile
experience of the crafts dealing with the virtuality of the present body.

The body of concrete individuals has been ominously absent in
the architecture of the postmodern crisis. Its vanishing-away has to do
with an architecture bound up in one or other of the structural-linguistic
currents that have dominated the scene during the last twenty years.

The Loosian plumber, but also the shoemaker or the tailor, do not
reappear solely as figures of the Viennese *fin-de-siècle* crisis confronting

ancients and moderns, but as referents of potential discourses on an architecture aiming at the subjects' corporeal materiality and their way of interpreting reality. Ozenfant and Jeanneret's right angle is not a geometrical figure but rather a way of fixing the position of the *homo erectus* who undertakes his or her personal activities within the complexity of modern metropolitan life.

The body in these discourses is not a defined and practical given reality, but rather an intersection of energies, an ectoplasm of imprecise limits whose identity is, at any one moment, problematic. This involves, in many instances, an archaeological, biological, psychological and mechanical research whose limits cannot be set without delicate critical tools which allow for approaching the body with tremendous caution.

The model of the plumber is, in this sense, symptomatic of a form of periphrastic approximation using mediations, indices, imprecise metaphors, elliptical protocols. In these partial attempts, language constitutes at once the necessary vehicle and the ambiguous tool through which we discover sensations, presences, productions.

There are those who speak of a new functionalism. Others, as already mentioned, speak of the return of the real, of a new phenomenology. Marcel Mauss, the French sociologist and father of modern anthropology, spoke of the techniques of the body as the only system our physico-biological constitution requires for an understanding of complexity and variety. The experiences, behavior patterns, and meanings that different cultures have developed to mediate between the subject and the material and symbolic worlds through which these bodies move, constitute the empirical basis of architectural production and design.

This primordial attention to the body forms the basis of an architecture closer to clothing, to wrapping, to a *mise en scène*—this is the hypothesis advanced by this collection of texts. There are, indeed, indications that this is not a banal proposition but one which appears to respond, despite the somewhat threadbare nature of the phrase, to *the spirit of the age*.

Ignasi de Solà-Morales
Barcelona, 1997

FIG. 1 Cindy Sherman, *Untitled Film Still #39*, 1979.

Though Plato and Hermes have plumbed it deeply, must we reach no further than their shallow sounding?

Broughton's Let. XII. 40 (1599)

Introduction

Nadir Lahiji and D.S. Friedman

Hygiene is the modern project's supreme act. The law of Hygiene in modernity belongs to the universe of postmodern experience, insofar as we allways belong to our own abjected body. Hygiene and its Other are at once the modern and postmodern project. For us *Plumbing* is the postmodern critique of a modernity that aggressively proceeds toward ever greater purity, always already alienated by its own ambiguous itinerary. Likewise, plumbing comes with its own radical ambiguity. Postmodern plumbing sounds modernity's pathological excess, which escapes symbolization. In such soundings the plumber eventually reaches an unplumbable limit, a spectral and inaccessible 'object' beyond which he or she can reach no more. Plumbing attempts to loosen or unsettle this traumatic kernel, which retroactively constitutes modernity's utopian promise—that whatever is unreachable can be achieved. Plumbing questions modernity precisely at the moment modernity attempts to transform this ambiguous, unplumbable 'object' into a positive ontolgical structure.

To begin our questioning we turn to the Viennese architect and critic Adolf Loos. One hundred years ago, on the eve of the twentieth century, Loos called the plumber the "beletting officer of culture," a pioneer of cleanliness and the first artisan of the state. "Increasing water usage is one of the most pressing tasks of culture," he wrote. "Thus may our. . . plumbers do their job as fully and completely as possible in leading us to this great goal."[1] Loos's great goal of course was modern civilization itself. But at the end of the twentieth century, as we once again undertake to plumb the depths of modernity, we find ourselves at its limits. One name for these limits is the hygienic body, the modern subject in its verticality. This verticality consists in its obstinate repression of the abject, the unclean, and the horizontal. In the collection of essays that follows, we present the dialectic of cleanliness and uncleanliness in various logics of modernity under the complex concept of "plumbing."

In the beginning of the twentieth century, Le Corbusier (with Ozenfant) invented the modern discourse by ruling that painting and architecture must comport with the law of the right angle and its geometry. Not just painting and architecture, though. Verticality, Le Corbusier rules, also underlies the workings of nature and the ethics of man: Insofar as man is *modern*, he is *ruly*. Historians from Siegfried Giedion and Colin Rowe up to our own time have further adjudicated Le Corbusier's rulings; they continue to invent twentieth-century modernity around the primacy of the visual, cleaning with bleach. Martin Jay calls this visuality the "scopic regime of modernity."[2] Verticality and its assumptions shape the discourse on theory and art, no less on power and knowledge. Modern ethics of uprightness reinforce the myth of the self-conscious, self-knowing subject.

Michel Foucault demonstrates that in the late eighteenth century the program of architectural hygiene and Jeremy Bentham's utilitarianism become one and the same project.[3] The trajectory of the modern passes through hygienic space to the space of social hygiene, by which we mean, after Foucault, the transparent space of institutional control and surveillance. In the cultural politics of modernity, discourse on Identity, Subject, Space, Gender, and Body all presuppose the discourse of verticality, which reaches its limits in the repression of the common abject—excrement, putrefaction, dirt, semen, menses, and so on. Ultimately, the plumb line has to fall; it has to establish a relationship to the horizontal.

One way or another the essays that follow answer once again the questions delimited by Loos and Le Corbusier, presented here in two new translations commissioned expressly for this volume: "Plumbers," by Adolf Loos, translated by Harry Frances Mallgrave; and "The Right Angle," by Ozenfant and Jeanneret (Le Corbusier), translated by Nadir Lahiji. Loos wrote "Plumbers" for the *Neue Freie Presse* in 1898 and included it in the first edition of *Ins Leere gesprochen* (Spoken Into the Void), which he released in 1921 through Georges Crès & Cie in Paris, after German publishers rejected it; eleven years later the Austrian firm *Brenner Verlag* published a second, revised edition. Ozenfant and Jeanneret published "The Right Angle" in the eighteenth issue of their short-lived avant-garde magazine *L'Esprit Nouveau* (1920-25).

Along the axes of the right angle Xavier Costa's essay "Ground Level" traces the genealogy of the plumb line in respect to both architectural and psychological constructions. From Vitruvius through Johann Joachim Winkelmann and Antonio Gaudí to Alfred Hitchcock, he explores crucial distinctions between the blind fall that "turns firm ground into an abyss" and the arrested fall of the lead weight that "suspends disorder and permits upright construction."

Uprightness in construction and morality manifest a common *urmotif*, which the acicular critic Adolf Loos projects onto the idea of universal plumbing. Plumbing is of interest to Loos not as a technology so much as a general critique of culture. In his essay "Adolf Loos: Ornament and Sentimentality," Harry F. Mallgrave argues that Loos cuts a paradoxical figure—he is a fiercely forward-looking classicist and an anti-bourgeois elitist who in his elevation of artisanal culture fails to predict its extinction under the relentless hegemony of a polite, bourgeois economy.

In *Fountain* (1917) Marcel Duchamp does nothing if not scandalize bourgeois politeness and its domestic sedimentation, the site of Helen Molesworth's essay "Bathrooms and Kitchens: Cleaning House with Duchamp." In her analysis of Duchamp, Molesworth de-hyphenates certain durable ruling oppositions—public-private, interior-exterior, male-female—arguing that *Fountain* disturbs the codes of both art and hygiene by irritating conventional boundaries, not least those demarcated by gender.

Mutable boundary relations also fall under Donald Kunze's scrutiny in his essay "*Poché*." For Kunze, the tripartite formulation of poché, *soupirail* (Michael Rifaterre's poetic theory of the "vent"), and space of representation "might be the basis for a more useful, if darker, architectural theory." In readings of Jacques Lacan, Giambattista Vico, Albrecht Dürer, Antonello da Messina, and Pablo Picasso, among others, Kunze demonstrates how this schema operates.

In his analysis of the interpenetrability of urban experience, Victor Burgin adopts a different but nonetheless apposite metaphor—"porosity"—

a term he takes up and extends from a reflection on Naples written by Walter Benjamin and Asja Lacis, which resonates in Benjamin's dedication to *One Way Street*. Burgin's essay "The City in Pieces" applies this metaphor in a broad, psychoanalytic critique of the "body" of the modern city, which he examines in a variety of visual and representational practices.

Porous membranes and vents likewise inhabit the oneiric reflections of Marco Frascari, who doesn't like the smell of contemporary architecture. In his essay, "The Pneumatic Bathroom," Frascari reconstructs the forgotten site of the *vita beata*, which he calls "The last locus of architectural union between 'voluptas' and venustas'." Around the double body of the pneumatic ethos, filled simultaneously with gasses and spirit, Frascari reformulates the bathroom as a "non-rational place of well-being," the heart of an architectural theory that shifts the focus of sensible building from optical-tactile intelligibility to audio-olfactory imagination.

In his essay "Siegfried Giedion and the Fascination of the Tub," William Braham locates Giedion's analysis of anonymous domestic bathroom fixtures in a polemic that seeks to reconcile the influences of Loos and Le Corbusier with those of Heinrich Wölfflin and Jacob Burkhardt; he argues that Giedion's use of Surrealist imagery, with which the historian suggests a correlation between the history of mechanization with the mechanization of visuality, amounts to a *faire voir*, a demonstration, that both supplements and exceeds Giedion's historiographic project.

Bathing presuppose the confluence of bodily and hygienic fluids that surface as a primary theme in artist-writer Margaret Morgan's narrative construction entitled "Too Much Leverage is Dangerous." These fragments of text and image consist of critical superimpositions of hygienic signs and genealogies—tool and body, modern art and modern family. She dissolves "gendered" activities such as plumbing into slippery relations between mother, daughter, father, and brother. "Control [is] infinitely more subtle than brute force," Morgan writes; in our attempt to open valves between these relations, too much leverage can be dangerous.

In "Architects' Bellies: The Plumbing of Masculine Conception," Claudio Sgarbi examines the iconography of architecture for signs of gender across diverse categories of representation, including Renaissance frontispieces, folk tales, contemporary film, and popular fiction. For Sgarbi, contemporary architecture is "the miscarriage of *couvade* (man's simulated motherness)"; according to Sgarbi, the preoccupation of contemporary practices with a strictly masculine conception of professional principles unnecessarily suppresses "the celebration of the otherness of human making."

Finally, in our own essay, we use the sink as a theoretical fulcrum to lever the problem of horizontality into the discourse on architecture. In our extension of the concept of Hygiene from the question this book asks of its contributors, we coin the term *hygienic superego* to signify the belonging together of the Law and Enjoyment, by which we mean the Law's injunction of Enjoyment as its obscene reverse; they are two parts of one and the same movement.[4]

The writers in this anthology, all cultural plumbers, sound out questions around related themes: Narcissism; hygiene and transgression; materiality; the erotic; ornament and dressing; gender; body ethics; art; optics, the porosity of space; the solubility of the subject. From the Latin *plumbum*—lead—"plumb" names the dense metal ball attached to line used to verify depth and verticality, a basic tool for building and navigation. The plumber, an expert worker in lead, brings special understanding to the problem of water and walls. Plumbers travel between purity and abjection. They order everyday fluids, manage flow, straighten things out, keep things clean, sound depths, right columns, fix pipes: plumbing leads to the bottom of things. Be warned, however, as Freud noted: "There is at least one spot in every dream at which it is unplumbable—a navel, as it were, that is the point of contact with the unknown."[5]

NOTES

1. Adolf Loos, "Plumbers," trans. Harry Frances Mallgrave, herein.

2. Martin Jay, "Scopic Regimes of Modernity," in *Vision and Visuality*, ed. Hal Foster (Seattle: Bay Press, 1988), 3–23; also see Martin Jay, *Downcast Eyes: The Denigration of Vision in Twentieth-Century French Thought* (Berkeley: University of California Press, 1993).

3. Michel Foucault, "The Eye of Power," in *Power/Knowledge: Selected Interviews and Other Writings, 1972-1977*, ed. Colin Gordon (New York: Pantheon Books, 1980), 146-165.

4. For a theoretical discussion of the relationship between the Law and Enjoyment in the work of Jacques Lacan, see Slavoj Žižek, *The Metastases of Enjoyment: Six Essays on Woman and Causality* (London: Verso, 1994); and also Slavoj Žižek, *Enjoy Your Symptom! Jacques Lacan in Hollywood and Out* (New York and London: Routledge, 1982).

5. Sigmund Freud, *Standard Edition of Complete Psychological Works*, ed. James Strachey, 4.III, quoted in Shoshana Felman, *Jacques Lacan and the Adventure of Insight: Psychoanalysis in Contemporary Culture* (Cambridge, MA: Harvard University Press, 1987), 167n.12.

documents

Plumbers

Adolf Loos

Translated by Harry Francis Mallgrave

One could easily imagine our century without the cabinetmaker—we would then be using metal furniture. We could just as well do without the stonemason—the cement contractor would take over his task. But without the plumber there would have been no nineteenth century. He has left his mark; he has become indispensable to us. And yet we give him a French name. We call him an *installateur*.

This is wrong. For this man epitomizes Germanic culture. The English were the guardians and protectors of this culture, and therefore we should give them priority in searching for a name for this man. Besides, the word stems from the Latin *plumbum*, meaning "lead," and the word is thus for both the English and ourselves not a foreign word but a borrowed term.

For a century and a half now we have been buying our culture second-hand: from the French. We have never resisted French leadership. Now that we realize that we have been duped by the French, now that we see that the English have been leading the French around on a string the whole time, we make a stand against the English, against Germanic culture. Being guided by the French was for us very pleasant; but the notion that the English are actually the leaders makes us nervous.

And yet Germanic culture has extended its triumphant progress over the face of the globe. Whoever obliges it becomes great and powerful: the Japanese. Whoever opposes it remains backward: the Chinese. We have to accept Germanic culture even if we Germans still very much bristle at the thought. It does no good to raise a hue and cry against the "English disease." Our living conditions, our existence depend on it.

The English have remained somewhat aloof from the great hustle and bustle of the world. Just as Icelanders have for thousands of years faithfully preserved the Germanic myth for us, the Romance wave that washed away the last vestiges of Germanic culture from German soil was broken at the English coast and Scottish cliffs. The Germans became Latinized in feeling and thought. Now they receive their own culture back from the English. And just as the German always adheres with well-known tenacity to habits once acquired, now he resists English culture because it seems new to him. Lessing earlier devoted much effort in trying to make the great Germanic way of thinking accessible to the Germans. In stages, a front had to be taken against the various Gottscheds, and only just recently the battle raged in the workshops of cabinetmakers.

Our Gottscheds, and with them all imitators of French culture and habits, are fighting a losing battle. Gone is the fear of mountains, gone is the fear of danger, gone is the fear of the dusty road, of the smell of the forest, of fatigue. Gone is the fear of getting dirty, our solemn fear of water. When the Latin view of the world prevailed, around the time of the great Ludwig, no one washed because no one ever got dirty. Only common people washed; the genteel were enameled. "That must be a beautiful pig, because it has to be washed every day," somebody probably said back then. In Germany today people almost certainly say the same thing. In fact I just recently read this comment in the *Fliegenden*—the response of a father to his small child, who had conveyed the instruction of a teacher to wash every day.

The Englishman has no fear of getting dirty. He goes to the stable, brushes his horse, mounts it, and flies across the broad heath. The Englishman does everything himself: he hunts, he climbs the mountain, he saws trees. Being a spectator holds no joy for him. Germanic chivalry found asylum on the English isle and now it is reconquering the world. Between Maximilian the last knight and our epoch lies the long period of Latin occupation. Charles VI on the Martinswand! Unthinkable! The full-bottomed wig and Alpine air! The Emperor would never have been allowed to scale the cliff of a mountain like a simple hunter. Had he voiced such a strange request at that time, he would at best have been carried up on a litter.

At that time plumbers had nothing to do and this is how they lost their name. Of course there were water systems, water for fountains, water for viewing. But water for bathing, douches, and water closets was not provided. One was very spare with water in washing. Still today in German villages with Latin culture one can find wash basins that we Anglicized city dwellers with the best intentions have no idea how to use. This was not always the case. Germany in the Middle Ages was famed for its water usage. The great public baths (only the *Bader*, the barber, still survives from them) were always crowded and everyone took a bath at least once a day. And even later when there was scarcely a bath found in royal palaces, the bathroom of the German burger's home was the most splendid and luxurious room in the house. Who has not heard of the famous bathroom in the Fugger house in Augsburg, that artistic jewel of the German Renaissance! And sport, games, and the noble hunt were enjoyed by everyone, not just by Germans, when the Germanic world view prevailed.

We are backward. Some time ago I asked an American lady what seemed to her was the most notable difference between Austria and America. She answered: *the plumbing!*—the utilities, the heating, the lighting, and the water pipes. Our faucets, sinks, water closets, and washstands are still far, far inferior to English and American fittings. That we, when we want to wash our hands, must first go down the hallway to fetch a pitcher of water, that there are toilets without wash sinks—that seems extraordinary to the American. In this regard America is to Austria what Austria is to China. Someone may object that we also have these devices in our country. Indeed, but not everywhere. Even in China there are English wash facilities for the rich as well as for foreigners. But they are unknown to most people.

A home without a bathroom! Impossible in America. The idea that at the end of the nineteenth century there is a country with a population of millions, all of whose inhabitants cannot bathe daily, would be outrageous in America. Even in the poorest sections of New York one can, for ten cents, sleep in a homeless shelter that is cleaner and more pleasant than our village inn. Thus in American there is but a single waiting room for all classes in which not the slightest odor is apparent, even with the greatest crowding.

In the 1830s a member of the "Young Germany"—it was Laube in *Die Kriegen*—made a great pronouncement: Germany needs a bath. Let us in fact consider this seriously. In truth we do not need art. We still do not have a culture. Here the state can come to the rescue. Instead of putting the cart before the horse, instead of spending money on the production of art, the state should first try to create a culture. Next to the academies it could build bath houses; together with professors it could appoint bath attendants. A higher culture will necessarily produce a higher art, which when it does occur will happen with or without the help of the state.

But the German—I am thinking only of the vast majority—uses too little water for bathing and for the home. He uses it only when he must, that is, if someone tells him that it is good for his health. A clever peasant from Schlesien and a clever clergyman from the Bavarian mountains prescribe water as a healthful remedy. That helps. People with the most ingrained fear of water now splash around in it. And they also become healthy. This is completely natural. Everyone knows the story of the Eskimo who complained to a traveler of an old chest pain. The traveler applied sticking-plaster to his chest and promised the skeptical patient that he would be cured by the next day. When the plaster was removed the pain was gone—and with it a thick layer of dirt that had clung to the plaster. A miracle cure!

It is sad that only through such means can most people be encouraged to wash and bathe. Were the need more prevalent, the state would have to take note of the fact. And if every bedroom did not have its own bath, the state would have to build giant baths, against which the Baths of Caracalla would look like a bathroom. The state even has an interest in raising its standard of cleanliness of its citizens. For only that nation that approaches the English in water usage can keep pace with them economically; only that nation that exceeds the English in water usage is chosen to overtake them in world dominance.

The plumber, however, is the pioneer of cleanliness. He is the first artisan of the state, the billeting officer of culture, of today's prevailing culture. Every English washbowl with its faucet and casting is a sign of English progress. Every English stove with its implements for grilling and roasting meat on the open flame is a new victory of the Germanic spirit. The revolution is even becoming apparent on Viennese menus. The consumption of roast beef, grilled steaks, and cutlets is always increasing. Whereas the consumption of wiener schnitzels and fried chicken (Italian dishes), together with the braised, boiled, and steamed French specialties, is continually in decline.

Our bathroom fixtures might well be our weakest point. Instead of lining the bathtub with white tiles, people in this country prefer colored ones because, as one manufacturer (not in the exhibition) naively assured me, the dirt would less likely be seen. Metal bathtubs are also enameled in dark colors instead of white, the only suitable color for them. Finally, there are metal bathtubs that are made to look like marble. People actually believe it for these marbleized tubs also find their buyers. Those brave souls who still look at things from the perspective of the American Indian (as is well known, the Indian decorates everything that he touches) are best provided for. We have rococo valves and rococo faucets, even a rococo washstand. We are truly fortunate in that a few firms have even sought to accommodate the non-Indian. At M. Steiner's display booth in particular, we found completely smooth and therefore elegant American shower heads—a new invention—and the fixtures of H. Esders are competent and correct in both form and color. From a purely technical point of view it is worth mentioning that in the age of the rotary valve, the crank valve can no longer be justified. That is an old custom that deserves to be discontinued. The crank valve is no less expensive but it wears out sooner and has many other drawbacks as a result. If our plumbers do not want it, the public might follow its own interests and insist on installing rotary valves.

Increasing water usage is one of the most pressing tasks of culture. Thus may our Viennese plumbers do their job as fully and completely as possible in leading us to this great goal—the achievement of a level of culture equal to that of other Western countries. For otherwise something very unpleasant, something very shameful, could take place. If both countries continue along at the present rate, the Japanese could attain Germanic culture before the Austrians.

L'ESPRIT NOUVEAU

REVUE INTERNATIONALE ILLUSTRÉE DE L'ACTIVITÉ CONTEMPORAINE
PARAISSANT LE 1ᵉʳ DE CHAQUE MOIS
ARTS   LETTRES   SCIENCES

Directeurs :

OZENFANT
ET
CH.-E. JEANNERET

LITTÉRATURE
ARCHITECTURE   PEINTURE   SCULPTURE   MUSIQUE
SCIENCES PURES ET APPLIQUÉES
ESTHÉTIQUE EXPÉRIMENTALE   ESTHÉTIQUE DE L'INGÉNIEUR   URBANISME
PHILOSOPHIE   SOCIOLOGIQUE   ÉCONOMIQUE   SCIENCES MORALES ET POLITIQUES
VIE MODERNE   THÉATRE   SPECTACLES   LES SPORTS   LES FAITS

Voir au verso les avantages
et les primes
réservés aux Abonnés.

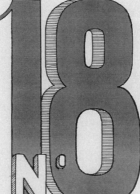

CE NUMÉRO
contient 102 pages,
64 illustrations
dont 8 hors-texte
et une reproduction
en couleurs
Tableau de Picasso

SOMMAIRE

Note de la Direction.
Ce mois passé,   OZENFANT.

Lettres

La Nouvelle poésie catalane, de
DOMENECH.
Les Livres | PAUL DUDRY.
Les Livres étrangers, PAUL DUDRY.
Les Livres d'art, MAURICE
RAYNAL.
Lettre aux Étudiants, R. ARON.

Beaux-Arts

L'angle droit, OZENFANT
et JEANNERET.

Architecture-Urbanisme

L'Ordre, LE CORBUSIER-SAUGNIER.

Musique

Noces,   ALBERT JEANNERET.
La musique espagnole, ALBERT
NAVILLE.

Sciences

Constitution de la matière, Dr.
ALLENDY.

ABONNEMENTS
SERVICE DE VENTE
Librairie Jean BUDRY & Cie
3, Rue du Cherche-
Midi, Paris VIᵉ

Arts décoratifs

Les pieds dans le plat (comment
on fabrique les meubles an-
ciens.)

A L'Étranger

Espagne,   VINCENT HUIDOBRO.

Cinéma

État du Cinéma, H. de COURTRY.

Théâtre

Le ballet " Création ", BORLIN,
CENDRARS, MILHAUD, LÉGER.

Actualités

Les faux du Louvre — Le dou-
nier Rousseau et le Professeur
d'anglais — Primitifs de haute
époque — Le bon docteur et
la Cocaïne — Deux expositions
à Prague — Fondation Barnes,
MAURICE RAYNAL.
Le hangar d'Orly.
Sport et Mécanique.
Les revues.
Les livres.

PRIX DU NUMÉRO

FRANCE :   6 frs. 00
ÉTRANGER :   7 frs. 00

ÉDITIONS DE L'ESPRIT NOUVEAU
SOCIÉTÉ ANONYME AU CAPITAL DE 150.000 FRANCS
3, RUE DU CHERCHE-MIDI
PARIS (VIᵉ)

Cover, *L' Esprit Nouveau* 18

The Right Angle

Amédée Ozenfant and Pierre Jeanneret

Translated by Nadir Lahiji

HAPPINESS

Man does nothing but search for happiness; if he kills himself, it is to pursue happiness into the world beyond or into the nothingness. Without going into metaphysical causes, one could say that the human being invented the work of art because it is useful for his happiness. But painting, sculpture, architecture, music, and poetry do not yield works of art if they do not yield happiness; they are feeble desires or simulacra. A match that does not light is only a simulacrum of a match; an aesthetic that searches for a single common law capable of being applied to both the work of art and its false semblance is a futility: Phidias does not explain Meissonnier.

THE CONSTANTS

The work that qualifies as art is the one whose emotive property is universal and durable; an affirmation such as this presupposes practical identity forever sufficient to human nature. Trivial details of modern analysis disproportionately increase the exception and eclipse the normal by placing the abnormal *en gros plan*. It is time to recall that the variation in the human physical and sentimental organization is infinitesimally vast; it is time to re-establish the axis around which these sinusoidal variables are but nuances; we have every right to believe in the homogeneity of man. This is

Meissonier

Mondrian

the reason why works of art from all epochs continue to move us. We will find the axial laws of works of art in the past; time alone will judge their *sine qua non* condition. Experience we acquire in our analysis of past works confers on our judgment of current works a certain soundness; in effect, the constancy of our organism permits us to establish certain laws of constancy that apply to the art of all times.

EMOTION

By our viewing of it and by the emotions of the senses it involves, a work of art moves us; it sets in our spirit the play of our heredities, of our acquired memory (conscious or unconscious); and by indefinable detours, it traces orderly paths in the fuzziness of our sensations and emotions, causing in our hearts a joyfullness similar to the one granted to our intellect by the mechanical law of the universe. These automatic associations put our unconscious into a state of delightful consciousness. This reaction of the senses—brute sensation scattered initially in physical well being—finally takes an interest the lucid faculties of our spirit, heartening at the same time our lowly nature and this secret God who inhabits the unknown in our being.

Schematically, this is all we can say if we persist in studying the problem of art solely from above. Let us try to take it up from below, when the work is still external to ourselves; upon its creation, it then fixes, arrests, relieves, and elevates us, and the spiritual emotion it produces in us persists even when our attention is exhausted and weary; but then, reposed, we meet it again, and it animates us anew.

THE CREATOR

It seems that we create out of a necessity for making order. We recognize organized beings by the fact that they order. Man is an ordering animal; he is an organizer because his knowledge of the world proceeds from his movements, and from movements relative to his body, which fall under the geometrical explanation that he gives it. Inside a nature that is always partial, appearing to him point blank in chaotic guise, man, who is in need of quasi-strategic security, is bent on creating an explicit environment for himself. On the other hand, seeking to satisfy his taste for knowledge, which is still a taste for classification—that is to say, a taste for order—he has conceived a system of explanation that adjusts itself as best as possible to natural phenomena. Finally, in pursuit of an ideal of purity, he has transcended empirical geometry and made of it a perfect system, without material contact with the real, a symbol of perfection, practically unrealizable and consequently inaccessible to errors, the refuge of the most pure poets. In all times, human work has been illuminated by this ideal: the work of the savage, the play of the infant, and Einstein.

Apogees

This ideal, which is not fulfilled by its previous conquests, becomes more and more imperious (appetite develops with eating). The tyrant, which we have brought upon ourselves, eagerly uses our tools and is never satisfied, since it seeks perfection itself. There are times when this geometric ideal becomes particularly despotic, when the perfecting of our tooling seems to render perfection itself attainable. This is the frenzy before the mirage: man, becoming conscious of his ideal, can no longer submit only to his instincts, like a bee that partitions its cells; it is with the full weight of reason that he formulates his ideal; epoch of apogee.

Then the inevitable: the letter kills the spirit; we live on material bliss, fruit of a partially realized ideal; the geometric function is nearly saturated. Decadence.

The march of civilization could be represented by the following graph in which the apogees are shown by the upper areas of the curve. Such a curve represents as well the regressions that follow the high points and the moments of sharp divergence that make the beginnings of a new cycle. The actual cycle begins with the long incubation that prepared the work of Encyclopedists, which made possible the scientific development of the nineteenth century. The mechanized revolution, which was the consequence of this development, provoked the blossoming of a violent taste for the geometrical thing and its derivatives.

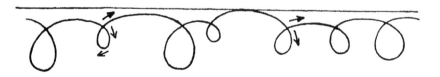

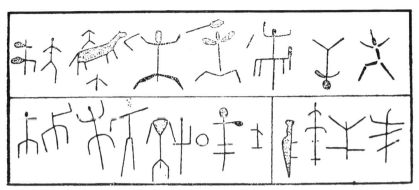

Primitive Figures

ORDER CREATES INTELLIGIBLE SIGNS

The spirit of order has created signs, conventional symbols of properly defined ideas, which are the raw materials that permit the construction of geometry and language, that by effective abbreviation render things intelligible to oneself and to others. An analogous need has created these signs in the domain of the art of seeing; they derive from very precise sources—they not only have to dignify, but also act physiologically on our senses. Signs could no longer be abstract and conventional symbols of writing or mathematics, escaping those who do not recognize the key to them, but figurations of facts relating to spirit, and conditioning in a manner as to effectively shock our senses.

Thus today, for example, a negative demonstration is provided to us by a whole movement of modern painting born recently in Holland, which seems to us to elude the necessary and sufficient conditions of painting (intelligibility and sensorial mechanism), by exclusively employing geometric signs limited to the rectangle. This restriction to a single element produces such a simplistic language that it can only allow mumbling—at the base, an excellent agreement of intention, but a vocabulary limited to unique proposition: "square, red square, blue square, yellow square, white square, black square, small black square, large white square, small, medium, etc. . ."

de Stijl cliché

THEO VAN DOESBURG
GENERALBASS DER MALEREI

By a denuded art we can tend to the purity of expression. Yet, one must choose the means that permit saying something that is worth saying; truth is not necessarily an extreme; the extreme is often the absurd: Meissonnier, Mondrain. Truth is there where it happens to be.

HIERATISM

By 'hieratism,' for lack of a better word, we mean the state of spirit that a civilization reaches coming out of the empirical stage, when it becomes conscious of what it could have only felt previously. We strip this term of the sacred signification that etymology confers upon it. Even if we allowed it to stay, it would be our right to use it this way, since science, formerly the apanage of the priest, has now changed hands. In order to avoid all ambiguity we secularize the term 'hieratism.'

Hieratism is the age of *connaissance,* knowledge of one's self, the moment of knowledge acquired often after a long period of research. It is, therefore, the moment when the human being, no longer shaken by exterior forces or by pure instincts, is in a position to manage himself and choose among the technical means those that permit him to satisfy the spiritual needs of new intellectual condition. Thus it was that in the realm of art, for example, the Egyptian priests determined to chose the means of the optical language among the numerous methods that the millennia had bequeathed them, signs (objects) satisfying at one and the same time the sensible (physiological) necessities as well as intelligibility. When Egyptian priests sculpted a god modeled after the hieratic type that they had created, they knew well that they were fabricating a machine for inciting sacred emotions. Their means were good, since their formal organizations still move mystically we who are not sensitive to old religious symbols. Osiris still silences the idlers in the Louvre, proof of the permanence of the work of art, the power of hieratism.

MEANS OF HIERATISM

The hieratic spirit therefore expresses itself by plastic equivalents that arrive through a thoughtful choice of elements, of whose properties it has an exact physiological and spiritual knowledge.

These elements are constituted by objects having particularly sensible properties; they are arranged following ordonnances that have particularly specific effects.

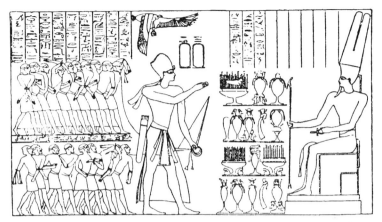

Egypt

THE STANDARD OBJECT

The objects that best represent the object-type, we establish, are the most perfectly banal; thus they satisfy the desire of the spirit to bring everything back to unity, which is one of its constants. Moreover, these banal objects enjoy perfect legibility, they are easily recognized, they clear away dispersions and inattention that would otherwise disrupt contemplation, the singular, the unknown, the misrecognized. They are perfectly legible because they have been recreated in the character of the most general and the most standard. And once again we find the manifestation of order that is the most banal and undeniable property of man. The tendency to unity is the noble sign of the standard object. We find evidence of these objects in the drawings of children and savages, on the walls of prehistoric caves, but also in some rare masterpieces produced over the millennia. And modern art? This is precisely why the review *L'Esprit Nouveau* attempts to research the destiny and means of Art.

Egypt

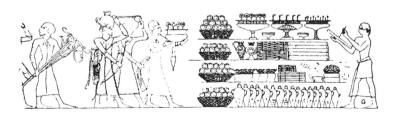

Egypt

The Orthogonal

The law of gravity governs all things on earth, as much man as the objects he creates. Instinct protests against instability, and even the appearance of instability worries him (the leaning Tower of Pisa). Art can only enter into opposition to this interior need of our nature. Moreover, on the contrary, art has to begin to satisfy this natural imperative of our sensibility. It is quite certain that there are examples of complicated exterior order the law of which escapes our senses; but art does not have to acknowledge that which escapes our senses.

The vertical is the visible characteristic of satisfied gravity; the plan of the application of this force is the ground that from the very beginning one is accustomed to represent by what is called the horizontal.

The vertical and the horizontal are among the sensitive manifestations of the phenomena of nature, constant verifications of one of its most directly apparent laws. The horizontal and the vertical consitute two right angles; among the infinite possible angles, the right angle is the angle type; the right angle is one of the symbols of perfection. In fact, the human being works according to the right angle (just look around you).

This explains and justifies the orthogonal spirit. It is the origin of human activity and it is the necessary condition of his most transcendental works of art.

If we disregard the parts of the preceding decades so often obliter-ated by the opinions of those who profess to be philosophers of art, and we embrace the whole of art in all its great periods, we will recognize the con-stant presence of the orthogonal.

THE OBLIQUE

Whereas the orthogonal is a perceptible sign of the permanent, the oblique is a sign of the unstable and variable. There is only one right angle, yet there is an infinite number of oblique angles. If the orthogonal gives the sense of the structural law of things, the oblique is only the sign of a passing instant. Herein lies the principal error of *Expressionism*, guided by the oblique, which, denying the work the susceptible balance and motion-lessness of duration, confers upon it an expressive dynamism of instability and testifies to the unresolved anxiety of spirits.

Expressionism, and for forty years before it, Impressionism, believed they could refute the millennia because they were "outdoing" Kodak. For the Impressionists the sign did not have any meaning; they banished the general and the essential in favor of the accidental. Confing themselves solely to the fragmentary aspects of nature, they copied or noted only the transient, which was nevertheless ordered; they intended to ignore this ordonnance. Order amused but did not interest them. Without even taking into account the vital value of this factor, they practiced the

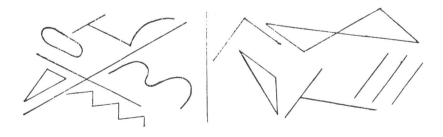

oblique. Futurism's race toward the fugitive moment would shipwreck the crew in the nothingness of the *movement*. All these cold-blooded movements lacked method and sense. Impressionism, Futurism, and Expressionism are all forms of expression that avoid the fact of creation—durable, humane, and compatible with plastic work.

* * *

At this moment, when the Cubist revolution is leading to a period of hieratism (knowledge of means, choice of signs, and geometric spirit), it appears that the orthogonal draws from its own universal fact an incontestable force. The orthogonal marks an enormous leap beyond the painting it has just surmounted, one that seems to regain its genuine and traditional destinies.

To be better convinced, those who would take an interest in this hurried and brutal conclusion might start carefully rereading this painful section, weighing perhaps with some surprise the fate, this time more pro-

Syria

found and imperative, that we customarily grant to a work of art when we create or judge it. This dangerous little game of *imitating nature, being sincere in front of nature* turns against laziness like a sharp double-edged weapon.

To those others who are totally circumvented by the later *Impressionist* period, who cannot get over it, and who cannot cast their gaze on the past or on a more general fact than that of painting—to those we say, taking our leave, Cezanne and Seurat (Cezanne obsessively so) were guided by geometry. These are the two Impressionist painters who will last precisely because they were not impressionists.

essays

FIG. 1 Cindy Sherman,
Untitled Film Still #2, 1977

Well, the plumb-line doesn't make a building. A number of other instruments are needed, a water-level for instance. But in the end the plumb-line isn't that bad—it allows us to gauge the vertical of certain problems.

Jacques Lacan
Seminar I: Freud's Papers on Technique 1953-54

At the Sink
Architecture in Abjection

Nadir Lahiji and D.S. Friedman

THE SINK AT THE EDGE OF THE FOYER IN THE VILLA SAVOYE contradicts everyday use: No spitting here, no washing your face. "As we further enter the vestibule of this temple and house," Colin Rowe reflects, "just how are we intended to interpret the so prominently displayed lavabo or sink? Scarcely as a functional accessory. For any details which one might associate with the act of washing (towels and soap) are conspicuously absent and would surely damage the pristine impact of this very obsessive little statement."[1] No towel in sight, Professor Rowe reaches for the alb: "Is it then a place of ritual purification, the equivalent of a holy-water stoop? Personally, I think that it is."[2] Like the bidet in *L'Art décoratif d'aujourd'hui*, Rowe sees this sink as a celebration of "the triumph of running water."[3] On closer inspection, however, we find that running water is secondary to its purpose. At Poissy, the real triumph of running water had to wait until the building was *in articulo mortis*: "Those who in 1965 visited the then derelict Villa Savoye certainly remember the squalid walls of the small service rooms on the ground floor, stinking of urine, smeared with excrement, and covered with obscene graffiti," Bernard Tschumi writes. "Not surprisingly, the long campaign to save the threatened purity of the Villa Savoye doubled in intensity in the months that followed, and finally succeeded."[4]

fig. 2 Le Corbusier, Villa Savoye, 1929

The "dismasted vessel" of the supreme "machine for living in" is momentarily submerged in a pool of defilement, stained by its own waste. "Society scares easily at those aspects of sensuality that it qualifies as obscene," Tschumi continues, citing St. Augustine: "'Inter faeces et urinam nascimus' (we are born between excrement and urine)."[5] Behind every cleanliness resides an execrable uncleanliness—clean dissimulates unclean. Clean and unclean do not exist in real opposition as two positive facts. Rather, they are two poles in a relationship of logical contradiction.[6] The unclean is not a positive entity; it is only the lack, the absence, of clean. The smeared body of the Villa Savoye reminds us that the clean body always comes with a remainder, an "excrement."

In twentieth-century modernity, the Villa Savoye functions as an apotropaic object that sustains the fantasy of distance from the unclean, understood as a horrible evil. As the Villa Savoye lies rotting on its bones, an undesirable odor invades the "civilization" of clear vision. This olfactory intrusion threatens to supersede the desiring eye (an important distinction in the Freudian sensorium to which we will return later). What the rescuers of the Villa Savoye preserve is not, in fact, Le Corbusier's *construction spirituelle*;[7] it is rather their own corporeal ego, which projects itself in order to repress the one thing that constantly threatens to return to haunt the body: the abject, the "leftover."

Holy water doesn't run; its job is to resist loss, whether by drain, sin, or evaporation. Anointing and baptism originate in practices related to strengthening life, to the human seed (which chrism imitates), to fecundity and virility, also to extending the life of the soul past death. Bathing and oiling the body imply not just surface cleanliness, but replenishment

FIG. 3 Le Corbusier, foyer
sink, Villa Savoye, 1929

through penetration to the body's depths. Life is liquid. Religious ablution is meant to pierce the skin on its way to the soul.[8] Colin Rowe is half right: saving the modern soul of the Savoyes and protecting them from dirt are one and the same problem. As that other modern prophet of hygiene, Adolf Loos, is at pains to demonstrate, twentieth-century soul-saving requires twentieth-century plumbing.

In his invention of twentieth-century architecture, Le Corbusier preaches directly to the eye. For the Savoyes he designs less a house—what about it after all is the least bit house-like?—than a modern domestic still - life. Monsieur Savoye sees the sink as he lays his hat and coat on the entrance table, beside the vase of flowers. Madame glances down at it as she climbs the ramp to the living room. The sink is a metonym for the body of the villa. Like other object-types in this composition—table, stair, ramp, telephone, vase, tiled chaise—its function is to be seen, not used. The sight of the sink gives the Savoyes pleasure. Their pleasure is scopophilic, voyeuristic; it fetishizes the sink. Here "seeing" has no subjec-tive dimension. The sink is a machine to separate the gaze from the eye. It is precisely the eye that it valorizes. The subject who looks at this sink is the phenomenological, self-conscious subject: the sink itself becomes a mirror in which "I see myself seeing myself." This is no ordinary sink. This is a poem about the "reign of hygiene."[9]

ABJECTION AND THE HYGIENIC SUPEREGO

To this sink we wish to juxtapose another, the one in Cindy Sher-man's *Untitled Film Still #2* (1977). [Fig. 1.] Rosalind Krauss notes that Sherman's camera in this work acts as a "proxy" for the watcher, whose psychic space is severed from the watched "by means of the signifier that reads as graininess, a diffusion of the image that constructs the signified—the concept of distance. . . ."[10] Hal Foster sees this work as an evocation of "the subject under the gaze, the subject-as-picture"; he observes that in *Untitled Film Still #2* "this gaze seems to come from within," capturing "the gap [of (mis)recognition] between imagined and actual body images that yawns in each of us. . . ."[11] Krauss's "severed psychic space" creates Foster's "gap." This yawning gap wants to swallow everything in the picture.[12] Take the sink, for instance: It is an unexceptional commercial fixture, little more than a common receptacle for water and spit; once in awhile the young girl uses it to soak delicates. The camera angle is too low to capture the drain, hidden by the porcelain bowl roughly at the level of her pelvis. We can see that her waste basket is full. She has lodged a sponge in the elbow of the chrome trap. She keeps her sink clean.

Presumably the sink is unaffected by the optical pumps that multiply in the space of our encounter with this scene—from young girl and "viewer" to mirror, from "viewer" to the back of the young girl's head, from her wig to her towel, across its fabric and drape, then through it to the flesh and the parts of the body that we cannot see but know to be there. What happens if we graft this optical pump onto a relation between the young girl's body and the medial sink, if we plumb these vectors for signs of the horizontal? "What relation between architecture and smell?" David Wills asks in his contemplation of Peter Greenaway's film, *The Belly of an Architect* (1987). "Should we insist on further evidence of the analogy between building and the human form, via the domus, the insistent economy of relations between interior and exterior, even the internal organic, and the play of penetration and expulsion, solidification and disintegration? An architecture of the digestive tract from ingestion to defecation"—or, in this case, from towel to bowel?[13]

In the composition of *Untitled Film Still #2*, the sink is a sink. Its utility seems to stand outside or below the psychological activity that takes place at the level of the mirror. In its very inconspicuousness we can conclude that unlike Le Corbusier's object-type, this sink does not separate the eye from the gaze. It is strictly a sink for use, in the use of which the young girl takes no pleasure. It is not a poem about hygiene, it is not a sink for looking at.[14] It is the primal scene of the abject. It refers to everything signified by the flesh and bones beneath the gaze, to what Foster calls their "extreme conditions"—"menstrual blood and sexual discharge, vomit and shit, decay and death. . . the body turned inside out, the subject literally abjected, thrown out," down the drain.[15] Sherman's sink stands in metonymic relation to the body of the young girl. In this middle position—between mirror and body, between vertical and horizontal—the image of the sink picks up speed, noun-becoming-verb, object-becoming-abject.

"Sink" in the verb form means to go down in stages, to fall gradually or drop to a lower level or condition. A "sinking feeling" suggests the weight of great disappointment, discouragement, or depression, as though from a loss of prestige or position. "To sink" means to pass slowly into sleep, despair, lethargy, weakness, or fatigue; or to become dangerously ill, to approach death, to fail or fall. In its transitive construction "to sink" means to cause to descend beneath a surface or to force into the ground; to reduce in quantity or worth; to debase the nature of something, to degrade it, ruin it, defeat it, or plunge it into destruction. First and second meanings of "sink" in its noun form alternate from one dictionary to the next, between "sewer or cesspool" and "any of various basins or receptacles connected with a drain pipe and water supply"; most dictionaries offer a third definition, in which "sink" refers to a place regarded as wicked, corrupt, or morally filthy.[16] To this last meaning our theoretical extension of the term "sink" opens to another stratum: "sink" operates in the field of signifiers that indicate a change in state during which the horizontal overcomes the sublimation of the vertical and emancipates the repressed condition of the body from the forces of gravity.

And what is the vestibule of Loos's Rufer House in Vienna if not a mise-en-scène for a sink? Loos hangs it off the tiled wall of a large, sunken nymphaeum, where it gazes out from its alcove, oddly outside everyday operations and the spaces of the household. Here again, no towel or soap, a sink only to look at.

FIG. 4 Adolf Loos, Rufer House, 1922, entrance foyer

Like Colin Rowe, Panayotis Tournikiotis reflects at on the position of the sink in the ritual composition of the Rufer House: "For Loos, the way one entered the house was of the greatest importance. The entrance could not be merely a door into a hall; it had to function as a zone of purification where one could disencumber oneself of the outside world and public life. Therefore, the entrance becomes a sequential event, with a cloak room to discard one's city clothes, a small room with a toilet, and a reception vestibule, sometimes furnished with a wash basin so one could literally wash one's hands of the outside before ascending a narrow stair to enter the sanctum of the home."[17] Tournikiotis forgets that the essence of this fixture as a conspicuous implement of hygiene consists not in its use but in its visuality; it cleans eyes, not hands.[18]

Visitors to the Villa Savoye have the cleanest eyes of all. In the gaze of "standard objects," Le Corbusier observes that "[they]. . . turn round and round . . . asking themselves what is happening, understanding with difficulty the reasons for what they see and feel; they don't find anything of what is called 'house.'"[19] Where then are we? In this purist still-life, which Le Corbusier strings along a line of circulation from the most public space in the villa (the entrance foyer) to the most private (the master bedroom), let us look at just three fixtures: first, the pedestal sink, which suggests the upright posture—plumbing, the vertical axis, perfection; second, the ramp, an oblique plane, "unstable and variable," but here composed in section as a path from the villa's "cave" to its "solarium"; and lastly, the tiled chaise, which visually separates the Savoye's bed from their bath, and which traces the outline of a reclining body. Each element diagrams a different axis of habitation—vertical (logos), oblique (eros), and horizontal (thanatos)—but insofar as Le Corbusier arrays these objects within a larger "scopic regime," they are all about verticality. We would argue that the sink (not the ramp, not the chaise) is the constitutive image in this series. Le Corbusier observes: "Circulation furnishes architectural impressions of such diversity that they disconcert visitors ignorant of the architectural liberties brought by modern techniques."[20] The sink in the foyer furnishes an architectural impression. Its real job in this picture is to ward off anxiety about dirt. It translates what we herein call the *hygienic superego* into a clean architectural body.[21] As Julia Kristeva states, however: "To each ego its object, to each superego its abject."[22] Our aim is to plumb this abject in architecture.

FIG. 5 Marcel Duchamp, *Fountain*, 1917   FIG. 6 Bidet, illustration from Le Corbusier, *L'Art décoratif d'aujourd'hui*, 1925

Modernism emerges from the belief that man is fundamentally a clean body. In the dialectic of the clean and unclean we might hypothesize an arc from Marcel Duchamp's *Fountain* to Le Corbusier's image of the bidet in *L'Esprit Nouveau* (later republished in *L'Art décoratif d'aujourd'hui*), to the sink in the Villa Savoye. Duchamp creates *Fountain* by mischievously detaching a gender-specific sanitary object from its regulatory circuits, the result of which opens onto the "civilization of the body" like a wound. Moreover, as Leo Steinberg notes in his seminal analysis of Rauschenberg's flatbed picture plane, Duchamp is the "vital source" of modern art's radical shift from vertical to horizontal orientation: "His *Large Glass*. . . is no longer an analogue of a world perceived from an upright position, but a matrix of information conveniently placed in a vertical situation. And one detects a sense of the significance of a ninety-degree shift in relation to a man's posture in some of those Duchamp 'works' that once seemed no more than provocative gestures: the *Coatrack* nailed to the floor and the famous *Urinal* tilted up like a monument."[23] On the other hand, the visual status of the sink in the composition of the Villa Savoye's foyer attaches itself to the fact that it is a working fixture, connected to the bureaucracy of hygiene, clean water in, dirty water out. This is architecture, after all; the sink must work.[24] The architecture of modern plumbing signifies the apparatus of uprightness, the ethics of the Good, and ordered regulatory systems, which issue primarily from representations of the identity of the Male body.

THE EGO AND THE VERTICAL

In a much-discussed footnote of Sigmund Freud's *Civilization and Its Discontents*, Freud speculates about man's first civilized act, arguing that the control of fire is a reward for the renunciation of his instinct to micturate on its flames.[25] Freud further argues in this account of the origin myth that human uprightness, the move from quadripedal to bipedal orientation, is coextensive with civilization's diminution of olfactory stimuli, which results in the repression of anal eroticism. Four-leggedness conceals animal genitalia, whereas man's upright posture leaves his sex exposed. Freud concludes that shame derives from the visible frontality of the genitals, which now require physical and psychological protection. With uprightness, the eye supplants the nose as the ruling organ of perception. According to Freud: "A social factor is also unmistakably present in the cultural trend towards cleanliness, which has received ex post facto justification in hygienic considerations but which manifested itself before their discovery. The incitement to cleanliness originates in an urge to get rid of the excreta, which have become disagreeable to the sense perceptions."[26]

Modern cleanliness departs from ancient ablution in its extension of hygiene to the psychological interior. Prohibition against dust and dirt marks the structure of the hygienic superego. This prohibition is aggressive; it propels modernism and identifies it. The clean body is also a plumbed body. In the psychological principles of hygiene, the plumbed body registers in the narcissism of the "Ideal Ego," and in the register of the Imaginary drive.[27] In the early years of this century it was precisely this vertical register of the Ideal Ego that the teachings of Jacques Lacan deconstructed. By now Lacan's "The Mirror Stage"[28] is common within contemporary cultural criticism, if it is not already a *doxa*.

The discourse of the plumbed body is the discourse of the Ego. In his seminar of February 17, 1954, entitled "Discourse Analysis and Ego Analysis," Lacan mentions a certain "absent friend" in the *Société*[29] who "with a lyrical impulse" calls Anna Freud "The Plumb-line of Psychoanalysis."[30] Not surprisingly, Lacan twists his response: ". . . well the plumb-line is not enough to make a building, a number of other instruments are needed, a water-level, for example."[31] Here, in the guise of an ironic architect, Lacan analogizes a well-established architectural principle. In the building trade, water level complements plumb line; the level is a necessary tool used to orient the perpendicularity of the building in relation to its floor. The water level signifies the horizontal axis of an ideal ground plane. In the relationship between plumb line and water level, something remains as leftover. Contemporary critical theorists situate this leftover in the notion of *informe* and abjection.[32]

Lacan's playful use of this architectural analogy subverts the teaching of Anna Freud, "the Plumb-line of Psychoanalysis." At the same time, however, his analogy subverts a certain method of "architectural thinking" in psychoanalysis itself. Plumb line and water level together constitute the dominant tradition of architecture that we know by the name of "the right angle." The right angle is present in the origin of the aesthetics and ethics of the upright body and its projection into building. It founds the architectural tradition that "massively privilege[s] the square at the expense of the hypotenuse, the oblique, or the diagonal."[33] The body in the right angle already represses the condition of its own possibility.

In Peter Greenaway's film, *The Belly of an Architect*, Rome is the site of the law of the return of these conditions, of the ruins and horizontality of the repressed body. When the American architect Stourley Kracklite casts himself from the window of the monument to Vittorio Emmanuel II, he throws his cancer-ridden body radically out of plumb. At the same moment, his wife's water breaks, delivering their child on the floor before the entrance to his exhibition of the work of E.-L. Boullée. Precisely here, in this suicidal defenestration, Greenaway plumbs the entropic

FIGS. 7–12 Film stills from Peter Greenaway's *The Belly of An Architect*, 1987

conditions repressed within the vertical. For Greenaway, as for David Wills in his reading of this film, "a crumbling Rome is. . . inevitably erotic." A city of olfactory monuments—"the belly of the Western world. . . or its sex. . . [or] the confounding of the two"—Rome is the city in which "eroticism is affirmation of the continuity that is death, by means of the prodigality engendered by decay and putrefaction."[34] In Rome, an architecture of the olfactory sense desublimates the architecture of visuality and its vertical axis, the axis out of which Kracklite falls in his fatal adjunction with Rome's horizontality.[35] In Rome, all right angles crumble.

The Abject in the Right Angle

Le Corbusier's lyrical and compulsive revival of the academic discourse of the right angle elevates it to a new status within the ethics and aesthetics of modernity. It prompts Salvador Dali, the surrealist, to react. In his essay, "*De la beauté terrifiante et comestible de l'architecture modern style,*" published in the surrealist magazine *Minotaure* in 1933,[36] Dali vehemently advocates art noveau, or "Modern Style" architecture. He writes: "I insist here on the essentially extra-*plastique* character of the Modern Style. For me every use of this style towards 'plastic' or pictorial ends imply the most flagrant betrayal of the movement's irrational and essentially 'literary' aspirations. The 'replacement' (question of wariness) of the formula of the 'right angle' or 'golden section' with the formula of convulsive-undulating, can only give birth in the long run to an aestheticism as sad as its predecessor."[37]

Dali's aesthetic of "regression," from the dominant right angle to the "modern style," coincides with the appearance in his writings, after 1933, of certain preoccupations—excrement, culinary activity, and regression to an oral, infantile, pregenital sexuality. Dali exhibits his rejection of the right angle in the surrealist Object. He fills his essay "Modern Style" with references to the delirious, sadomasochistic, extra-plastic, edible character of Art Nouveau architecture and fiercely objects to its replacement by the "plastic" object, in which the right angle is the dominant element. "Dali views the origins of this architecture in terms of '*faim originale,*' which submits architectural elements of the past to a '*trituration convulsive-formelle*' (convulsive-formal grinding) under the banner of 'fonctionnement des desires.' Dali sees those 'modern style' buildings as the 'realisation de desires solidifiés' (realization of solidified desires) and cites the presence in them of 'characteristic dream elements: condensation, displacement, etc.' All those ideas are finally labeled by Dali as 'cannibalisme des objets.'"[38]

Dali shores up this defense of the "modern style" in another essay entitled "The Stinking Ass": "Perhaps no image has produced effects to which the word ideal can more properly be applied than the tremendous image which is the staggering ornamental architecture called the 'Modern Style.' No collective effort has produced a dream world so pure and so disturbing as the 'Modern Style' buildings, these beings, apart from architecture, the true realization in themselves of desire grown solid. Their most violent and cruel automatism pitifully betrays a hatred of reality and a need for seeking refuge in a ideal world, just as happens in infantile neurosis."[39] For Dali art nouveau architecture hysterically expresses a social repression, "the repression of the 'symbolic-psychic-materialist function' of art nouveau by the functionalist ideal of modernist art and architecture," as Hal Foster acutely observes; for Dali, the perversity of art nouveau scandalizes these "'intellectualist aesthetics.'"[40] The functional regime of the right angle replaces the hysterical body of desire—infantile, feminine, unconscious, paranoid-critical. The modernity of desire yields to the modernity of discipline.[41]

In his many autobiographies, Dali likes to recall his first meeting in 1932 with a "brilliant young psychiatrist," Dr. Lacan.[42] Dali owes his understanding of early psychoanalytical notions of perversion and regression to Lacan. In turn, Lacan, who read Dali on the "paranoid-critical method," owes his theory of *Fantasme* to the surrealists. An article by Lacan follows one by Dali in the first issue of the magazine *Minotaure*. Dali's acquaintance with early Lacanian theory equips him to write "I am because I hallucinate, and because I hallucinate I am."[43] Dali's cogito denies the rationality of the subject in the right angle of Le Corbusier, who also contributes an essay to the magazine *Minotaure*, one in which he reveals his doubt about the surrealists.[44]

The "plumb-line of psychoanalysis" propagates "ego psychology," which disregards the letter and spirit of Freudian teaching. In ego psychology, the vertical axis serves as the structural scaffold of the ego, its agent of synthesis and its "mechanism of defense" and adaptation. In Lacan's teaching of the theory of "The Mirror Stage," the Imaginary ego is the agent of alienation and separation. This teaching, which fundamentally subverts the verticality of the ego and its uprightness, is Lacan's "return to Freud."[45] Yet why does Lacan begin his seminar by urging his students to read Anna Freud's *The Ego and the Mechanisms of Defense*, which he rejects? What does he mean when he states that "in the end the plumb-line isn't that bad—it allows us to gauge the vertical of certain problems"?

The problem we want to gauge is the vertical axis itself, especially its double determination within the tradition of the right angle. As with all remote probes, our soundings eventually reach a level that we can no longer measure, the level Freud identifies as "the navel" of dream. The vertical of the right angle dominates not only the tradition of architecture but also the ethics of modernity. Modernity is split from the beginning into plumbable and unplumbable depths. At one and the same time, this unplumbable point is both the condition of the possibility of the vertical and the very limitation of our modernity defined from the inside. Psychoanalysis points out this internal limit, which, as Mladen Dolar says, was always-already there.[46]

"I Stand therefore I Am"

Le Corbusier expropriates the notion of the right angle from nineteenth-century French academic teaching, which demonstrates the vertical of the right angle visually, through a didactic graphic known as the *aplomb*. The *aplomb* represents the ideal human figure and its posture:

> [The *aplomb* is] a pose with the engaged leg bearing nearly all the weight, and approaching a right angle at the knee. The almost totally disengaged leg trailing behind was so completely extended, at the end of movement, that it is straight enough to suggest the hypotenuse of a triangle defining the entire pose. Practically, as a working method, the aplomb, or *ligne milieu*, was a weighted drop line of the carpenter's variety, that swung at the ground between the ball and the heel of the engaged leg when hung from the pit of the throat (Lomazzo credits Polyclitus with the discovery of the importance of the instep in creating a classical balance). A figure so constructed may be said to conform to a right-angle pose, where the aplomb defines the limits of forward movement, brought to an aesthetic and physical arrest, and creating at the ground a right triangle whose hypotenuse is provided by the profile of the back and extended leg.[47]

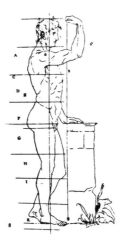

FIG. 13 "The aplomb,"
J.F. Bosio, *Elements of Drawing*, Philadelphia, 1816.

In his modern adaptation of this image, Le Corbusier transposes the gestural body of the right angle into the abstract body of the vertical, a principle he (as Pierre Jeanneret) memorializes with Amédée Ozenfant in an essay entitled "L'angle droit," originally published in their 1920s avant-garde magazine *L'Esprit Nouveau*.[48] After Lacan, one might be tempted to call Le Corbusier "the plumb-line of architecture."

Young Jeanneret, working with Ozenfant, first tries to gauge the vertical of the problem of painting. Verticality and its dominant mode of vision for Le Corbusier and Ozenfant is the very reason behind painting. In the same essay, "L'angle droit," it is the plumbing of the painting that has been gauged vertically. In the section entitled "The Orthogonal" they write:

> The vertical is the visible characteristic of satisfied gravity; the plan of the application of this force is the ground that from the very beginning one is accustomed to represent by what is called the horizontal.
>
> The vertical and the horizontal are among the sensitive manifestations of the phenomena of nature, constant verifications of one of its most directly apparent laws. The horizontal and the vertical constitute two right angles; among the infinite possible angles, the right angle is the angle type; the right angle is one of the symbols of perfection. In fact, the human being works according to the right angle (just look around you).

In the same essay, under "The Oblique," Jeanneret and Ozenfant again reconfirm the law of nature:

> Whereas the orthogonal is a perceptible sign of the permanent, the oblique is a sign of the unstable and variable. There is only one right angle, yet there is an infinite number of oblique angles. If the orthogonal gives the sense of the structural law of things, the oblique is only the sign of a passing instant. Herein lies the principal error of *Expressionism*, guided by the oblique, which, denying the work the susceptible balance and motionlessness of duration, confers upon it an expressive dynamism of instability and testifies to the unresolved anxiety of spirits.[49]

In the structure of Le Corbusier's thought, the vertical enjoys the status of a first principle, the immutable expression of a certain "natural" necessity, the condition of man walking on the earth. For Le Corbusier, the vertical is the axis of form;[50] it is foundational in entering the world of vision. Likewise is the vertical situated in the structure of Gestalt psychology and its interpretation of the upright posture in the phenomenological movement of consciousness. In this movement the unity of the Ego arises from the intentionality of the individual. Man has not yet entered into social relations. He lacks nothing. Lacan calls this unity the "Imaginary" because it is "founded on the essential illusion of a totalized body-image."[51]

Within the movement of Gestalt psychology, Erwin Strauss argues that the upright posture is "the leitmotiv in the foundation of the human organism": "in getting up, man gains his standing in the world."[52] Here we want to establish the fact that Le Corbusier's anthropological image of ideal man and its upright posture has affinities with the phenomenological picture Freud portrays of the evolution of man from the horizontal to the vertical axis. This view is common within early twentieth-century phenomenology, which presents the subject and the organization of the ego's perceptual unity in the limited field of consciousness. We can situate Le Corbusier squarely within this tradition: in itself, the vertical is the ethical condition of man, signifying his moral uprightness. The sea, the water level, similarly constitutes the horizontal, forever kept apart from yet connected to the vertical by ninety degrees. For Le Corbusier, true verticality is the most poetic of all angles—it is the *only* poetic angle. In this obsessive preoccupation with the vertical, Le Corbusier

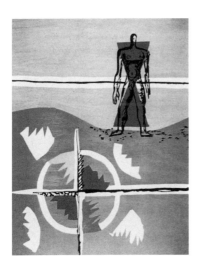

FIG. 14 Image from Le Corbusier, *Le Poème de l'angle droit*, 1955.

avoids the danger and risk of obliquity. Just listen to the "*Le poème de l'angle droit*," which he would pen thirty years after the essay with Ozenfant. In section "*A. 3 milieu*" Le Corbusier writes:

L'univers de nos yeux repose	The universe of our eyes rests
sur un plateau bordé d'horizon	upon a plane edged with horizon
La face tournée vers le ciel	Facing the sky
Considérons l'espace inconcevable	let us consider the inconceivable space
jusqu'ici insaisi.	hitherto uncomprehended.
Reposer s'étendre dormir	Repose supine sleep
—mourir	—death
Le dos au sol. . .	With our backs on the ground. . .
Mais je me suis mis debout!	But I am standing straight!
Puisque tu es droit	since you are erect
te voilá propre aux actes.	you are also fit for action.
Droit sur le plateau terrestre	Erect on the terrestrial plain
des choses saisissables tu	of things knowable you
Contractes avec la nature un	sign a pact of solidarity
pacte de solidarité: c'est l'angle droit	with nature: this is the right angle
Debout devant la mer vertical	Vertical facing the sea
te voilá sur tes gambes.	there you are on your feet.[53]

André Wogenscky, apologist for *Le poème de l'angle droit*, notes that the right angle constitutes "a pact with nature."[54] For Le Corbusier the right angle is the axiomatic expression of an anthropological fact; it "civilizes," but without discontent. With the right angle Le Corbusier accounts for natural order at the expense of culture. Man is erect, therefore he is "fit for action." The erect body is not only the "subject" of space, it is also the origin of its coordinates, master of the horizontal and vertical field. Le Corbusier wants the condition of repose to equal death, but of course it does not. On the contrary, repose—the horizontal—implicates what Leo Steinberg identifies as "a different order of experience":

> The pictures of the last fifteen to twenty years insist on a radically new orientation, in which the painted surface is no longer the analogue of a visual experience of nature but of operational processes. . . . What I have in mind is the psychic address of the image, its special mode of imaginative confrontation, and I tend to regard the tilt of the picture plane from vertical to horizontal as expressive of the most radical shift in the subject matter of art, the shift from nature to culture.[55]

Le Corbusier is the architect of the cogito of the right angle. He reconstructs space at the level of the intersection of the vertical of the body and the horizontal of the ground—"vertical facing the sea, there you are on your feet." No statement, we think, better expresses Le Corbusier's cogito than this one: *I stand therefore I am.* Compare this to Georges Bataille's.[56] Bataille writes: "Placed before you, I feel myself to be the contrary of him who tranquilly watched the dismasted vessels from the shore, because in fact, in spite of everything, I cannot imagine anyone so cruel that he could notice the one who is dismasted with such carefree laughter. Sinking is something altogether different, one can have it to one's heart's content."[57] From this Denis Hollier formulates a cogito for Bataille: "I sink therefore I am."

Bataille's dictum is "no beauty without defilement";[58] man never attains complete verticality. The idea of sinking is embedded in the horizontal, which Bataille brings to the surface for the first time as the transgressive axis of twentieth-century philosophy. For Le Corbusier, vertical and horizontal are two positive facts in real opposition, by which he organizes his harmonious cosmology into perfect symmetries and neat pairs of

opposites; but for Bataille, vertical and horizontal stand in logical contradiction. Horizontal is the void of vertical, its zero degree. Horizontal is the
lack, the absence of vertical, which makes "vertical" possible. If verticality
refers to the axis of transcendence and therefore to "objectification, con-
ceptualization, representation, distinction, homogeneity, knowledge, history (as written or as narrative), and, more generally, to the domain of
theory, especially in the sense of *theoria*: to see," then horizontality refers
to immanence, and thus to "ritual, difference, horror, silence, heterogene-
ity, abjection. . . ."[59]

In the right angle there is already an implicit "natural" pact
between architecture, which comes later, and the vertical body raised on its
feet. The body is already there, a priori, before any geometrical intervention occurs. Le Corbusier axiomatically inscribes a right angle on a geometrical human body, a body without subjectivity. But what if the upright
body has no natural architecture to begin with? And what if the body cannot be inscribed in the coordinates of the right angle? Le Corbusier's vertical body inheres an optimistic and jubilant view of civilization, populated
by the ruling oppositions from his universe of absolute differences: vertical versus horizontal, life versus death, male versus female—in other
words, a gendered world, but not yet a sexual one. *There you are on your
feet*, erect, in the field of verticality. The architect waxes a polished anthropological narrative. He is helpless to tell us at what cost this civilizing posture came about, or that something in this formulation is repressed.[60]

THE SUPEREGO AND THE HYGIENIC GAZE

We find the registers of the right angle in the cone of vision that
emanates from the eye at the apex of the upright body. This perspectival
representation of geometral optics constitutes the "scopic regime" of
modernity, as Martin Jay demonstrates.[61] "Everything is geometrical to our
eyes," Le Corbusier declares in *Précisions*, adding that "biology exists only
as organization, and this is something that the mind understands only
after study. Architectural composition is geometric, an event primarily of a
visual nature; an event implying judgment of quantities, of relationship;
the appreciation of proportions."[62] Le Corbusier's vision does not admit of
a void. "Instead this space inside [his] cosmic envelope is everywhere vec-
tored," Rosalind Krauss argues, "scored by ordinate and abscissa, marking
out the numberless sites of an always potential *Prägnanz*."[63] Particles of

geometry—"universal constants"—"underlie everything that gives itself to be seen."[64] All these indices of existence—vision, geometry, ethics—Le Corbusier fuses into a single sovereign schema, the vertical. The vertical is the constitutive, defining image of his modernity, which Krauss aptly identifies as "a machine for the multiplication of the geometric."[65] "Architecture is run by the right angle," Le Corbusier proclaims; "it is dangerous for architecture to leave this firm and magnificent terrain, to be defeated by the acute or obtuse angle: everything becomes ugliness, constraint, wastefulness."[66]

Le Corbusier's construction of the upright body is the last theoretical moment in an epistemic genealogy that extends back to the end of the nineteenth century, by which time modern ethics had already turned the reality principle into usable pleasure. But the transformation really begins a hundred years earlier, with the rise of utilitarianism. In his *Précis des leçons d'architecture* (1802–05), J.N.L. Durand adopts a utilitarian credo: "[I]n all times and in all places, the entirety of man's thoughts and action have had their origin in two principles: the love of well-being and the aversion to every sort of pain."[67] Succeeding thinkers would modify Durand's fundamental definition of modern society: pleasure comes not only from use but from cleanliness. Le Corbusier transforms this pleasure principle into the hygienic superego.

In her seminal essay "The Sartorial Superego," Joan Copjec argues that for modernists there was no principle beyond pleasure: "Well, then, does man's construction of architecture, like everything else, have its origins in pleasure and pain; or does it originate. . . in the principle of use? Durand answers economically that it originates in both, and he thereby erects modern architecture on the same equation that Jeremy Bentham used to formulate his utilitarianism. . . . Durand did not start out from the proposition that pleasure is usable; he began his *Précis* instead with the assumption that use is pleasurable."[68] These economic affinities have a common psychological contour. In the "Eye of Power," Michel Foucault argues that architecture in the late eighteenth century is integral to the program of Benthamian reform, which seeks to introduce a technology of "generalized surveillance," the *Panopticon*, an architectural instrument of control with which to lighten and economize institutional discipline.[69] In the transparent society, it is in "the name of health and cleanliness [that] all sorts of spatial arrangements are subjected to [panoptical] control."[70]

Thus for Foucault, the supervisory gaze is also hygienic. Distribution of clean space presupposes social hygiene. The pathological fear of "darkened space" that haunts the late eighteenth century ultimately gives rise to the modern space of hygiene, nowhere more purely demonstrated than the white architecture of Le Corbusier, governed by the Law of Ripolin, "itself an eye. . . , not simply the look of cleanliness but the cleaning of the look."[71]

The hygienic superego is the reverse of the utilitarian law of social and institutional transparency; likewise, the "optical unconscious" is the obverse of the law of the hygienic gaze. Avoidance of pain and aversion to dirt engender the superego, which Freud describes in *Civilization and its Discontents*:

> What happens in him to render his desire for aggression innocuous? Something very remarkable, which we should never have guessed and which is nevertheless quite obvious. His aggressiveness is introjected, internalized; it is, in point of fact, sent back to where it came from—that is, it is directed towards his own ego. There it is taken over by a portion of the ego, which sets itself over against the rest of the ego as superego, and which now, in the form of 'conscience,' is ready to put into action against the ego the same harsh aggressiveness that the ego would have liked to satisfy upon other, extraneous individuals.[72]

"I Sink therefore I Am"

Cleanliness is the response to a guilt modernity has had to internalize. Freud writes: "The super-ego is an agency which has been inferred by us, and conscience is a function we ascribe, among other functions, to that agency. . . . The sense of guilt, the harshness of the superego, is thus the same thing as the severity of the conscience. . . . As to a sense of guilt we must admit that it is in existence, before the super-ego, and therefore conscience, too."[73] The process of modernization in the economic developments of the nineteenth century brings about the civilization of cleanliness. Modernization, working as an external agency, forces twentieth-century modernism to internalize this process, to redirect it as a form of superego, and exert its authority as a project undertaken in the name of hygiene. The superego of the hygienic movement constructs modernity by plumbing the destructive instinct of the pleasure we take in dirt and pollution.

Accordingly, in *Vers Une Architecture*, Le Corbusier declares: "Every man's mind, being molded by his participation in contemporary events, has consciously or unconsciously formed certain desires; these are inevitably connected with family, an instinct which is the basis of society. Every man to-day realizes his need of sun, of warmth, or pure air and clean floor; he has been taught to wear a shiny white collar, and women love fine white linen."[74] To this observation we need only add the warning Adolf Loos broadcasts to his countrymen in the essay "Plumbers": "Increasing water usage is one of the most pressing tasks of a culture. May our Viennese plumbers therefore do their jobs as fully and completely as possible in order to lead us to this great goal—the attainment a cultural level equal to the other countries of the civilized Western world. For otherwise something very unpleasant, something very shameful could take place."[75]

Le Corbusier celebrates the clean lines of American silos and factories; Adolf Loos, the clean lines of American plumbing; both writers elevate principles of efficient production and pleasure in utility. On the other hand, their contemporary Georges Bataille writes about the factory not as a beautiful or clean building, but as "lugubrious filth," as another emblem of wastefulness and the excess of *dépense*. In his "Critical Dictionary," under the heading of "Dust," Bataille examines the language of a ubiquitous material that threatens to clog the transparency of social hygiene:

> The storytellers have not imagined that the Sleeping Beauty would be awakened covered by a thick layer of dust; no more have they dreamed of the sinister spiders' webs that at the first movement of her brown hair would have torn. Nevertheless the sad *nappes de poussière* endlessly invade earthly dwellings and make them uniformly dirty; as if attics and old rooms were planned for the next entry of obsession, of phantoms, of larvae living and inebriated by the worm-eaten smell of the old dust. When the big girls 'good for anything' are themselves, each morning, with a big feather duster, or even with a vacuum cleaner, they are perhaps not entirely ignorant that they contribute as much as the most positive savant keeping off the evil phantoms that sicken cleanliness and logic. One day or another, it is true, dust, if it persists, will probably begin to gain ground over the servants, invading the immense rubbish of abandoned buildings, of deserted docks: and in the distant epoch there will be nothing more to save us from nocturnal terrors.[76]

Yve-Alain Bois elaborates: "But dust, Bataille also says, pours immense rubbish ('*immenses decombres*') into 'abandoned buildings, deserted dockyards,' which is to say the area called 'Zone'. It would even seem that its irreversible invasion must end by chasing the 'servant' away and emptying all 'earthly habitation' of their occupants, transforming them into 'deserted dockyards' (dust in the Zone: there again you have a double index). On an urban scale, the Zone is what dust is at the scale of the single dwelling: it is the waste that inevitably accompanies production (which is necessarily, we should remember, over production)."[77] Dust evokes eternal decay, the dirt and nocturnal terrors of abandoned houses, but not only that. Briony Fer, in his reflection on domestic decay, adds to these associations the quality of gender: "Woman as a servant, or as a mother, is charged (and I mean Charged in both senses of responsibility and impugned guilt) with the management of dirt. Dirt and cleanliness are the women's prerogative."[78] It is the horror of this prerogative that Cindy Sherman plumbs in her work of the early 1980s.

I sink, therefore I am. Every day we bend out of our uprightness and spit into the drain: How do we plumb the secret pleasure we take in malodor? The sink represents a paradox in the hygienic movement when we consider it in relation to "spitting" or oral hygiene, as Denis Hollier informs us. For Marcel Mauss, spitting is a "bodily technique," "not sacrilegious, but rather therapeutic."[79] Building on Mauss's insight, Hollier writes that "for Bataille and [Michel] Leiris, hygiene excuses nothing. On the contrary, it is their *bête noire*. In their hands, the word hygiene has precisely the impact of spitting. Dirtiness is proper to man, from which it follows that the less a thing is clean (*propre*), the more human it is."[80] And to put it in the dialectal maxim of the obscene law of the superego, "the cleaner you are, the dirtier you are."[81]

NOTES

1. Colin Rowe, *The Architecture of Good Intentions: Towards a Possible Retrospect* (London: Academy Editions, 1994), 60.

2. Ibid.

3. Ibid. Here Rowe reproduces the photograph of the bidet Le Corbusier uses to illustrate the chapter in *L'Art décoratif d'aujourd'hui* entitled "Other Icons, The Museums." See Le Corbusier, *The Decorative Art of Today*, trans. James I. Dunnet (Cambridge, MA: MIT Press, 1987), 16.

4. Bernard Tschumi, "Architecture and Transgression," in *Architecture and Disjunction* (Cambridge: MIT Press, 1994), 73. For an historical account of the saving of the Villa Savoye, see G. E. Kidder Smith, "Letter to the Editor," *Journal of the Society of Architectural Historians* 52 (December 1993): 511.

5. Tschumi, "Architecture and Transgression."

6. "Contradiction is a logical relationship that does not have any real existence, while real opposition is a relationship between two poles that are equally positive. The latter relationship is not between something and its lack, but between two positive givens." Slavoj Žižek, *Looking Awry: An Introduction to Jacques Lacan through Popular Culture* (Cambridge, MA: MIT Press, 1992), 161.

7. "[The interpenetration of inner and outer space] became possible to achieve. . . in a dwelling. This possibility was latent in the skeleton system of construction, but the skeleton had to be used as Le Corbusier used it: in the service of a new conception of space. That is what he meant when he defined architecture as a *construction spirituelle*." Siegfried Giedion, *Space, Time and Architecture: The Growth of a New Tradition*, 5th ed. (Cambridge, MA: Harvard University Press, 1967), 529.

8. Richard Broxton Onians, *The Origins of European Thought* (Cambridge: Cambridge University Press, 1951), 189–91, 213, 215, 219–23.

9. "However, they are also poems about hydraulics. . . ." Colin Rowe, *The Architecture of Good Intention*, 60; see also Sigmund Freud, *Civilization and its Discontent*, Standard Edition, ed. James Strachy, intro. Peter Gay (New York and London: W.W. Norton, 1961), 40.

10. *Cindy Sherman 1975–1993*, text by Rosalind E. Krauss with an essay by Norman Bryson (New York: Rizzoli, 1993), 56.

11. Hal Foster, *The Return of the Real: The Avant-Garde at the End of the Century* (Cambridge, MA: MIT Press, 1996), 146–52.

12. It wants to swallow the whole bathroom. Michel Leiris calls the bathroom "the other sacred pole of the house—the left-hand pole, tending toward the illicit" (the right-hand pole is the parents bedroom). In his note to this passage from Leiris's "The Sacred in Everyday Life," Denis Hollier points out the anthropological significance of "the two poles, the right and the left, of the sacred": "Caillois, as well, fixes on the polarity of the sacred to which he devotes a chapter of *L'Homme et le sacre* (1939): 'The right hand and adroitness manifest divine purity and favor, the left-hand and clumsiness manifest pollution and sin.'" See Michel Lieris, "The Sacred in Everyday Life," in *The College of Sociology* (1937–39), ed. Denis Hollier, trans. Betsey Wing (Minneapolis: University of Minnesota Press, 1988), 25 n. 4.

13. David Wills, "Rome, 1985," in *Prosthesis* (Stanford, CA: Stanford University Press, 1995), 206; also see David Wills, "Designs on the Body: Film/Architecture/Writing," in *Assemblage* 19 (1992): 97–105, an earlier version of this essay.

14. "Not a machine for looking but a machine for looking at. . . ." Mark Wigley, "Architecture After Philosophy: Le Corbusier and the Emperor's New Paint," in *Journal of Philosophy and the Visual Arts: Architecture & Philosophy*, ed. Andrew Benjamin (London: Academy Editions, 1990), 85–86.

15. Foster, *The Return of the Real*, 149.

16. We have adapted these definitions from the *American Heritage Dictionary*, 3d ed., *s.v.* "sink"; and *Webster's New Universal Unabridged Dictionary*, 2d ed., *s.v.* "sink."

17. Panayotis Tournikiotis, *Adolf Loos* (New York: Princeton Architectural Press, 1994), 71.

18. Wigley writes that whitewash is "not simply the look of cleanliness but the cleaning of the look." Wigley, "Architecture After Philosophy," 86.

19. Le Corbusier, *Precisions: on the current state of architecture and city planning*, trans. from the French by Edith Schreiber Aujame (Cambridge, MA: MIT Press, 1991), 136.

20. Ibid.

21. For the Freudian notion of the super-ego, see Sigmund Freud, *The Ego and the Id*, Standard Edition, ed. James Strachey, intro. by Peter Gay (New York and London: W.W. Norton, 1961). We model the term *hygienic superego* after Joan Copjec's "Sartorial Superego," which she discusses in "The Sartorial Superego," chap 4 in *Read My Desire* (Cambridge, MA: MIT Press, 1994). Later in this text we develop the Lacanian extension of this concept around Copjec's analysis.

22. Julia Kristeva, *Powers of Horror* (New York: Columbia University Press, 1982), 2.

23. Leo Steinberg, "Other Criteria," in *Other Criteria: Confrontations with Twentieth-Century Art* (London: Oxford University Press, 1979), 85.

24. "The bidet which forms a leading illustration in *L'Art décoratif d'aujourd'hui* must principally enjoy a polemical and ritual status; and the spatial complexity of the bathrooms at Garches renders them somewhat the same category of event. For all their elaboration, they function." Colin Rowe, *The Architecture of Good Intention*, 60.

25. "Psycho-analytic material, incomplete as it is and not susceptible to clear interpretation, nevertheless admits of a conjecture—a fantastic-sounding one—about the origin of [the control over fire]. It is as though primal man had the habit, when he came into contact with fire, of satisfying an infantile desire connected with it, by putting it out with a stream of his urine. The legends that we possess leave no doubt about the originally phallic view taken of tongues of flame as they shoot upwards. Putting out the fire by micturating—a theme to which modern giants, Gulliver in Lilliput and Rabelais' Gargantua, still hark back—was therefore a kind of sexual act with a male, an enjoyment of sexual potency in a homosexual competition. The first person to renounce this desire and spare the fire was able to carry it off with him and subdue it for his own use. By damping down the fire of his own sexual excitation, he had tamed the natural force of fire. This great cultural conquest was thus the reward for his renunciation of instinct. Further, it is as though woman had been appointed guardian of the fire which was held captive on the domestic hearth, because her anatomy made it impossible for her to yield to the temptation of this desire. It is remarkable, too, how regularly analytic experience testifies to the connection between ambition, fire, and urethral eroticism." Sigmund Freud, *Civilization and its Discontents*, 42 n. 4.

26. Ibid., 54 n. 1. In the same place, Freud writes: "The fateful process of civilization would thus have set in with man's adoption of an erect posture. From that point the chain of events would have proceeded through the devaluation of olfactory stimuli and isolation of

menstrual period to the time when visual stimuli were paramount and the genitals became visible, and hence to the continuity of sexual excitation, the founding of the family and so the threshold of human civilization. . . ." For a critical discussion of this chapter in Freud, see Leo Bersani, *The Freudian Body* (New York: Columbia University Press, 1986).

27. For elaboration on the Imaginary drive, see Richard Boothby, *Death and Desire: Psychoanalytical Theory in Lacan's Return to Freud* (New York and London: Routledge, 1991).

28. See Jacques Lacan, "The Mirror Stage as Formative of the Function of the I," in *Écrits* (New York and London: W.W. Norton, 1977).

29. Société française de psychanalyse (SFP). Lacan in 1953 resigned from SPP (Société psychanalytique de Paris) and established his own SFP with several psychoanalysts whom he trained.

30. Jacques Lacan, *The Seminars of Jacques Lacan, Book I: Freud's paper on technique, 1953–1954*, ed. Jacques-Alain Miller, trans. John Forrester (New York and London: W.W. Norton, 1991), 63.

31. Ibid.

32. On the notion of *informe* after Georges Bataille, see Rosalind E. Krauss, *The Optical Unconscious* (Cambridge, MA: MIT Press, 1993); on the notion of abjection, see Julia Kristeva, *Powers of Horror, An essay on Abjection*; also see Hal Foster, *The Return of the Real*; for a discussion of the relevance of the abject in contemporary theory see "The Politics of the Signifier II: A Conversation on the *Informe* and the Abject," in *October 67* (Winter 1994): 3–21.

33. See David Wills, "Designs on the Body: Film/Architecture/Writing," in *Assemblage* 19 (1992): 97–105. Wills attempts a deconstruction of this tradition through his analysis of Peter Greenaway's film, *The Belly of an Architect*. Also see David Wills, "Rome, 1985," in *Prosthesis*.

34. Wills, "Rome, 1985," 195, 176.

35. Ibid., 206–07.

36. Salvador Dali, "*De la beauté terrifiante et comestible de l'architecture modern style*," in *Minotaure* No. 3–4 (December 1933): 69–76. For a translation of this article in English, with a preface by Dalibor Veseley, see "Art Nouveau: Architecture's Terrifying and Edible Beauty," *Architectural Design* 2/3 ("Surrealism and Architecture," 1978): 139–42.

37. Dali, "Art Nouveau: Architecture's Terrifying and Edible Beauty," 139 [translation modified by the editors].

38. See Haim Finkelstein, "The Incarnation of Desire, Dali and the Surrealist Object," *Res* 23 (Spring 1993): 126–127.

39. Dali, "The Stinking Ass," *Quarter* 5 1 (1932): 53.

40. Hal Foster, *Compulsive Beauty* (Cambridge, MA: MIT Press, 1993), 183–86.

41. Ibid., 190.

42. For more details, see Hanjo Berressem, "Dali and Lacan: Painting The Imaginary Landscape," in *Lacan: Politics, Aesthetics*, eds. Willy Apollon and Richard Feldstein (Albany: State University of New York Press, 1996).

43. Quoted in Berressem, "Dali and Lacan," 275.

44. Le Corbusier, "Louis Sutter, l'inconnu de la soixantaine," *Minotaure* 9 (October 1936): 62–65.

45. See Philippe Julienne, *Jacques Lacan's Return to Freud: The Real, the Symbolic, and the*

Imaginary, trans. Devra Beck Simiu (New York and London: New York University Press, 1994).

46. See Mladen Dolar, "'I Shall Be with You on Your Wedding-Night': Lacan and the Uncanny," in *October* 58 (Fall 1991).

47. Richard Moore, "Academic *Dessin* Theory in France after the Reorganization of 1863," *Journal of the Society of Architectural Historians* 36 (October 1977): 171.

48. Pierre Jeanneret and Amédée Ozenfant, "L'angle droit," in *L'Esprit Nouveau* 18 (n.d.). See the translation in this volume.

49. Ibid.

50. See Krauss, *The Optical Unconscious*.

51. Robert Samuels, *Between Philosophy and Psychoanalysis: Lacan's Reconstruction of Freud* (New York: Routledge, 1993), 2.

52. Erwin W. Strauss, "The Upright Posture," chapter 7 in *Phenomenological Psychology*, trans. Erling Eng (New York: Basic Books, Inc., 1966), 139, 143; also see Erwin Strauss, "Born to See, Bound to Behold: Reflections on the Function of the Upright Posture in the Aesthetic Attitude," in *The Philosophy of the Body*, ed. Stuart Spicker (New York: Quadrangle, 1970), 334–359, cited in Rosalind E. Krauss, "Cindy Sherman: Untitled," in *Cindy Sherman 1975–1993*, 94 n.35.

53. Le Corbusier, *Le Poème de l'angle droit* (Paris: La Fondation Le Corbusier and Editions Connivences, 1989), paginated in the original art work, "29–30"; translated in the appendix by Kenneth Hylton, no pagination.

54. André Wogenscky, in *Le Poème de l'angle droit*, no pagination.

55. Steinberg, "Other Criteria," 84; also see Krauss's notes *s.v.* "Verticality/Horizontality" in *The Optical Unconscious*, 327.

56. For further discussion of the relationship between Le Corbusier and Georges Bataille, see Nadir Lahiji, "The Gift of the Open Hand: Le Corbusier Reading Georges Bataille's *La part maudite*," *Journal of Architectural Education* 50/1 (September 1996): 50–67.

57. Denis Hollier, "The Dualist Materialism of Georges Bataille," *Yale French Studies* 78, "Special Issue on Bataille" (1990): 138.

58. See John Lechte, "Surrealism and the Practice of Writing, or the 'Case' of Bataille," in *Bataille, Writing the Sacred*, ed. Carolyn Bailet Gill (London and New York: Routledge, 1995), 118.

59. Ibid., 120. Also see Bataille, "The Penial Eye," in Georges Bataille, *Visions of Excess* (Minneapolis: University of Minnesota, 1985), 79–90.

60. See note 26 above.

61. Martin Jay, *Downcast Eyes: The Denigration of Vision in Twentieth-Century French Theory* (Berkeley: University of California Press, 1993).

62. Le Corbusier, *Precisions*, 133.

63. Krauss, *The Optical Unconscious*, 186.

64. Ibid.

65. Ibid., 161.

66. Le Corbusier, *Precisions*, 151–152.

67. We owe this reflection on Durand to Joan Copjec, "The Sartorial Superego," in *Read My Desire*. Here Copjec cites Durand, *Précis des leçons d'architecture à l'Ecole Royale Polytechnique* (Paris, 1918), 6.

68. Copjec writes that "[Durand's] argument is essentially this: because we seek pleasure, we

therefore seek to surround ourselves with useful things, since they alone can and do necessarily provide us with pleasure—or, at least, with the only pleasure worth considering. For, in fact, there is more than one pleasure in Durand's text, though only one is accepted as legitimate, the other is discounted as a false pleasure." Copjec, "The Sartorial Superego," 82.

69. Michel Foucault, "The Eye of Power," in *Power/Knowledge: Selected Interviews and Other Writings, 1972–1977,* ed. Colin Gordon (New York: Pantheon Books, 1980).

70. Michelle Perrot, "The Eye of Power," 150.

71. Mark Wigley, "Architecture After Philosophy: Le Corbusier and the Emperor's New Paint," 85–86, in relation to which see Le Corbusier, "A Coat of Whitewash, the Law of Ripolin," in *The Decorative Art of Today;* for a discussion of the pathology of "darkened space," see Anthony Vidler, "Dark Space," in *The Architectural Uncanny: Essays in the Modern Unhomely* (Cambridge, MA: MIT Press, 1992); for critical insight into white architecture see Mark Wigley, *White Walls, Designer Dresses: the Fashioning of Modern Architecture* (Cambridge, MA: MIT Press, 1995).

72. Freud, *Civilization and Its Discontents,* 84. For an interpretation of this passage, see David Wills's "Berchtesgaden, 1929," in *Prosthesis;* for the Lacanian construction of the Freudian super-ego, see also Slavoj Žižek, *Looking Awry,* 159–60: "The superego is, so to speak, as agency of the law exempted from its authority. It does itself what it prohibits us from doing. We can explain its fundamental paradox thus: the more innocent we are, i.e., the more we follow the superego's order and renounce enjoyment, the more guilty we feel, for the more we obey the superego, the greater is the enjoyment accumulated in it and, thus, the greater the pressure it exerts on us," to which Žižek attaches this endnote: "The Lacanian formula 'the only thing of which the subject can be guilty, ultimately, is ceding his desire,' presents an exact inversion of the paradox of the superego, and is thus deeply Freudian."

73. Freud, *Civilization and Its Discontents,* 100.

74. Le Corbusier, *Towards a New Architecture,* (New York: Dover, 1978), 277.

75. Adolf Loos, "Plumbers," trans. Harry Frances Mallgrave, herein.

76. Georges Bataille, *s.v.* "Dust," in "Critical Dictionary," *Documents* (October 1929). See also *Oeuvres complètes,* vol. 1 (Paris: Gallimard, 1970), 197. This translation was rendered by Anthony Vidler in *The Architectural Uncanny: Essays in the Modern Unhomely* (Cambridge, MA: MIT Press, 1992), 218.

77. Yve-Alain Bois and Rosalind E. Krauss, "A User's Guide to Entropy," in *October* 78 (Fall 1996): 83.

78. Briony Fer, "*Poussier/peinture,* Bataille on Painting," in *Bataille: Writing the Sacred,* ed. Carolyn Bailey Gill (London: Routledge, 1995), 162.

79. Denis Hollier, "The Use-Value of the Impossible," in *Bataille: Writing the Sacred,* 144.

80. Ibid.

81. See Slavoj Žižek, *Enjoy Your Symptom! Jacques Lacan in Hollywood and Out* (New York and London: Routledge, 1982), 185; see also note 72.

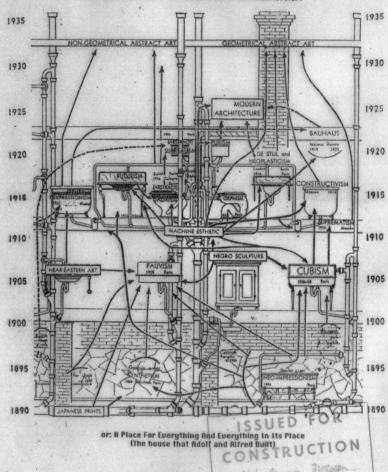

BARR/LOOS:
PORTRAIT OF A HISTORY OF MODERN ART AS SANITARY SYSTEM

or: A Place For Everything And Everything In Its Place
(The house that Adolf and Alfred Built)

Too Much Leverage is Dangerous

Margaret Morgan

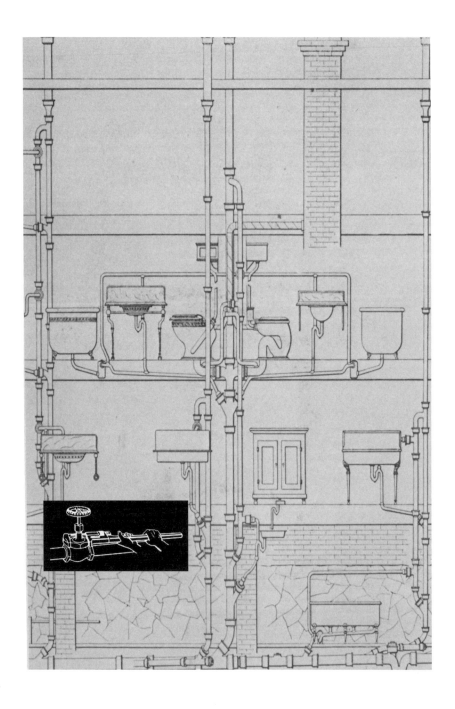

It dripped. The flesh of the upper arm barely concealed a well-developed muscle beneath. She pushed. Up and down, each thrust of rhythmic motion turned her face a deeper shade of purple, forcing her breath from her body, making her sweat. Her ears rang. Gorged with blood, each capillary filled to bursting. She plunged deeper, then with less depth but greater speed, each motion a perfect seal between the rubber of the apparatus and the steel below. The trap was open, she had thrust its lid aside herself. This palpitating flesh was not the flesh of orgasm, the lips of this woman weren't ecstatically apart. Rather it was a woman, my mother, in the throws of temper, her mouth quite shut, a slit of a line to hold in her rage. I remember watching, motionless and at some distance, the ammoniac fumes still searing my nostrils. "It's those tampons," she said, "those bloody tampons." Were I one of those sharp-witted, precocious adolescents I might have punned on her indignation. Instead I stood there dumbfounded and humiliated, watching as the plunger disgorged gob after gob of my guiltiness from the bowels of the house at the back of the yard. This was the gully trap, the big drain that connected our net to the street and the larger system. This was not the dusty storm water channel that my girlfriend and I, at a younger age, had crawled through during the drought. This was the wet drain, the one in use, the one between my mother and I. Tampons, I never use them now. I don't like them. They inhibit my flow. I like to see what I bleed. And as for those stupid cylinders of cardboard with which to shove them up, I'd take my finger any day.

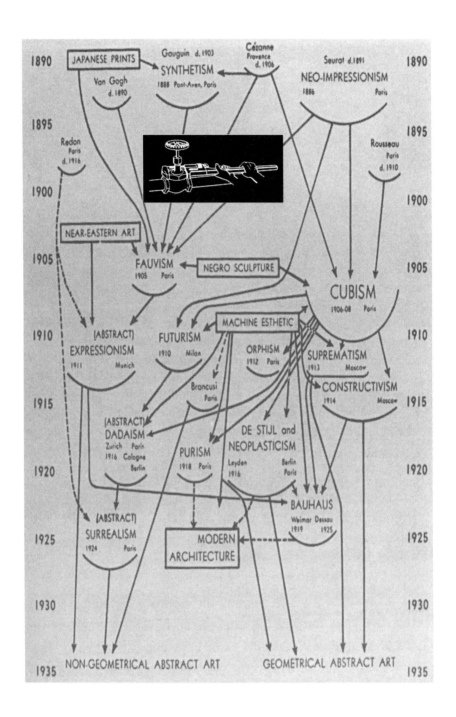

From under the door, a crack of light interrupted the darkness. If you stared for long enough its violet afterimage would blink round the room, fading only as your gaze returned to the slides you were meant to be watching. The room seemed cooler for being in darkness and the projector's whirring reassured you, its sound a mechanical ballet. You were never lulled to sleep. You had too much invested in red squares and red rooms and the crop the gleaners were harvesting. You desired the Fife Player, little boy and woman as he was, in the same way, you surmised, as the historian who lauded him. You returned the stare of Manet's model and you liked to imagine her bullfighting. Years later the blonde lashes of a friend would recall those of the model and, like a crack of light, the image would float before you. Your gaze scanned these surfaces, looking for your reflection in the folds of red drapery, the oscillating fields of colour, the impossible monument to the Third International. In that classroom at lunch time, you burned with the pleasure of your knowledge, of your familiarity with the subject, of the place for you in its lexicon. In many ways you were relieved there'd been no room in that working-class curriculum for such frivolities as art. You were only too happy to be far from the usual social intercourse of the classroom, the boys' mucking up, the girls' cigarettes. A sanctuary for fantasy, that extracurricular space became home. It was only later, at art school, that most non-vocational of endeavours, that you learnt the contingency of your imaginings. In a place where your class and gender distinguished you, your accent and manner betrayed you as not belonging but for your status as metaphor.

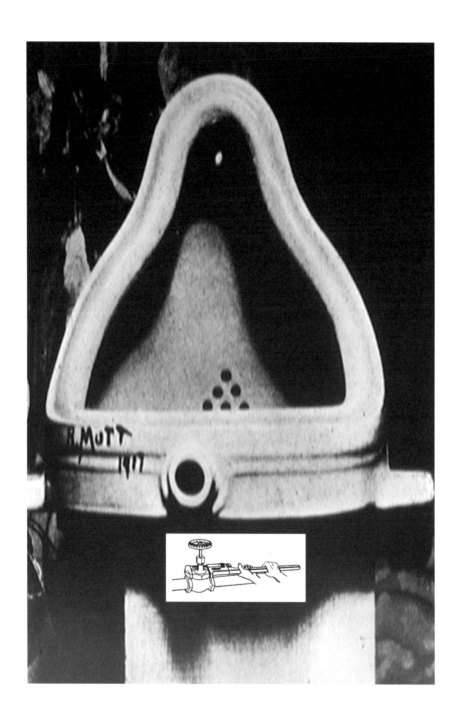

Today was the day. No more pencils, no more books, it was Muck-up Day, the last day of the last year of school. Wet lipped, he anticipated his final achievement. A simple lever, a novel construction, for such things he had aptitude. For once, he'd come first. On points alone, he knew he'd win: the element of surprise, the elegance of the design, his forward planning. He knew the other boys would approve. He savoured the prospect of his spectacular deployment, the shells cracking, the yokes flying, a sulfurous miasma filling the cubicle. He rehearsed his strategy, checking the set-up, testing the pulley. At last his prey entered the adjacent stall and, suppressing squeals of glee, he let go, releasing the hidden cord that propelled his load onto the target. Obliged to retaliate, grinning wildly and with albumen still dripping from his eyes, his friend thrust his head down the toilet, flushing as he pushed, convulsing in paroxysms of delight and revulsion. They tumbled in that confined and vertiginous space, losing their bearings, falling against gravity, slipping in the spills of their own undoing. It didn't matter that by mid-morning their uniforms were ruined. They were meant to be ruined, this their final denouement. They knew it was the last time they'd ever need to wear them. Smeared with flour, egg and unnamable concoctions from the bathroom, they wore their dishevelled garb like revolutionaries, the clumps of sticky poultice their badges of honor, its smears of yellow and brown, bruises from battle. Summer, already bleaching the sky white with heat, had cooked the mucky glue onto their clothes and faces, making cracks and fissures with each gesture or movement, leaving dissolute trails in their wake as they ran from the school yard at the three o'clock bell.

They were swollen from unrelieved pressure and incorrect usage. They were my hands and I was no tradesperson. Bearing what my pectorals and biceps could not, my hands suffered each misguided fit and turn. To me leverage was an abstraction; it was only at the end of the job I began to understand, at a bodily level, that control was infinitely more subtle than brute force. Joints grinding, body in torsion, the wrench a dull lump in my pocket, I learnt the lessons of the unskilled. My father, so my mother told me, had been highly skilled. She kept his tools as homage to as much, maintaining them just as he would have liked: oiled, wrapped, neatly ordered, a place for everything and everything in its place. She kept them with the rest of his things in a large suitcase in the linen closet in the hallway. It was always in darkness, this place, because you didn't need to go there, and because to turn on the light would have been a waste. Sometimes, surreptitiously, I would open the suitcase that housed his things. I would flip through his books, never reading, only looking, looking for the pressed flowers he'd left for someone to find there. I'd fondle the brittle leather of his shaving case, unzip it to inspect the razor within. I'd turn the handle of the bitless screw driver, weigh the hammer in my hand, gingerly finger the sharp edge of the plane. Those tools are still with me; I carry them in the cavities of my body. You know, Audre Lorde is wrong: they are not the Master's Tools, they never were. A tool is a tool is a tool and it belongs to me as much as anyone. I want something more than an old saw.

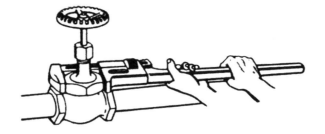

air chamber bagstopper ball and socket ballcock basin coupling belly trap
bend boot bend bending dresser bent bolt bib cock bladder bleed bleeding
cock blind man's rule blowoff blowpipe boiler coupling boiler screws bosh
boss boss and flange cran box head buck bucket head closet cock cock-and-
ball cock-and-pail cock box cock case high cock cock bib cock frost cock
gland cock hose cock plug cock sludge tapering cock tumbling cock cock's
eye see bird's eye collar concussion conductor conduit coupler bent coupler
nut coupling straight coupling bent coupling cramp-and-ratchet nose cran
crapper crease creepers crevice crooked thread cry of tin cundy dead man
devil diaphragm ballvalve dog ear dolly dook dope doubling down-comer
drain dress bending dresser tongue dresser drip box driving mandrel
drunken thr   elbow joint
street elbov   fire plug fit-
ter's union   esser flush
box flux fol   e bill goose
neck gully   ast hopper
closet hopp   ap bending
iron dookin   joint elbow
joint spigot   t knee knee
bend knob   ong hopper
longthread   y gravy bar-
rel nipple r   ow packing
gland pap pig's lug pillared cock pillar sink fittings pin-hole pipe bending
pipe hook pipe screwing pipe socket pipe expansion overflow puff plain
elbow plug plug cock plumb plumber's union podge podger see tommy
pricker-hole quirk raggle raglet raked flashing rest bend riser running nipple
screw screwdown stopcock shute head sill cock skeleton waste skew sliding
collar slip collar slop stone sludge cock slurry smudge snake's mouth snow
box soaker socket sodder sow's lug spaghetti spicket spigot spigot and
faucet spigot and socket spile peg splash stone stepped apron stick stink
trap stopcock screwdown stopcock street bend street elbow string flashing
stub nipple stud stuffing box surface box swagging tool swan-neck sweat
table waste tailpiece tail pipe tampin tampion tapering cock tell-tale pipe
three branch hand tilting fillet tinker's flea toggle tommy tongue dresser
trap belly trap stink trap trumpet tumbler-cock turncock turnkey turnpin UG
stopcock under and over underhand joint union coupling navy coupling up
and over upright joint valley gutter closet valve back pressure valve screw

FIG. 1 Marcel Duchamp's studio, with *Fountain* suspended in doorframe, c. 1917.

Bathrooms and Kitchens:
Cleaning House with Duchamp

Helen Molesworth

IT MAY STRIKE THE READER AS TEDIOUS TO READ YET ANOTHER (alternative) narrative of modernism. But rethinking modernism may be more crucial now then ever, and not only because the legacy of modernism remains the stomping ground of postmodern and post-structuralist academic discourse. For as the future unfolds, increasingly described in the language and images of cyborgs, and as increasingly intimate relations between machines and humans form the conditions of daily life for most of the industrialized world, understandings of the old relations between women and machines, between wholes and parts, and between desire and filth will demand clearer articulations.

These articulations may be aided by looking back and looking closely at modernism's deep involvement with issues of domesticity, from Marcel Duchamp's ready-mades to Meret Oppenheim's fur-covered teacup, *Object* (1936); from Pablo Picasso and Georges Braque's use of real wallpaper to the Futurists' cookbook; from Robert Rauschenberg's inclusion of old socks in the combines to Andy Warhol's Brillo boxes. While I am wary of merely establishing an iconographical system that will allow us to identify "domestic moments" within modernism, the pervasiveness of this concern appears increasingly apparent.

In art history the discourse of the avant garde has been blind to such readings. The discipline tends to narrate the agenda of the avant garde as one of critiquing ideas such as originality and authorship, and the institutional frameworks of art. In so doing, it has missed an extended, richly associative and imaginative meditation upon the problems and effects of the radical transformations taking place in both the concept and the actual space of home in the twentieth century. It is within the framework of domesticity that this essay reads the oeuvre of Marcel Duchamp. The ready-mades (which are everyday domestic objects) tell a story of the women's work of shopping and cleaning as much as they present a challenge to traditional notions of art. The avant garde has many narratives; this one takes the desire to reconcile art and life seriously, for there is nothing more everyday than housework.

1. Shock/Absorption

Absorb: to take in without echo, recoil, or reflection: to absorb shock.
Absorption: assimilation: incorporation.

Modernism and modernity have often been narrated through the trope or experience of shock. There is the shock of technology (the train, the shattering technologies of the two World Wars), and the "shock of the new" delivered by avant-garde art practices motivated by the artists' desire to disturb the complacency of the bourgeois class through an aggressive use of culture. Other narratives of modernity mark the dramatic shifts in the configuration and understanding of space and time, linked to the massive shift in modes of production from the artisanal to the industrial.[1] Psychoanalysis attempted to describe the new subjectivity which emerged from these shifts in narratives of extreme fragmentation and loss such as castration, neurasthenia, the compulsion to repeat, and the death drive. Yet it seems important to place these developments, both discursive and socio-cultural, in a dialectical relation to the "other" of shock, its (mechanical) counterpart, absorption.

Increasing mechanization occurred in domestic space at an extraordinary pace from the turn of the century through its first two decades. Siegfried Giedion mapped this shift in his famous *Mechanization Takes Command*, in which he argued that the home developed a "mechanical core" structured around the kitchen and the bathroom. During this period the average North American home took in a barrage of lightweight machinery (much of it electric), from eggbeaters to vacuum cleaners. In addition, the home was re-structured around water availability in order to incorporate standardized plumbing, was wired for electricity, saw the rise of centralized heating, and experienced the introduction of the telephone.

Yet none of this is ever described as shocking, or even disruptive, by either the women's magazines of the period, or by subsequent histories of domestic space. Rather, due to the curious matrix of forces that comprise the home, the experience, or subject effect, of the mechanization of domestic space was *absorption*. The home was not thought of as a work or public space, rather, it was conceived of as a place of rest for men, a space of reprieve from increasingly congested and loud urban spaces. But, the home was in fact a work place all along, one which had developed its own new managerial strategies in time with those of industry: for instance the continuous work surface, a connected counter-top that ran around the perimeter of the kitchen, allowed for an easy incorporation of new tools and technologies to aid in the efficiency of household labor.[2] Household labor, of course, was performed almost exclusively by servants and the "mistress of the house," people whose histories and narratives were not traditionally recorded at the turn of the century. For the most part, the mechanization of the home happened quietly. Its "public" face existed in the burgeoning phenomena of advertising which directed kitchen wares at the "new" women consumers, and in the spectacular world fairs and expositions that displayed such marvels as electric kitchens and porcelain plumbing fixtures.

Yet beyond these material conditions, domestic space was able to absorb technology and its effects for another reason. Discourses of shock rhetorically posit a whole which has been disrupted or fractured. Domestic space, however, was always already fragmented. For instance, the back door architecturally marks the liminal nature of the kitchen, the threshold of public and private, space for the back and forth movement of servants and delivery men. It is a fluctuating public/private, inside/outside passageway. Consider industrial designer Henry Dreyfuss's assessment of the 1910s and 1920s, in a chapter of his book *Designing for the People* titled "Through the Back Door": "It was not surprising that when they [designers of new domestic technologies] tried to introduce their new designs into the sacred American living room they were rebuffed at the front door. But they persisted and finally gained entrance through the back door. Their first achievements were in the kitchen, the bathroom, and the laundry, where utility transcended tradition."[3] Promises of less work and increased comfort lubricated the mechanization of the domestic sphere until the kitchen was filled with new technology, without any disruption of "business as usual."

In addition, domestic work is a fractured, never-completed labor, structured by competing needs and desires—cooking, cleaning, child care, entertaining, the maintenance of comfort and pleasure, mending and repairs. No "whole" product exists at the end of the day; instead, the home is structured by the continuous flow of part-objects (e.g., food, dirty dishes, laundry) in various states of production and consumption. This relation to labor and its (semi-)products also may have ameliorated the effect of "shock" in terms of mechanization.

Through the effects of mechanization and female consumerism, the apparently firm boundaries of the home seem to shift, troubling the more traditionally assumed divisions of public/private, inside/outside. These divisions, while historical, remain overwhelmingly present in today's cultural criticism. Often such binary oppositions are shored up by the division masculine/feminine, further bolstered by the (equally suspect) binary nature/culture. Frequently, however, thinking these binary opposi-tions along gendered lines serves to preserve such distinctions rather than disturb them. In *Bodies and Machines*, Mark Seltzer has argued that part of the "logic and erotics" of machine culture is that machine-and-human relations form "a miscegenation of the natural and the cultural: the ero-sion of the boundaries that divide persons and things, labor and nature."[4] This "miscegenation" is most clearly articulated today by the fantasies that comprise cyborg culture, virtual reality, the "net," and the field of ergonomics. Indeed, these recent developments may help to shed a new light on the early twentieth-century experience of women in the mecha-nization of domestic space as an ur-phenomenon of contemporary machine-body "marriages."

The relation between the ready-made and the history of the mech-anization of domestic space, which this essay will articulate, is a way to trouble more traditional narratives of modernism, structured by shock and the logic of binary thinking. After all, how stable are the narratives of whole/part, inside/outside, clean/unclean, public/private, machine/per-son? And how might bathrooms and kitchens, housework, machines, and ready-mades elucidate these problematics?

2. THE BATHROOM

In 1917 the American Society of Independent Artists held an exhibition in New York under the rubric, "no jury, no prizes," and for the small fee of five dollars anyone who wanted could enter an artwork. Marcel Duchamp was the head of the hanging committee. Under the pseudonym R. Mutt, he submitted an inverted and signed urinal entitled *Fountain*. When the committee of the Independents refused *Fountain*, Duchamp resigned immediately. By now, this story is one of the more infamous tales the twentieth-century avant garde tells about itself. Art historian Thierry de Duve has argued that the *Fountain* acted as a fulcrum in the crisis of legitimation set into play by the Independents' slogan, "no jury, no prizes."[5] For if the sole criteria for entering the exhibition was five dollars, then what constituted or legitimated art was in jeopardy. I would like to argue that Duchamp manipulated this crisis, in part, by tapping into the *mana* of the urinal.

Mana, an anthropological term borrowed from the Melanesians, is a loose concept used to describe the "distinctive character of every sacred being." In his seminal, *The Elementary Forms of Religious Life*, Emile Durkheim argued that because "*mana* is not fixed in anything," it must be conceived of in terms of a visible object.[6] Hence, part of *mana's* power is that "no one possesses it entirely and that all participate in it," and furthermore that it can be transferred from one object or person to another.[7] In this regard, the *mana* of the urinal is the "*mana* of the washroom."[8] The sacredness and power of the washroom is that it is a privileged site of bodily cleanliness, and conversely, it is necessarily a site of dirt and the unclean body.

By placing a urinal in the middle of an art exhibition, Duchamp's *Fountain* threatened the other art work in the exhibition with the *mana* of the urinal, the *mana* of clean and unclean bodies. The *mana* of the urinal could have permeated all of the these other entries, destabilizing its position as art, bringing to a head the crisis of legitimation already set into play by the lack of "criteria" established by the Independents. Needless to say, history proved the Independents wrong; ultimately the *mana* of art transformed the urinal into the *Fountain*. But at what cost? Perhaps the urinal's passage to the *Fountain*, its purification and elevation to the realm of art, only delayed the questions it first posed.

Never exhibited in 1917, lost under mysterious circumstances, known primarily through a photograph of it taken by Alfred Steiglitz, the *Fountain*'s tale is in large part one of reception.[9] However, in this essay I want to engage the historical specificity of the *Fountain*. *Fountain* was not exactly denied admission to the Independent's exhibition. As Duchamp notes, it was "suppressed," placed behind a partition in the hall during the entirety of the exhibit.[10] It is ironic that the hanging committee took the urinal so literally as to place it in a site hidden from "public" view. In effect they treated it as if it were a functional object, or (even worse, perhaps) an art object that ran the risk of being mistaken for a urinal.

Today, the ubiquitous nature of the urinal delays the acknowledgment of its identity as a machine. A urinal is neither electric nor "high-tech," but it is a machine, one based on a system of water pressure, valves, and the development of standardized components. In 1917 urinals were hardly as common as they are today. The concept of a public urinal was first introduced only sixty years prior to *Fountain*, by George Jennings, at the Great Exhibition of 1851 in London. It met with considerable objection, particularly the grave anxiety that it would be offensive to women and children.[11] In addition, toilets and urinals' connection to a reliable system of disposal was far from guaranteed, since the development of the "wash down method," that created two to three gallons of water pressure, still used in contemporary flush toilets, was not developed until 1889.[12] This partly explains why many homes in the United States were still using versions of chamber pots at the turn of the century. It has been argued that the entrance of the modern toilet into the middle class American home was not complete until the 1920s.[13] That these radical changes took place in Duchamp's lifetime may contextualize his famous quip: "The only works of art America has given are her plumbing and her bridges."[14] It certainly adds credence to art historian Craig Adcock's claim that *Fountain* "is in many ways an archetypal emblem of modernity and mechanical perfection."[15] This sense of the newness and importance of the bathroom was also noted in an article in the February 1917 issue of *House and Garden*, "Bathrooms and Civilization." The language of this small article gives an indication of the triumphant nature of plumbing's introduction into the middle-class home. "The bathroom is an index to civilization. Time was when it sufficed for a man to be civilized in his mind. We now require a civilization of the body. And in no line of house building has there been so great progress in recent years as in bathroom civilization."[16] The effect of mechanization and plumbing on codes of hygiene could not have been more dramatically expressed.

In *Purity and Danger*, anthropologist Mary Douglas argues that disruptions in systems of order are at the heart of cultural relations and significations regarding the clean and unclean, and that "pollution behaviors" are reactions which "condemn objects or ideas that confuse or contradict classifications."[17] "Dirt avoidance," Douglas continues, "for us is a matter of hygiene or aesthetics."[18] *Fountain* runs amok with both categories by refusing both the bodily pleasure of bladder release and the traditional expectation of visual pleasure attached to artworks. We can see fully how the *mana* of the *Fountain* is able to disturb the categories of both art and hygiene.

The marriage of aesthetics and hygiene is consummated with the development of the modern bathroom and kitchen. (We need only think of those pre-fab materials whose primary distinguishing characteristic is their easy-wipe surfaces.) But, we must not forget that the urinal is a specifically public artifact, and the exposure of the "private" activity of bodily waste disposal makes the public washroom fraught with certain anxieties *vis à vis* hygiene. Mechanization plays a crucial role in this development. Outhouses were often constructed for multiple use, however this multiple use would have normally taken place within the intimate structure of the family or a community of workers or friends who knew one another.[19] Urinals don't make peeing public as such, for male urination already had a public component. Rather, through the standardization both of the space and the receptacle, peeing is privatized as its publicness is sanctioned. This tension between public and private is exacerbated by Duchamp's infamous *Fountain*. You can't pee in it. The male viewer must contend with its definitively "public" placement in the middle of an art gallery. The inversion of the urinal makes its use doubly problematic, for if a man were to use it he would be splashed by his own urine, experiencing what one art historian has referred to as a "mirrorical return."[20]

The threat of dirtiness that emanates from the *Fountain* exists in a discursive and punning register as well. Rapid mechanization went hand in hand with the development of germ theory. Popular science magazines, as well as women's magazines, preached the virtues of higher levels of sanitariness as a way to ward off the omnipresent status of invisible germs. Two sites that were particularly fraught in this regard were the public rest room and the public drinking fountain.[21] Both were seen to harbor the germs of all those who preceded before the user. Duchamp's punning takes on new valences; not only does the up-ended urinal look like a fountain, not only is there play with the morphological similarity between a stream of male urine and the jet stream of water from a fountain, and not only are drinking and peeing intimately connected, but both activities had become mechanized, public, and subsequently tinged with dread in the popular print media of the time.

For Douglas, the danger of pollution behavior is also signified by attacks on form. Whole forms signify social completeness. Bodily waste and trash are then seen as markers of incompletion, fragmentary, the part to the whole. Similarly, *Fountain* is a fragment, a part-object disconnected from its pipes and plumbing. It is a receptacle for bodily waste, whose fragmentary nature helps to constitute the producing (clean) body as a whole. Here the concept of the "mirrorical return" problematizes the wholeness of the producing body, for body and fragmentary waste product would be rejoined, complicating the whole or part status of either. *Fountain* pressures the boundaries of public/private, for with the advent of the urinal, what was once a public act is cordoned off, made a curious mix of private *and* public. This newly codified form of behavior perhaps pointed to the complicated status of public and private in institutions of art, a site where a public comes together in order to have a private experience of art.[22] In this regard, *Fountain* points to the ways in which the development of certain technologies were shifting the cultural terms of propriety and cleanliness.

But what of *Fountain's* status as a ready-made? Take, for instance, art historian Rosalind Krauss's distinction between the ready-made and the sculpture. The ready-made, she argues, is a "freestanding object" taken off the shelf of the supermarket or the department store, self-contained, able to present itself as a totality. Sculpture, however, belongs to the realm of part-objects, in that sculpture always has as its referent the body. Even when a sculpture appears autonomous, its force emanates from the tacit acknowledgment that it's a part-object which has "migrated off the body."[23] The urinal, situated as it is in a web of interdependency and interconnectedness, does not stand alone. The *Fountain* demands to be hooked up, both to a body and to a plumbing network. In this regard, it slips out of the realm of the ready-made as defined by Krauss, but does not sit comfortably as sculpture. Krauss's definition of the ready-made is one that uses solely the parameters of (high) art production (sculpture vs. ready-made). Art historians have acknowledged that the ready-made offered a devastating challenge to the traditional boundaries of high art production, yet the discourse of the ready-made has remained firmly within the traditional disciplinary boundaries of art history. It may be this limitation that allows for such a neat distinction between sculptural and ready-made objects, a distinction that refuses the bodily relations implied by *Fountain*.

By stalling the urinal, Duchamp suspended and magnified the moment of machine-body interaction. In the breakdown of the machine its workings and its social conditions become manifest. In other words, when the urinal was stalled, frozen into the *Fountain*, it pointed everywhere to dirty bodies and full bladders. Its total and complete unusability set into play certain desires about cleanliness (and its potential impossibility), and certain fantasies about the spaces where clean and unclean happen: the home, the institution, the art gallery.

Because domestic machines have now been absorbed into the fabric of daily life, the moments of engagement between bodies and have become more common. Gilles Deleuze and Felix Guattari have called these moments of interaction "plugging in" or "hooking up." They describe the world as a continuous production of part-objects (shit, piss, semen, milk) that get cut off and consumed by other part-objects (the mouth, the urinal, the anus). "Every object presupposes a flow," they write in *Anti-Oedipus*; hence, "every flow presupposes the fragmentation of the object."[24] The urinal is a site at which the body is "hooked up" to a machine, relieving the body of its excess, engaging in a ritual act of cleanliness and bodily release. And part-objects only have part functions. Peeing as the other of drinking, flushing as the other of peeing.

The intersection of art, hygiene, the body and the machine found in the work of Duchamp allows for the proximity of two theoretical models: an anthropological model which describes the construction of clean and unclean in terms of attacks on forms, shifts in boundaries, and the relation of the fragment or part to the whole; and a theory of body-machine interactions structured around a perpetual connecting and disconnecting of part-objects, and a grafting of the human and the machine. I would like to raise some questions about the relationship between these two systems of thought. To what extent are boundaries shifted, or transgressed, in the human-machine engagement, either hooking up or grafting? If certain boundaries are indeed shifted, can the interactions of bodies and machines then be seen as a mutual challenge to the form of each? In this regard, can the anxiety about the preservation of the "natural" in the face of the "technological" be read, in part, as anxiety about a form of pollution behavior? Or are categorical distinctions between the natural and machinic in large part disturbed by the absorption of machinery into the home?

3. THE KITCHEN

In 1913 Christine Frederick wrote *The New Housekeeping*, a book which took the principles of "scientific management" from Frederick Winslow Taylor's 1911 book of the same name, and attempted to apply them to the North American household.[25] In 1912 the book had been serialized, and widely read, in the popular women's magazine *Ladies Home Journal*. Frederick desired to turn the kitchen into an organized work space, and manage all household work (laundry, mending, child care) in a manner akin to the factory. She studied specific tasks to evaluate the amount of time and the number of motions used to complete them. She then divided each task and assigned optimum performance times and methods. Ideally, these findings were to culminate in the restructuring of the kitchen in order to provide more efficient work patterns, so that no footsteps would have to be retraced.

Taylor's and Fredericks' "scientific management" sought to eliminate waste (of time, effort, space, and money). In this context, the double valence of the word "waste" cannot be overlooked. The desire to eliminate waste, both literally and rhetorically, is in part a desire to consolidate a culture's understanding of cleanliness. That the kitchen should become a site for Taylorization suggests the doubleness of the kitchen's simultaneous roles as both waste producer (garbage, dirty dishes, etc.) and waste manager (work process, trash removal, cleaning).

The transformation of the kitchen into a "factory" had several ramifications. Most importantly it firmly acknowledged domestic labor as *work*, work that required proper equipment, time schedules, and a system of labor management. The "factorization" of the kitchen is a powerful instance in which the separation between work and home became particularly ambiguous. Still referred to as a safe and quiet haven for men upon their return from work, in actuality the home had increasingly become a workplace like the one from which they had just come—mechanized and managed.

The old adage, "a woman's work is never done," describes the endless, ostensibly nonproductive nature of domestic labor, which must be repeated over and over again with no tangible "product" at the end of any given task. The commodity object, in as much as it makes the double demand to be bought, and to be used up, mirrors the cyclical, nonproductive labor of housework. The repetition that is absolutely structural to housework is mirrored by the endless stream of commodity production and consumption. If, as Mark Seltzer has argued, "the real innovation of Taylorization becomes visible in the incorporation of the *representation* of the work process into the work process itself—or, better, the incorporation of the representation of the work process *as* the work process itself,"[26] then the Taylorization of the home found its representational corollary in the commodity. Doing time-motion studies of housework was, in part, an attempt to *represent* housework, to make it visible in the form of an image. The most "successful" form of this imaging was through advertising. Advertisements were able to image housework literally (albeit in a falsely idealized fashion), but more importantly they were able to represent the act of consumption as a form of work itself.

The relation between commodities and the Taylorized home is bolstered by the woman's role as prime consumer. Frederick's book contains several chapters instructing women on the most efficient means of consumption, how and what to buy, when and where to buy. Then in 1929 she wrote a best-selling book, *Selling Mrs. Consumer*. Although manufacturers promised that the mechanization of the home would lessen the time required for housework, the dramatic rise in standards of cleanliness in the home actually increased the amount of time women spent on housework.[27] The new expectations of the mechanized and hyper-clean kitchen and home led to a burgeoning market for household products. "The new tasks associated with consumption were not necessarily physically burdensome, but they were time consuming, and they required the acquisition of new skills."[28] Consumption itself had become a form of work. Perhaps no one understood this better then Duchamp. After his famous note to himself, "Marcel, no more painting; go get a job," Duchamp got a part-time job making ready-mades.

The ready-made has been firmly canonized within the narratives of the avant garde, as being set against painting, the institution of art, and uniqueness.[29] Such historical accounts refuse to look at the content of, or relations between, Duchamp's "first" ready-mades: the hat rack, the bottle rack, the shovel, the kitchen stool with the bicycle wheel, and the comb. All are house-bound items, all tools for storing, cleaning, grooming, drying. And the ready-mades that exist outside of this iconographic register relate to it through their titles, titles by which Duchamp "meant to carry the mind of the spectator towards other regions more verbal."[30] For instance, both *Why Not Sneeze Rose Sélavy?* (1921) and *Pharmacy* (1914) evoke the body and its personal hygiene. By locating the ready-made within the sphere of the domestic, Duchamp questions the "work of art," by evoking the larger cultural problematic regarding the signification of work solely in terms of production. Thus, Duchamp's ready-mades, traditionally viewed as a wry send-up of the artisanal art practice in favor of industrial production, can also be seen as deeply invested in the new cultural phenomenon of consumption as work. For Frederick, like so many domestic science practitioners of her generation, made clear that consumption was a form of work, work that demanded knowledge, research, and organization. "Whether Mr. Mutt with his own hands made the fountain or not has no importance. He CHOSE it."[31] And in that act of choosing, there is the implicit understanding that he *bought* it.

Consumption has two meanings: to buy and to use up. Duchamp understood that housework has no product per se, but it is the domain of perpetual management: buying, using up, and disposing of objects, time, and food. By denying (ready-made) objects their use-value, Duchamp pointed not only to the new form of work, consumption, but also to the destructive nature of that work as well. He attempted to show how antithetical consumption is to the Protestant work ethic of production.

Mark Seltzer has described the "look" or representation of consumption as that which is "set in motion by the 'tinkling of the apparatus'—the mechanism that incites and measures, registers and personates 'the consumer.'"[32] The mechanisms or machines of Duchamp, by exploring consumption versus production, allow for a model of body-machine interactions that are structured by the phenomenon of incorporation, taking in, absorption into the fabric of the subject/consumer, rather than organized by production, which elaborates the practice of making, expelling, creating an other to the self, an other from the body.

4. BECOMING WOMAN, BECOMING MACHINE

Duchamp's first "machine" image was the *Coffee Mill* (1911), originally made as a gift for the decoration of his brother's kitchen. For the most part, the painting is in keeping with the broken or stalled quality of the ready-mades, yet one can trace a certain biomorphic quality in what otherwise appears as a "technical" drawing. The connections are not quite precise, the lines which indicate movement are a tad too sinuous, the color in the piece a bit lush. *Nine Malic Molds* (1914-1915) offers a similar feel; even before their final placement in *The Large Glass* (1915-1923) they were arranged in an upright cluster evoking human forms, and given the title *Cemetery of Uniforms and Liveries.*

These images are a striking counterpart to Duchamp's paintings of "women" during this period: *Nude Descending a Staircase* (1912, 1916), *Bride* (1912), and *The Passage of the Virgin to the Bride* (1912). While the ready-mades explored a strategy of "brokenness," these paintings work through the dynamics of transformation. The mechanization of women is viscerally apparent. All the images play with notions of movement and transformation, they attempt the difficult articulation of a transient state, a state *between* woman and machine. The most salient feature of these works is their sense of metamorphosis, or becoming. Duchamp has said he had a desire "to break up forms—to 'decompose' them."[33] And "decomposition" is as much a process as it is an endpoint.

Deleuze and Guattari have explored the difficult notion of becoming in the simultaneous language of negation and giddy metaphysical possibility. For them "a becoming is not a correspondence between relations. But neither is it a resemblance, an imitation, or at the limit, an identification."[35] Becoming is a temporal structure within which "what is real is the becoming itself, the block of becoming, not the supposedly fixed terms through which that which becomes passes."[35] Like the hook-ups between bodies and machines described earlier, becoming offers a model of human relations to technology based on transience and fluidity. In this sense, *Nude Descending a Staircase* is in a state of becoming robotic *and* becoming woman, neither one nor the other. The supine allure of the tilted head moves without disruption into the angularity of those piston-legs. And that open circle of dashed lines, a convention for marking direction or divisions in technical drawing, is here left incomplete, a broken ellipsis: suspension. What is suspended, however, are not the workings of the machine, as in the ready-made or *The Large Glass*; instead, the painting attempts to present, through an act of re-presentation (isolation, suspension), a moment of transformation. This goes beyond the epistemological quandary of how to represent movement on a two-dimensional plane. This painting explores the fleeting temporality of our hook-ups with machines (and how those hook-ups make us part-machinic), from the simple hand-handle-coffee mill-machine, to the complex becoming-machine-becoming-woman-machine that happens when the virgin becomes a bride and begins her daily kitchen routine.

Why did Duchamp place women in this role of becoming? The effects of the mechanization of the kitchen may point to an answer. The home's absorption of machines offered a different dynamic of human-machine relations than that experienced in the factory. The continual stream of partial activities with machines on an intimate and bodily scale (prosthetic machines—hand extensions for beating and grinding, ear extensions for the phone) shows women quietly becoming part machine, part human. This occurs, in part, due to the absence of shock involved in the process of mechanizing domestic space, and the fragmented nature of domestic labor.

Women, placed in the role of buffer or mediator, appear in Duchamp's paintings as ur-cyborgs.[36] We can think here of Lawrence Steefel's description of Duchamp's "mecanomorphic" period as "concerned with the human figure and its transmutation. . . into schematized robot-like personages."[37] In a related fashion, the ready-mades show the stalled relations between bodies and machines, relations that have "migrated off the body." The ready-mades are art objects that sit in wait for someone to engage them, implicating the bodies that circulate through art galleries and museums.

What then are the implications of a theory of trash and dirt based on the fragment, and a theory of desire and machines structured by the part-object? Is this merely a morphological similarity, or does it point to the reconfigured role of domesticity in the "machine age"? I turn again to Deleuze and Guattari:

We think the material or machinic aspect of an assemblage relates not to the production of goods but rather to the precise state of intermingling of bodies in a society, including all the attractions and repulsions, sympathies and antipathies, alterations, amalgamations, penetrations, and expansions that affect bodies of all kinds in their relations to one another. What regulates the obligatory, necessary, or permitted interminglings of bodies is above all an *alimentary and sexual regime*.[38] (my emphasis)

The regimes of the alimentary and the sexual most often take place in domestic spaces and are almost always structured by notions of domesticity. (The alimentary is not isolated in Deleuze and Guattari; the first example of a desiring machine in *Anti-Oedipus* is a child suckling at its mother's breast.) Duchamp exhibits an uncanny ability to make sense of women's roles, during a period when they came to stand as allegorical representations of electricity,[39] and when the image of the phone operator, almost always a woman, sitting amidst connecting wires, technological communication literally being mediated through her body, became extremely popular.[40] Duchamp's obsession with domestic space was, in part, an understanding that the boundaries between bodies and machines were no longer clearly delineated, and that women were perhaps not only representations of this phenomenon, but were practicing, in everyday life, different versions of machine-body relations.

Duchamp's works understood that these relations presented a model of desire structured around the notion of continually free-floating connections between part-objects. He certainly made clear the necessity of hooking up one's body to the machine or art work at hand. This hooking-up is intimately linked to the idea of absorption, for both imply a perpetual shifting of boundaries. It is within this fluid space of absorption and hooking-up that modernism can perhaps begin to rethink its narratives of the relations between bodies and machines, housework and ready-mades.

This text has been deeply influenced by the work and teachings of Mark Seltzer, to whom it is dedi-
cated in appreciation. It has also been criticized, in the very best sense of the word, by Susan Choi,
Moyra Davey, Hal Foster, and Frazer Ward. All this being said, the text's flaws remain my own.

NOTES

1. See primarily the work of Georg Luckás, *History and Class Consciousness*, trans. Rodney Livingstone. (Cambridge: MIT Press, 1971); Wolfgang Schivelbusch, *The Railway Journey, The Industrialization of Time and Space in the 19th Century* (Berkeley: University of California Press, 1986); and Stephen Kern, *The Culture of Space and Time 1880–1918* (Cambridge: Havard Unversity Press, 1983).

2. See Siegfried Giedion, *Mechanization Takes Command* (New York: W.W. Norton and Co., 1969) and Witold Rybczynski, *Home, A Short History of an Idea* (New York: Penguin Books, 1986). It must be noted here that domestic science has a long tradition in America starting in 1841 with Catherine Beecher's *Treatise on Domestic Economy*. She was the first to propose the notion of the ideal kitchen, and situated women's housework within a particularly moral framework, i.e., the good home produces the good citizen. This essay will focus solely on the "second wave" of domestic science and its relation to scientific management. It is interesting to note that the two waves are related, particularly in their ambivalent relationship to the radical feminist movements which coincided with them.

3. Henry Dreyfuss, *Designing for the People* (New York: Simon and Schuster, 1955), 76, cited in Ellen Lupton and J. Abbott Miller's *The Bathroom, The Kitchen and The Aesthetics of Waste: A Process of Elimination* (New York, Princeton Architectural Press, 1992).

4. Mark Seltzer, *Bodies and Machines* (New York: Routledge, 1992), 21.

5. Thierry deDuve "Given the Richard Mutt Case" in Thierry deDuve, ed. *The Definitively Unfinished Marcel Duchamp* (Cambridge, MA: MIT Press, 1991).

6. Emile Durkheim, *The Elementary Forms of Religious Life*, trans. Joseph Ward Swain (New York: The Free Press, 1965), 79 and 223.

7. Ibid., 217.

8. *Mana* is not a term that has traditionally held any critical valence in theoretical work. I use it here in an attempt to think about the odd power and resonance of the ready-made. In this regard, *mana* is a term that is offered to help us think about the plethora of people's relations to objects, not to see them solely in relation to commodity fetishism. In the case of the ready-made, mana allows us to register the clean/unclean charge not only of *Fountain* but many other ready-mades.

9. In 1950 the *Fountain* was exhibited and viewed for the first time at the "Challenge and Defy" exhibit in New York. Using a replica of the *Fountain* (the original had been mysteriously lost) Duchamp hung it right side up on the wall at a level where "little boys could use it." In 1953 this replica was installed upside down from a doorway with mistletoe hanging from it. For the most part, however, the *Fountain* primarily came to be known through the famous Alfred Steiglitz photograph. The best strictly chronological history of the reception of the *Fountain* is William Camfield, *Marcel Duchamp: Fountain* (Houston: Houston University Press, 1989). For an account of how Duchamp became "Duchampian" in the 1960s, and of importance the non-chronological in the history of the avant garde see Hal Foster, "What's Neo about the Neo-Avant-Garde?" *October 70* (Fall 1994).

10. Pierre Cabanne, *Dialogues with Marcel Duchamp*, trans. Ron Padgett (New York: Viking Press), 54–55.

11. Lawrence Wright, *Clean and Decent, The History of the Bath and Loo* (London: Routledge, 1980), 138.

12. Ibid., 144.

13. Ellen Lupton and J. Abott Miller, "Hygiene, Cuisine, and the Product World of Early 20th Century America," *Incorporations* (New York: Zone, 1992), 499.

14. Camfield, *Marcel Duchamp: Fountain*, 39.

15. Craig Adcock, "Duchamp's Eroticism: A Mathematical Analysis," in *Marcel Duchamp Artist of the Century,* eds. Rudolf Kuenzli and Francis M. Naumann (Cambridge: MIT Press, 1989), 151.

16. "Bathrooms and Civilization" *House and Garden* Vol. XXX No. 2 (February 1917): 90, cited in Ellen Lupton and J. Abbott Miller, *The Bathroom, The Kitchen and The Aesthetics of Waste: A Process of Elimination* (New York: Princeton Architectural Press, 1992).

17. Mary Douglas, *Purity and Danger* (London: Ark Paperbacks, 1985), 36.

18. Ibid., 35.

19. Ronald S. Barlow, *The Vanishing American Outhouse* (El Cajon: Windmill Publishing Company, 1989).

20. This "phenomenon" is repeatedly mentioned in the literature. According to William Camfield it was first noticed by Ulf Linde whom he quotes as follows in *Marcel Duchamp: Fountain*, "if anyone tried to use it in the normal way, the 'product' would run out the hole which faces the spectator, and the latter would have to suffer the experience of a 'mirrorical return.'" 106.

21. See Andrew McClary, "Germs are Everywhere: The Germ Threat as Seen in Magazine Articles 1880–1920," *Journal of American Culture* 3 (Spring 1980).

22. For more on the status of public and private with regard to museums and aesthetic experience, see Frazer Ward's *Performance, Publicity, Pathology: Vito Acconci and Chris Burden* (Ph.D. dissertation, Cornell University).

23. Rosalind Krauss, "Bachelors," *October* 52 (Spring 1990): 54.

24. Gilles Deleuze and Felix Guattari, *Anti-Oedipus Capitalism and Schizophrenia*, trans. Robert Hurley, Mark Seem and Helen R. Lane, (Minneapolis: University of Minnesota Press, 1989), 5–6.

25. Christine Fredrick, *The New Housekeeping, Efficiency Studies in Home Management* (New York: Doubleday, Page and Co., 1913); and Frederick Winslow Taylor, *The Principles of Scientific Management* (New York: W.W. Norton and Co., 1967).

26. Seltzer, *Bodies and Machines*, 159.

27. See Ruth Schwartz Cowan, *More Work for Mother: The Ironies of Household Technology from the Open Hearth to the Microwave* (New York: Basic Books, 1983).

28. Ruth Schwartz Cowan, "The 'Industrial Revolution' in the Home: Household Technology and Social Change in the Twentieth Century," *Technology and Culture* 17 (January 1976): 13.

29. Peter Bürger's *Theory of the AvantGarde* has done much to shape the reception of this "neo-avant garde." Many art historians, following Bürger's dismissal of the neo-avant garde as mere empty morphological repetition of the avant garde's originally critical practices, have shunned the first wave of Duchamp reception in America (i.e. Jasper Johns, Robert Rauschenberg). They have focused instead on the productivist paradigm of the ready-made as understood by Minimalism, Conceptual art, and Institutional critique. For

instance, Benjamin Buchloh argues that the ready-made "negated not only figurative representation, authenticity, and authorship, while introducing repetition and the series (i.e., the law of industrial production) to replace the studio aesthetic of the hand-crafted original." Buchloh sees the history of the ready-made as being almost exclusively bound up with the modernist ethos of production. (He cites Pop art as an example of the ready-made's relation to consumption, but he emphasizes Pop's serial mode of production.) For the argument about the ready-made's relation to nominalism see Rosalind Krauss, "Notes on the Index," in *The Originality of the Avant Garde and Other Modernist Myths*, (Cambridge, MA: MIT Press, 1988) and Thierry deDuve, *Pictorial Nominalism*, (Minneapolis: University of Minnesota Press, 1991). For a discussion of the ready-made's relation to the problematics of fetishism see Hal Foster, "The Future of an Illusion, or the Contemporary Artist as Cargo-Cultist," in *Endgame* (Cambridge, MA.: MIT Press, 1987) and Buchloh's "Conceptual Art 1962–1969: From the Aesthetic of Administration to the Critique of Institutions," *October* 55 (Winter 1990).

30. *Essays on Assemblage*, ed. John Elderfield (New York: The Museum of Modern Art, 1992), 36.

31. *Art in Theory 1900–1990 An Anthology of Changing Ideas*, ed. Charles Harrison and Paul Wood (Oxford: Blackwell, 1993), 248.

32. Seltzer, *Bodies and Machines*, 115.

33. Marcel Duchamp, "The Great Trouble with Art in this Country," in *The Writings of Marcel Duchamp*, ed. Michel Sanouillet and Elmer Peterson (New York: De Capo Press, 1973), 124.

34. Gilles Deleuze and Felix Guattari, *A Thousand Plateaus*, trans. Brian Massumi (Minneapolis: University of Minnesota Press, 1987), 237.

35. Ibid., 238.

36. For an account of women as cyborgs in the present see Donna J. Haraway, *Simians, Cyborgs, and Women, The Reinvention of Nature* (New York: Routledge, 1991), especially "A Cyborg Manifesto," therein.

37. Lawrence Steefel, *Duchamp's "Glass" in the Development of his Art* (New York: Garland Publishing, Inc., 1977), 107.

38. Deleuze and Guatarri, *A Thousand Plateaus*, 90.

39. See Martha Banta, *Imaging American Women* (New York: Columbia University Press, 1987) especially "Scaling up to War," therein.

40. See the exhibition catalog Ellen Lupton, *Mechanical Brides: Women and Machines from Home to Office* (New York: Princeton Architectural Press, 1993). Both the catalog and the exhibition contained many documentary photographs of women as telephone operators. The image of the woman as phone mediator emerges at the turn of the century and continues into the present.

Ground Level

Xavier Costa

What does a building rest upon? A leveled ground, which is any ground razed to match the horizontal surface of water. The instrument to measure and to create a leveled ground is the plumb line, a piece of lead attached to a line and suspended. It refers both to the instrument that guides upright construction and to a sounding device used by anglers. In other terms relative to plumbing, the reference to water sounding and angling recurs.[1] The affinity between plumb lines and water is observable in the act of leveling—as in "plumb and level," which in architecture denotes something rightly set, properly built. Indeed, the term level derives from *libra*, a scale or balance. Something level is right and justly made by reference to a reflecting surface of still water. Only the surface of water is level, as only a suspended weight is always plumb. Uprightness, verticality, must be measured and guided by a plumb line; the concept and the instrument are inseparable.

Perpendicularity thus means "in accordance to the suspension of the plumb line and the level horizontality of still water." Plumb and level require each other's presence to define verticality, weight and perpendicularity. The plumb line is suspended hovering over a virtual water surface, which in turn seems to await the plunge of a plummet. The basic geometrical concepts of horizontal plane and vertical line are thus incarnate in the material qualities of weight and suspension, and of water stillness and bal-

ance. A still water plane reflects images of what is suspended over its surface. The problem of reflection and image is exposed in the mythological figure of Narcissus, whose story and iconography stand for the reflexive construction of identity. In Caravaggio's depiction, the upright subject of Narcissus depends on his "foundation," which is made of reflected and desired images—in Gaston Bachelard's words, "I am what I desire." [2]

FIG. 1 Caravaggio (attrib.) *Narcissus*, Rome, 1600

CHOROBATIC INSTRUMENTS

Although Vitruvius mentions the need for walls and foundations to be plumb and level, he only describes leveling methods and tools in the eighth of his *Ten Books on Architecture*, dealing with water supply to country houses and cities. Vitruvius describes three leveling instruments: *dioptrae, librae aquariae* (water scales), and the *chorobate*.[3] The first refers to a group of instruments for visual mensuration, such as astrolabes or theodolites. In Claude Perrault's seventeenth-century French translation of the *Ten Books*, the water scale is illustrated as being a T-square piece suspended from its upper middle part, so acting as a plumb line and a balance at the same time [Fig. 2]. The source for the illustration was an instrument still used by French plumbers in Perrault's time.

Yet the builder's instrument to measure and know perpendicularity is the *chorobate*, an eloquent version of the plumb line [Fig. 3]. Vitruvius describes a *chorobate* as a twenty-foot-long plank supported by two short legs, fastened by cross pieces. Several plummets hang from the plank to coincide with marked lines when in level position. In addition, a channel is cut on top of the plank that is to be filled with water so as to confirm the proper positioning if "blowing winds" happen to disturb the plumb lines. The Greek term *chorobate* literally translates as "treading over regions," thus describing plumb-and-level verticality as disengaged from regions or *klimata* —the term for regions as sources of body-influencing emanations. Local influence is manifest in inclination. Inclination predisposes, shapes

FIGS. 2 &3 Chorobate and water scale, from Claude Perrault, *Abrégé des dix livres d'architecture de Vitruve*, 1674

prejudice and foretaste among those exposed to a certain climate. The greater the inclination, the stronger the influence of a place—thus a vertical, upright subject denotes autonomy from climatic forces. Able to tread over different localities, chorobates procure vertical guidance.[4] Chorobatic architecture levels its bed, eliminates local accidents and incorporates the illusion of a water surface, a water flood. Violence is made to the climatic site, its inclination being resisted in a trans-regional act of leveling. Yet this is not an abstract geometric procedure; it rather implies that the building rests upon a plane equivalent to that of water and of scales.

WATER SCRUTINIZED

In his *Reflections on the Imitation of Greek Works in Painting and Sculpture* (1755), Johann Joachim Winckelmann articulates a theory of art revolving around the concepts of *outline, contour* and *drapery*, terms that incorporate a visuality based on watery metaphors—understanding classical sculpture is compared to scrutinizing a surface of water, in which interior meaning is hidden yet not completely invisible. The faint outline of John Flaxman's engravings or the subtle rippling of drapery in classical sculpture are the beginnings of a full form, the rest of which remains concealed under the visible surface. Surface treatment thus attracts the viewer's attention and directs vision to deeper yet less visible realms. Winckelmann compares this phenomenon to looking onto the surface of water.[5]

Besides the well-known comparison of the classical Laocoon's noble soul to a calm sea beneath an agitated surface, Winckelmann refers to other, more elaborate comparisons between modeling sculpture and sounding a body of water. When discussing his *Arbeitmethoden* ("working methods"), he recommends the French Academy in Rome's method of copying a model. Such translation may be reduced to a problem of "finding" the hidden figure, as the following passage from *Reflections* describes:

> ... the artist attaches, above the statue that he wishes to copy, a rectangular frame of corresponding dimensions from which he suspends plumb lines at equal intervals. These lines indicate the outlines of the figure more clearly than was possible with the former method of drawing lines on a surface where every point is outermost. The plumb lines also give the artist a more exact measurement of some of the larger prominences and depressions as indicated by the distance of the plumb lines from the surface, and the artist can thus proceed somewhat more confidently.[6]

The procedure was to be repeated for several contours or intersecting planes, thus seizing the figure's volume. The sculptor would then transfer the plumb line's depth into the block of marble, "sounding" its interior to find the concealed figure—"for the copying of antiquities, which one must treat with great care, the plumb lines still have their value since no easier or more reliable way has been discovered." This method, however, involves a visual distortion not unlike the very phenomenon of refraction in water. [7]

The plumb line method of surveying or recording an existing figure had been applied to architectural measured drawings throughout the sixteenth and seventeenth centuries. A common graphic device to incorporate measurements in a drawn section or elevation consisted in adding plumb lines next to each architectural element to be measured along a vertical line. This technique recurs in the plates of major treatises, and it is used to measure the contour of architectural elements against the vertical line of the plummet. In the works of some authors such as Andrea Palladio, this graphic plumb line does not hang from the elements it serves to measure, an indication that the complex network of plumb lines is supported by a separate frame alien to the architecture being surveyed [Fig. 4].[8]

The recurring metaphor for Winckelmann is that the sculptor is uncovering a submerged figure, which is progressively revealed either by sounding devices or by gradually removing it from water, as in his interpre-

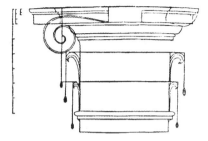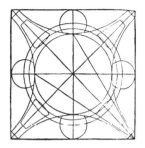

FIGS. 4 & 5 Illustration from Andrea Palladio, *I quattro libri d'architettura*, 1570

tation of Michelangelo's working method. The sculptor would lay the model in a container proportioned to its size. Gradations were marked on the container's sides and these lines were then transferred to the sculptor's block in a different scale. Water was poured into the container and then gradually removed so as to reveal a succession of contours that could be transferred to the block and thus progressively model the three-dimensional figure. The very notion of contour, so carefully studied in Winckelmann's theory of art, implies a surface able to define an otherwise inapprehensible figure.[9]

In these examples, which deal primarily with sculpting technique, the very activity of sculpting is the transfer of a given model into the block of marble, as a copying routine. The model is of interest only in terms of the transferal technique being applied to it—for instance, the model as a submerged and "invisible" form that needs to be gradually revealed or approximated, whether this is literally effected as in Michelangelo's case, or virtually implied as in the technique of the plumb lines "sounding" the model.

Winckelmann's study of meaning in art is inseparable from his attentive scrutiny of the surface through water metaphors, in which a surface reveals something by partially concealing it, by not letting it come forth in full terms. This approach mirrored contemporary thought: in the late eighteenth century, the Platonic contempt for reflections as deceitful appearances was reelaborated into a theory of character and physiognomics, which proposed a more complex relationship between what is visible and what remains concealed beneath (yet manifested by) surface traits—themselves a reflection.

FIG. 6 Antoni Gaudí, photograph of the Güell chapel model (exterior view, draped version)

GAUDÍ'S MODEL

A variation of Winckelmann's *Arbeitmethod* was applied to architectural design by Antoni Gaudí in his project for the Colonia Güell chapel. He worked on the project from 1898 for ten years before construction work began, yet only the crypt was ever completed. Gaudí devised a singular method to build an inverted model by suspending it from a false ceiling that acted as ground level. The "inversion" of the model also applied to the study of tectonic stresses: as the masonry chapel would have all of its components working in compression, so the model could all be in tension, and built by using lines and weights made with little bags filled with lead.[10] These weights allowed him to measure the stress at each point. The dense web of cables and weights was covered with a piece of fabric to indicate the enclosure.

Gaudí's model follows Winckelmann's sculptural method, in which the process of architectural modeling is a "sounding" of a submerged world. The diffuse and ghostly corporeality of the model alludes to a figuration that has been only vaguely grasped, an invisible body marking its contours and its weight on a net. Whereas the chapel is a masonry building that celebrates the materiality of its components, the model is bordering on immateriality. According to the sculptor's method, Gaudí's suspended model is not so much a literal (though inverted) representation of the building itself, as it is a sounding apparatus that allows for "finding" the searched figure. In the Colonia Güell project, the place of contact between project and building is the surface or screen of a ground level. The mirroring effect is the agent that permits the transfer from image-project into object-building—which is thus organized by an effect of "screen-transfer."

VERTIGO

To build is to build up, following the direction of the plumb line, whereas downward movement is blind fall. To fall, *cadere*, is to approach

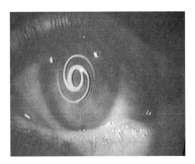 

FIG. 7 (left) "Eye spiral," and FIG. 8 (right) "James Stewart hanging by his arms looking down," film stills from Alfred Hitchcock's *Vertigo* (1959)

what is accidental, coincidental, by chance. If blind fall turns firm ground into an abyss, the arrested fall of the plumb suspends disorder and permits upright construction.

Blind fall in suspension, the position of the plumb line, may organize space, as in Alfred Hitchcock's film, *Vertigo,* a cinematic investigation of suspended experience of space and vision. *Vertigo* opens on a full-screen image of a woman's eye. From her retina, the geometrical figure of a pendulum's luminous trace appears, as if a plumb line had been hovering over the screen surface—so that the spectator's view is virtually directed *downward* in relation to the screen, where the woman's eye mirrors one's own. Suffering from acrophobia, each time the film's hero looks down, an abyss opens under his feet and paralyzes him. Looking downward is thus equated to losing control, to losing one's stand. Looking downward, one is captivated and paralyzed by the space one occupies. This may be termed as an experience of *distich* space, a space in which the observer is not the active generator of a perspective order, but rather a stain in a space defined by light.[II] The film relates this plunging gaze of its hero with the "doubling" of his object of desire—the woman who literally plunges into the abyss, and which he recovers by painfully reconstructing her image. In other terms, *Vertigo* is the story of a creation (by making an image, a reflection, a double) directed by the downward-looking position of the plumb line.

Writing on Hitchcock's late-1950s films in *Cahiers du Cinéma*, Eric Rohmer noted a common trait among them—their heroes tend to appear as victims of a paralysis relative to their positioning in a certain space. Hitchcock's heroes yield, become captive to the influence of a place, and

FIG. 9 "Falling man," film still from
Alfred Hitchcock's *Vertigo* (1959)

from this captivation the plot is built up. In *Vertigo*, this paralysis is translated as arrested fall, as a phenomenon along the vertical axis that also organizes the spaces in which the observer-hero is.[12] *Vertigo*'s hero may be
compared to the decisive gesture in the architecture of Mies van der Rohe
of moving from a common window-in-wall architecture (as in the alcove-
window of his early Riehl house, where the window design includes a
bench, a static point of view) to a glass-wall or screen architecture (as, say,
in the Stuttgart Glass Room or in the Barcelona German Pavilion). If in the
first example the observer-user is a generator of perspectival order due to
the positioning of the window, in the second example, the observer
becomes a stain on a surface of light, dazzled and captivated by the reflecting effect that organizes that space.

The plumb line comes out as a device that permits sounding into
an invisible (or barely visible, yet refractive) domain where that which is
to be translated or transported resides. In this sense, the plumb line is
in effect an angler's device that permits the capturing and "pulling-out" of
an architectural project which is formed from the position of a suspended,
downward-looking observer, to become visible only through a labor of
transferal or translation from one medium to another. The plumb line thus
embodies this condition and refers to a virtual "ground level" that separates
two domains (the image's and the object's) only related by the mirroring
effect of the screen. As in the figure of Narcissus, and also as in *Vertigo*,
this is a position of yielding to the place, of paralysis rather than of perspectival control. If the window stands for the architectural element that permits controlled, perspectival definition of space by the observer, then the
reflecting screen implies captivation by space, as in suspension, in an
arrested blind fall.

NOTES

1. Philibert Delorme, for instance, provides an illustration of the mason's tools that includes a plumb line and two plumb-rules, in all of which the plummet is modeled as an urn. *Premier tome de l'architecture* (Paris, 1567) Francesco Colonna's *Hypnerotomachia Poliphili* (Venice, 1499) includes in an illustration of hieroglyphs two plumb lines that are meant to signify construction; and in Luca Pacioli's *De divina proportione* (Venice, 1509), some illustrations, attributed to Leonardo, represent geometric volumes suspended from lines. Sebastiano Serlio also included two plummets in the frontispiece of his sixth book, published together with the other five as *Tutte l'opere d'architettura* (Venice, 1584).

2. Gaston Bachelard, *L'eau et les rêves. Essai sur l'imagination de la matière* (Paris: José Corti, 1942), 34. "Devant les eaux, Narcisse a la révélation de son identité et de sa dualité" (Facing water, Narcissus has the revelation of his identity and his duality).

3. Vitruvius, *On Architecture*, trans. and ed. Frank Granger, vol. 2, (Cambridge, MA: Harvard University Press, 1931) bk. 8, ch. 5, pp. 178–181. After dedicating the chapter entitled "On the Method of Leveling" to instruments, Vitruvius continues to consider the construction of aqueducts, leaden and earthen.

4. "Klima" and "inclination" share a common root. This relationship is a subject of extensive study throughout the late seventeenth and eighteenth centuries. For an overview of this modern debate, see G.-L. Fink, "Von Winckelmann bis Herder: Die deutsche Klimatheorie in europäischer perspective" in *Johann Gottfried Herder 1744–1803*, ed. G. Sauder (Hamburg: Meiner, 1987), 157–175.

5. Johann Joachim Winckelmann, *Reflections on the Imitation of Greek Works in Painting and Sculpture* (La Salle, Ill.: Open Court, 1987). It was published in 1755 as *Gedanken uber die Nachahmung der griechischen Werke in der Malerei und Bildhauerkunst.*

6. Ibid., 49. Winckelmann means "floats up to and extends just under the plane with which it becomes imperceptibly bound, it does not come forth." See also Barbara M. Stafford, "Beauty of the Invisible: Winckelmann and the Aesthetics of Imperceptibility," *Zeitschrift für Kunstgeschichte* 43 (1980): 65–78; and Martin Kemp, "Some Reflections on Watery Metaphors in Winckelmann, David and Ingres," *Burlington Magazine* 110 (1968); also, Barbara M. Stafford, "Les idées 'innées': la conception winckelmannienne de la création," in *Winckelmann: la naissance de l'histoire de l'art à l'époque des lumières: Actes du cycle de conférences prononcées à l'Auditorium du Louvre du 11 décembre 1989 au 12 février 1990*, ed. E. Pommier (Paris, 1991).

7. ". . . with this method the true proportions of the figures are hard to ascertain. The artists can attempt to show them by means of horizontals placed across the plumb lines. But the light reflected from the figures through these squares strikes the eye at an angle that increases when the squares are seen from a higher or lower point of view, and thus makes them appear larger." Winckelmann, *Reflections*, 49.

8. Andrea Palladio, *I quattro libri dell'architettura* (Venice, 1570) bk. 1, p. 36. This graphic device is repeatedly used throughout the illustrations. Similar examples may be found in Cosimo Bartoli's illustrations to Leon Battista Alberti's architectural treatise.

9. See Winckelmann, *Reflections*, 49–55.

10. For Gaudí's project, see José Luís Sert, *La cripta de la colonia Güell* (Barcelona: Polígrafa, n.d.); also Isidre Puig Boada, *L'església de la colonia Güell* (Barcelona: Lumen, 1976). Although he only briefly mentions Gaudí's model, Robin Evans studies its implications in Robin Evans, "Mies van der Rohe's Paradoxical Symmetries," *AA Files* 19 (1990): 56–68.

While most studies and monographs on Gaudí mention and illustrate the model, none of them dwells in detail on its implications.

11. On blind fall, see Jacques Derrida, "My Chances/Mes Chances: A Rendezvous with some Epicurean Stereophonies," *Talking Chances*, ed. J.H. Smith and W. Kerrigan (Baltimore: Johns Hopkins, 1984). On *distich* space, see Rosalind Krauss, *The Optical Unconscious* (Cambridge, MA: MIT Press, 1993), 87.

12. See Eric Rohmer, "L'Hélice et l'Idée," *Cahiers du Cinéma* 93 (1959).

The City in Pieces*

Victor Burgin

IN HER BOOK ABOUT WALTER BENJAMIN'S PARIS ARCADES PROJECT, Susan Buck-Morss tells the story of how, in 1924, Benjamin traveled to Italy "in order to bring to paper his [thesis] *The Origin of German Tragic Drama*, with which he hoped to secure an academic position at the University of Frankfurt."[1] This was the year of Lenin's death, and the year of the first surrealist manifesto. An eventful year in politics and art, it was no less eventful for Benjamin's personal life. In Italy he met, and fell in love with, Asja Lacis, "a Bolshevik from Latvia, active in post-revolutionary Soviet culture as an actress and director, and a member of the Communist Party since the Duma revolution."[2] In 1928, having failed to win the approval of the university, *The Origin of German Tragic Drama* was nevertheless published.[3] Benjamin dedicated it to his wife, from whom he separated that same year. In this same year Benjamin also published *One Way Street*,[4] a montage of textual fragments in which he juxtaposes observations of everyday life with descriptions of his dreams. One of the longer fragments is titled: "Teaching Aid—Principles of the Weighty Tome, or, How to Write Fat Books."[5] *One Way Street* is not a Weighty Tome. No academic monument, it has more the appearance of a city plan: avenues of open space cross its pages, between compact and irregular blocks of text. Benjamin's dedication to *One Way Street* reads:

*This essay first appeared in Victor Burgin, *In/Different Spaces: Place and Memory in Visual Culture*, University of California Press, 1996.

This street is named
Asja Lacis Street
after she who
like an engineer
cut it through the author

I

When, in 1924, Benjamin first told Lacis about the academic the-sis he was working on, her horrified response was, "Why bury oneself with dead literature?"[6] In Benjamin's subsequent production, funerary con-struction gives way to a lighter and more open textual architecture. When, in 1925, he and Lacis wrote an essay together about the city of Naples, the central image (which Susan Buck-Morss tells us was "suggested by Lacis") is that of "porosity." Naples rises where sea meets cliff. Lacis and Ben-jamin wrote:

> At the base of the cliff itself, where it touches the shore, caves have been hewn. . . . As porous as this stone is the architecture. Building and action interpenetrate in the courtyards, arcades, and stair-ways. In everything they preserve the scope to become a theater of new, unforeseen, constel-lations. The stamp of the definitive is avoided. No situation appears intended forever, no figure asserts its "thus and not otherwise." This is how architecture, the most binding part of the communal rhythm, comes into being here.[7]

Benjamin and Lacis find that: "Buildings are used as a popular stage. The are all divided into innumerable, simultaneously animated the-aters. Balcony, courtyard, window, gateway, staircase, roof are at the same time stage and boxes."[8] Or, again: "Housekeeping utensils hang from bal-conies like potted plants. . . . Just as the living room reappears on the street, with chairs, hearth and altar, so . . . the street migrates into the liv-ing room."[9] The permeability that Lacis and Benjamin saw in the streets of Naples is also to be found in *One Way Street*, a street that will eventually lead to the *Passagen-Werk*. We will remember that Benjamin named his street *Asja Lacis Street*, "after she who, like an engineer, cut it through the author." Just as Benjamin recounts his dreams in *One Way Street*, so his laconic dedication to the book itself was a dream image: the image of a book that is a city street, cut through the body of the author by his lover. Benjamin's written body is penetrated by Lacis, just as the body of what might have been *his* text on Naples became porous, translucent, permeable to *her* voice. The lapidary inscription commemorates an erotic event in which the categorical distinctions that separate body, city, and text dissolve.

The (con)fusion of representations of body and city has a history. In the third book of Vitruvius, dedicated to the design and construction of temples, the Roman architect describes how the outstretched limbs of a "well-formed man" subtend the circle and the square. The purpose of the description—the basis of a widely known drawing by Leonardo da Vinci— is to urge that buildings should display the same harmonious relation of parts to whole as Vitruvius found in the human form.[10] The body is not simply that which is to be contained by a building, the body *contains* the very generating principle of the building. In an article of 1974,[11] Françoise Choay describes how, in the work of Leon Battista Alberti and other architect-theorists of the Italian Renaissance, the Vitruvian doctrine was woven into a mythology of origins. For example, humanist authorities wrote that the first men derived their units of measure from the palms of their hands, their arms, and their feet. Or again, that Adam, driven from the Garden of Eden, protected himself from the rain by joining his hands above his head—a gesture that subsequently led him to construct the first roof. That the human body is seen as the origin not only of the building, but of the entire built environment, is apparent from the descriptions and drawings of anthropomorphized cities that appear in illustrated books during the Renaissance. Choay describes an image from a book by Francesco di Giorgio Martini as showing

> a personage whose head is adorned with a fortress which he supports with his arms. His body is inscribed in a rectangle marked *città*. His legs are spread, and his feet and elbows are figured by towers. His navel marks the enter of a circular public place, on the periphery of which is situated the principal church.[12]

Such fantasy constructions were already implied in the writing of Alberti, who had found that "the city is like a large house and the house like a small city,"[13] but that ultimately, "every edifice is a body."[14]

If, in Renaissance Italy, the city could be conceived of as a body, it was because the city had recently coalesced from a condition in which it was virtually undifferentiated from the countryside. In a book of 1974, translated in 1991 as *The Production of Space*, Henri Lefebvre observes:

> The city in Vitruvius is conspicuous by its absence/presence; though he is speaking of nothing else, he never addresses it directly. It is as though it were merely an aggregation of 'public' monuments and 'private' houses. . . . Only in the sixteenth century, after the rise of the medieval town (founded on commerce, and no longer agrarian in character), and after the establishment of 'urban systems' in Italy, Flanders, England, France, Spanish America, and elsewhere, did the town emerge as a unified entity—and as a *subject*.[15]

The text in which Alberti inaugurates the concept of the corporeal city[16] postdates, by about fifteen years, his treatise on painting, *De Pictura*, which contains the first written description of a method of drawing in linear perspective. Perspective provided, quite literally, the "common ground" on which the identification of architectural space with corporeal space could "take place." In the Renaissance, the inaugural act in constructing a painting was to lay out the horizontal plane that united the illusory space of the image with the real space of the viewer. This is the familiar grid of receding squares, accelerating toward a vanishing point, which in many paintings rises to the finished surface thinly disguised as a tiled floor. The side of each square in the underlying perspective grid represented a common unit of measurement, the *braccio*, equivalent to one-third of the height of a standing man. By this means, the correct stature of a depicted figure could be determined relative to any point in the illusory depth of the represented space. The size of all other objects—not least the built environment—could then be determined by reference to this common corporeal measure. Man, here, is literally "the measure of all things." For all that the erect male body may have been at the origin of this space, however, it quickly ceded its place to its disembodied metonymic representative, the eye—in what Lefebvre calls "the spiriting-away or scotomization of the body."[17] As a consequence, as Luce Irigaray remarks, "Man no longer even remembers that his body is the threshold, the porch of the construction of his universe(s)."[18]

At the dawn of modernity, disembodied geometric and mathe-matical principles came to dominate all visual representational practices. The same abstract order that informed painting and architecture was brought to enhance the instrumentality of such things as navigational charts, maps, and city plans. In conformity to the exigencies of a militant and expansive mercantile capitalism, the image of the convergence of parallel lines toward a vanishing point on the horizon became the very figure of Western European global economic and political ambitions. This optical-geometric spatial regime—the panoptical-instrumental space of colonialist capitalist modernity—would govern Western European representations for the ensuing three centuries. It has been widely remarked that this representational space, inaugurated in the Renaissance, entered into crisis in the early part of the twentieth century. We have become familiar with the arguments from industrialization, urbanization, and technology: Fordism and Taylorism, factory town and Garden City, steam train and airplane, telephone and radio, all were implicated in a changed "common sense" of space. On the basis of the "artistic" evidence, also, few would disagree that the early twentieth century was a time of major change in Western representations of space, and space of representations. Exhibits presented in evidence here typically include such things as analytical cubism, the twelve-tone scale, jazz, and Bauhaus design. It is in terms of such arguments that I understand Lefebvre when he writes: "Around 1910 a certain space was shattered. It was the space of common sense, of knowledge [*savoir*], of social practice, of political power. . . the space, too, of classical perspective and geometry. . . bodied forth in Western art and philosophy, as in the form of the city and town."[19] Lefebvre also observes, however, that "'common sense' space, Euclidean space and perspectivist space did not disappear in a puff of smoke without leaving any trace in our consciousness, knowledge or educational meth-ods."[20] A certain space was shattered, but nevertheless it did not disap-pear. The "nevertheless" does not signal that disjunction between knowledge and belief to which Sigmund Freud gave the term *Verleugnung*, "disavowal." For our terminology here, we might better turn to Mao Tse-Tung: the relation between the existing instrumental space of political modernity and the emergent space of aesthetic modernism is one of "nonantagonistic contradiction."

II

Benjamin and Lacis, themselves out of place in Naples, found all things in Naples to be dis-located, as when "the living room reappears on the street." This particular image, retrospectively determined by a short history of surrealism, returns in Benjamin's long essay of 1938 about Paris at the time of Charles Baudelaire. Here, Benjamin remarks on the tendency of the *flâneur* to "turn the boulevard into an *intérieur*." He writes: "The street becomes a dwelling for the *flâneur*; he is as much at home among the façades of houses as the citizen is in his four walls. To him the shiny, enameled signs of business are at least as good a wall ornament as an oil painting is to a bourgeois in his salon."[21] This passage, in retrospect, helps to reveal a fundamental ambiguity both in Lacis and Benjamin's essay about Naples and in Benjamin's dedication to *One Way Street*. The *flâneur* who turns the street into a living room commits an act of transgression which reverses an established distinction between public and private spaces. Benjamin and Lacis, however, saw the porosity of urban life in Naples as the survival of precapitalist social forms that had not yet succumbed to the modern segregation of life into public and private zones. Again, Benjamin's terse dedication to *One Way Street* pictures a fusion of spaces in the same instant that—through the image of penetration—it asserts the individual integrity of those spaces. Like an arrested filmic lap-dissolve, which refuses to decide either origin or destination, the image forms through condensation. It also forms through displacement to, or from, the image of Baron George-Eugene Haussmann's infamous *percements* that ripped through working-class districts of Paris like the cannon fire they were designed to facilitate.[22] An ambivalence inhabits this textual fragment: as if two different spaces—one sealed, the other permeable—compete to occupy the same moment in time. In both the essay on Naples and the dedication to *One Way Street*, the metaphor of porosity competes with a dialectic of interior and exterior which belongs to a different register. This ambivalence marks the representational space of modernism in general.

One of the most visible images of the modern dialectic of interior and exterior is the wall of steel and glass, of which the glass and iron structures of the Paris arcades are a prototype. We may take the specific example of the administrative office, for a model factory complex, built by Walter Gropius and Adolf Meyer for the Werkbund exhibition in Cologne in 1914. As Richard Sennett has described it:

In this building you are simultaneously inside and outside. . . . From the outside you can see people moving up and down between floors. . . . You can see through walls, your eyes move inside to outside, outside to inside. The confines of the interior have lost their meaning. . . . Gropius and Meyer have used glass in and around the doors so that you can literally look through the building to people entering from the other side of a cubist portrait.[23]

It is no doubt this sort of "image of the modern"[24] that Benjamin has in mind when he celebrates "the twentieth century, with its porosity, transparency, light and free air."[25] The modernist architect to whom he pays explicit homage, however, is not Gropius but Le Corbusier, the designer of the "radiant city."[26] Le Corbusier's project of 1930 for the Ville Radieuse is the source of the now cliché perspectivist vision of urban modernity as made up of evenly spaced towers rising from a limitless expanse of park land. The project evolved from Le Corbusier's plan for the Ville Contemporaine, to contain three million people, which was exhibited in Paris in 1922. Kenneth Frampton describes the Ville Contemporaine as "an elite capitalist city of administration and control with garden cities for the workers being sited, along with industry, beyond the 'security zone' of the green belt encompassing the city."[27] We may remember, then, that as much as modernity is the locus of transparency in architecture, it is also at the origin of the social isolation in and between high-rise apartment houses, the death of the street as a site of social interaction, and the practice of "zoning," which establishes absolute lines of demarcation between work and residential areas, and between cultural and commercial activities. The transparent wall, used by such socialist modernists as Gropius to unite interior with exterior, was destined to become the very index of capitalist corporate exclusivity.

III

Lefebvre finds both that, around 1910, "a certain space was shattered" and that "it did not disappear." The phallocentric abstract space of capitalist modernity survived to inhabit the representational space of aesthetic modernism. Indeed, it survives to the present day. It is not that one spatial formation was replaced by another. It is rather as if a superior "layer" of spatial representations itself became permeable, "porous," and allowed an inferior layer to show through. Lefebvre himself supplies the appropriate analogy. He notes that early in the genesis of a biological organism, "an indentation forms in the cellular mass. A cavity gradually takes place. . . . The cells adjacent to the cavity form a screen or membrane which serves as a boundary. . . . A closure thus comes to separate within from without, so establishing the living being as a 'distinct body.'" This "closure," however, is only ever relative: "The membranes in question remain permeable, punctured by pores and orifices. Traffic back and forth, so far from stopping, tends to increase and become more differentiated, embracing both energy exchange (alimentation, respiration, excretion) and information exchange (the sensory apparatus)." Closure, then, rather than belonging to the natural order, is a creation of the social order. Thus Lefebvre writes: "A defining characteristic of (private) property, as of the position in space of a town, nation or nation state, is a closed frontier. This limiting case aside, however, we may say that every spatial envelope implies a barrier between inside and out, but that this barrier is always relative and, in the case of membranes, always permeable."[28] The transgressional magic of the *flâneur* is to make the interior appear on the "wrong side" of its bounding wall, the wrong side of the façade. Certainly, the transformation is an illusion, but then the interior itself is an illusion—in a double sense. First, Benjamin points out that the bourgeois interior emerges into history, in the nineteenth century, as a reified fantasy:

> For the private person, living space becomes, for the first time, antithetical to the place of work. . . . The private person who squares his accounts with reality in his office demands that the interior be maintained in his illusions. . . . From this springs the phantasmagorias of the interior. For the private individual the private environment represents the universe. In it he gathers remote places and the past. His drawing room is a box in the world theater.[29]

In an essay about the domestic architecture of Adolf Loos, Beatriz Colomina writes:

> In Loos's interiors the sense of security is not achieved by simply turning one's back on the exterior and becoming immersed in a private world— "a box in the world theatre," to use Benjamin's metaphor. It is no longer

the house that is a theater box; there is a theater box inside the house, overlooking the internal social spaces, so that the inhabitants become both actors in and spectators of family life—involved in, yet detached from their own space. The classical distinctions between inside and outside, private and public, object and subject, are no longer valid.[30]

To develop Colomina's insight, I would say that it is not that these distinctions are no longer valid, but rather that they have been displaced—as in the Paris arcades, which pierce the façade only to reproduce the façade in the form of glass entrails within the body of the building.[31] Further, Lefebvre's example of the biological organism would indicate that, in any real sense, the absolute distinction between interior and exterior can never be valid. It will always belong to "reality," never to the order of the Real. Here, then, is the second sense in which the interior is an illusion. Extending the analogy of the biological organism to the social space of the built environment, Lefebvre reminds us that an apparently solid house is "permeated from every direction by streams of energy which run in and out of it by every imaginable route: water, gas, electricity, telephone lines, radio and television signals, and so on," and that similar observations apply in respect of the entire city. Thus, he writes: "As exact a picture as possible of this space would differ considerably from the one embodied in the representational space which its inhabitants have in their minds, and which for all its inaccuracy plays an integral role in social practice."[32] If the built environment is conceived of in terms of the body, then a different body is at issue here.

An Arnold Newman photograph from 1949 shows the components of a prefabricated house laid out on what appears to be the concrete runway of an airfield. Every shape in the intricate pattern of this carpet of components is equally visible. No hierarchy, formal or functional, governs the relations between the parts. Contiguity alone links wood, metal, and glass; frames, planks, and pipes. This is nothing like a house, yet nothing but a house. If the houses destined to be its neighbors had been laid out alongside, it would have been impossible to tell where one ended and the other began. At the beginning of his book of 1974, *Économie libidinale*, Jean-François Lyotard similarly lays out the surfaces of the body. In a long and violent passage, glistening with mucous and blood, he unfolds not only that which is seen, "the skin with each of its creases, lines, scars . . . the nipples, the nails, the hard transparent skin under the heel," but also the most intimate and deep interior linings of the body. Moreover, as nothing but proximity links one surface to another, we pass indiscriminately to other contiguous bodies. We pass, for example, from these lips to other lips, and to the lips of others. We pass from the palm of the hand, "creased like a yellowed sheet of paper," to the surface of an automobile steering wheel. Even further, Lyotard reminds us, we must not forget to add colors to the retina, or to add to the tongue "all the sounds of which it is capable," including "all the selective reserve of sounds which is a phonological system." All of this, and more, belongs to the libidinal body. This "body" bears no allegiance to what Lyotard terms the "political economy" of the organic. The "political body" is a hierarchically organized assembly of constituent organs—jointly ruled by mind and heart—which seeks to resist death and to reproduce itself. It is a body clearly differentiated from other bodies, and from the world of objects. It is this body under the Law which may become the site of "transgression"—illustrated, for Lyotard, by a Hans Bellmer drawing in which a fold in a girl's arm stands in place of the crease of the vulva. It is not such transgressive metaphor that is at issue but a more corrosive metonymy. Lyotard writes: "We must not begin with transgression, we must immediately go to the very end of cruelty, construct the anatomy of polymorphous perversion, unfold the immense membrane of the libidinal 'body,' which is quite the inverse of a system of parts." Lyotard sees this "membrane" as composed of the most heterogeneous items: human bone and writing paper, steel and glass, syntax and the skin on the inside of the thigh. In the libidinal economy, writes Lyotard: "All of these zones are butted end to end . . . on a Moebius strip . . . a moebian skin [an] interminable band of variable geometry (a concavity is necessarily a convexity at the next turn) [with but] a single face, and therefore neither exterior nor interior."[33]

Gropius and Meyer's design for the 1914 Werkbund Exhibition may render interior and exterior mutually visible, but it does not thereby abolish the hierarchical distinction between the two: it is, after all, an administration building. The glass walls of the corporate towers that follow may be transparent, but they are no more porous than are their "glass ceilings." Such façades retain their classical function[34] of both leading the eye toward a vanishing point, or point of interest, and of marking a *boundary*. Lefebvre seems to leave the transparent wall out of account when he notes: "A façade admits certain acts to the realm of what is visible, whether they occur on the façade itself (on balconies, window ledges, etc.) or are to be seen *from* the façade (processions in the street, for example). Many other acts, by contrast, it condemns to obscenity: these occur *behind* the façade. All of which seems to suggest a 'psychoanalysis of space.'"[35] The façade of which Lefebvre speaks here is opaque. By his account, if nothing is concealed then there is no need for psychoanalytic theory. This would be to reduce psychoanalysis to a theory of repression, but modern psychoanalysis is no more *necessarily* concerned with repression that the modern façade is necessarily opaque. Lefebvre's observation about the façade is the only passage where he suggests the possibility of a psychoanalysis of space. There are nevertheless many points in Lefebvre's complex and densely argued book where his ideas invite development in terms of psychoanalytic theory. Most fundamentally, he writes that space is "first of all *my* body, and then it is my body counterpart of 'other,' its mirror-image or shadow: it is the shifting intersection between that which touches, penetrates, threatens or benefits my body on the one hand, and all other bodies on the other."[36] The full psychoanalytic implications of such a remark— most obviously, in relation to Lacan's idea of the "mirror stage"—remain to be developed. Indeed, insofar as they apply to considerations of space, they are as yet little developed within the field of psychoanalysis itself.

IV

The problematic of space is encountered from the beginning of Freud's therapeutic practice and metapsychological theory: both in real terms, as in the question of the therapeutic setting, and in metaphorical terms, as in his topographical models of mental processes. It is perhaps because of this early ubiquity that the topic of space as such came to receive little, and late, direct consideration in psychoanalysis. To my knowledge, Paul Schilder's essay of 1935, "Psycho-Analysis of Space,"[37] is the first to address the topic explicitly and exclusively. Schilder finds that "space is not an independent entity (as Kant has wrongly stated) but is in close relation to instincts, drives, emotions, and actions."[38] His remarks here anticipate an isolated work-note made by Freud in 1938: "Space may be the projection of the extension of the psychical apparatus. No other derivation is probable. Instead of Kant's *a priori* determinants of our psychical apparatus. Psyche is extended: knows nothing about it."[39] Schilder's findings in respect of psychical space emerge from his work on, in the words of the title of his book of 1935 (a book that is one of the sources of Lacan's idea of the mirror stage), "the image and appearance of the human body."[40] In "Psycho-Analysis of Space" Schilder writes:

> There is at first an undifferentiated relation between an incompletely developed body-image and the outside space. Clearer differentiations take place around the openings of the body. There is a zone of indifference between body and outside world which makes distortions of body-space and outside-space by projection and appersonization possible.[41]

"Appersonization" is the process in which "we may take parts of the bodies of others and incorporate them in our own body-image."[42] In a pathological setting, such interchange of body parts is a characteristic of the "psychoses." Amongst what Freud calls the "defense psychoses," autism and schizophrenia bear most directly on the corporeal relation to external reality. In her book of 1972 on *Autism and Childhood Psychosis*, the British psychoanalyst Frances Tustin notes: "The common psychiatric division of psychotic children [is] into those suffering from Early Infantile Autism and those suffering from childhood Schizophrenia."[43] Tustin finds this distinction "too rigid." For expository clarity however, outside of a clinical setting, it is convenient to retain the distinction. Schematically, the terms *autism* and *schizophrenia* name the opposing extremities of a continuum of modes of psychocorporeal relation to external reality. The middle range of this schematic continuum would encompass "normal" socially acceptable ways of relating to the world. At one extreme limit, autism represents a total closing down of that relation: the autistic subject may appear "dead to the world." At the opposite extreme, schizophrenia represents a total opening of the relation: to the extent that the schizophrenic body is scattered in pieces throughout its world. Both autism and schizophrenia are normal states of very early infancy, the time when there is as yet little substantive distinction between an outer world of "real" objects, and the inner world of those "objects" that are the psychical representations of sensations from, primarily, bodily organs and the mother's body. Pathological autism and schizophrenia represent a fixation at, or regression to, such early object relations. We should however remember that, as Freud remarks: "The frontier between the so-called normal states of mind and the pathological ones is to a great extent conventional, and . . .

is so fluid that each one of us probably crosses it many times in the course of a day." As Octave Mannoni succinctly puts it: "We are all more or less healed psychotics."[44]

A book of drawings by Antonin Artaud, published in France in 1986,[45] is accompanied by an essay by Jacques Derrida which is, in effect, an extended reflection upon the rarely used French word *subjectile*—a word that appears, appropriately rarely, in Artaud's writings. The 1978 edition of the *Petit Robert* dictionary defines *subjectile* as "surface serving as support (wall, panel, canvas) for a painting." This is not how the term functions for Artaud. Rather, as Derrida notes, the *subjectile* is that which lies "between the surfaces of the subject and the object."[46] It is the place where may be traced "the trajectories of the *objective*, the *subjective*, the *projectile*, of the *introjection*, the *interjection*, the *objection*, of *dejection* and *abjection*, etc."[47] Derrida describes a graphic work by Artaud in which,

> with the aid of a match, Artaud opens holes in the paper, and the traces of burning perforation are part of a work in which it is impossible to distinguish between the subject of the representation and the support of this subject, in the *layers* of the material, between that which is above and that which is below, and thus between the subject and its outside, the representation and its other.[48]

Reading this, I was reminded of a recurrent television news image: the image of a house, or apartment, whose walls have been pierced by rocket fire, or shells. For all its repetitions, the image never fails to "pierce" me. This has nothing to do with Roland Barthes's *punctum*, nor the *studium*. This is neither a private nor an ethical reaction. Something quite different is at issue. Discussing the child's anxiety at being separated from its mother, Freud notes that at the origin of the distress is the child's perception of the mother as the one who will satisfy its needs. Thus, rather than being reducible simply to object loss, "The situation . . . which [the child] regards as a 'danger' and against which it wants to be safeguarded is that of a . . . *growing tension due to need*, against which it is helpless" (italics in the original). Even more fundamentally, regardless of need, anxiety derives from "the economic disturbance caused by an accumulation of amounts of stimulation which require to be disposed of. It is this factor . . . which is the real essence of the 'danger.'"[49] In the contemporary environment of mass media, particularly television, we are all of us subject to anxiety arising from, amongst other things, exposure to pain we are helpless to alleviate. The helpless distress we may feel—comparable to infantile "transitivism"—bears witness to the congenital instability of psychocorporeal boundaries which is at the source of both empathy and jealousy, compassion and aggression. It indicates the fragility and permeability, the porosity of the layers between one embodied subject and another. In the physical encounter, the porosity is of the boundary of skin which contains the body ego, the "skin ego."[50] In the mediatic encounter, there is permeability between "layers," such that interior and exterior, here and there, are simultaneously affirmed and confused. I am thinking of the corneal and retinal layers that both receive and transmit the image; the phosphor-coated layer of glass that—in receiving the bombardment of electrons that encode the image—effectively pierces the layer, the screen that is the wall of my living room; the pierced layer of the wall *in* the image within or behind the television screen—within that building, behind that wall, where someone in their living room perhaps once watched television.

V

The Paris arcades of which Benjamin spoke, and the modernist buildings that they presaged, did not mark the emergence of a historically unprecedented space. Such examples rather represent the imperfect partial development of an image of space latent in all of us: the pre-Oedipal, maternal, space: the space, perhaps, that Benjamin and Lacis momentarily refound in Naples. In this space it is not simply that the boundaries are "porous," but that the subject itself is *soluble*. This space is the source of bliss and of terror, of the "oceanic" feeling, and of the feeling of coming apart; just as it is at the origin of feelings of being invaded, overwhelmed, suffocated. The generation of Europeans to which I belong grew up in a world of fixed borders, of glacial boundaries: frozen, it seemed for eternity, by the cold war. Now, in the time of thaw, borders everywhere are melting, sliding, submerging, reemerging. Identities—national, cultural, individual—are experiencing the exultant anxieties that accompany the threat of dissolution. Benjamin's Europe was one of strong borders, a fact that was to prove tragically fatal to Benjamin himself. Today's national borders are largely inconvenient to world capitalism—they have long been routinely ignored by transnational corporations and by a money market become a global computer network, operating at the speed of light. As weak and emergent nations struggle to maintain their faltering identities by drawing their borders more tightly around them, stronger established nations are losing the political will to effectively police their uncertain limits. The boundaries of today's Europe are increasingly porous. The recent history of Germany is an example. A space in transition, it represents the economic and political equivalent of "osmosis"—the movement of a fluid through a semipermeable membrane, from the weaker to the stronger solution. However, as "The Wall" crumbled inside Germany, osmosis at Germany's borders—fluid transmissions from the weaker to the stronger economy—revived a pathological horror of mixing, the modern history of which has been so effectively cataloged by Klaus Theweleit.[51] The rhetoric of neofascism, by no means unique to Germany, sounds familiar—but it now resounds in a different space. Rhetoric was originally an art of space—of gesture and of staging—as well as an art of speech. The space of the stage, the antique source of perspectival space, has changed.

In explaining the principle of drawing in perspective, Leonardo asked his reader to imagine he were looking through a window and tracing the outline of what he saw upon the surface of the glass. Paul Virilio describes the television screen as "an introverted window, one which no longer opens onto adjoining space."[52] Today, the perspectivist's "window on the world," and proscenium arch, remain the habitual frames of our representations—even in television. But such means of circumscribing the mise-en-scène appear out of their time; dislocated remnants from another time, a sort of nostalgia. The truth of this is nowhere better seen than in the images of computer-generated "virtual" realities with which we have recently become familiar. Their impeccably Euclidean "wire-frame" spaces invoke nothing so much as illustrations from seventeenth-century treatises on perspective, creating much the same uncannily nostalgic effect as a polystyrene bowl that has been molded to bear the impression left in wet clay by a potter's fingers. Benjamin remarked that the arrival of photography in the nineteenth century "gave the moment a posthumous shock." Much of this shock was the shock of the uncanny: the strangeness of the automaton, the android, the replicant; the shock of the unfamiliar familiarity of this new old representational space. The photograph, we are now accustomed to observe, lends itself easily to fetishism: that psychical structure that is the preferred commodity form of capitalism, the most favored psychoaesthetic currency in which modernity and "postmodernity" alike are traded. Photographs, therefore, are most amenable to "disavowal" as the mechanism by which we may defend ourselves against their more distressing (un)realities. As Octave Mannoni expresses the form of disavowal, "I know very well, but nevertheless."[53] "I know very well that this (unpleasurable) reality exists/existed, *but nevertheless* here there is only the beauty of the print."[54] Since Laura Mulvey's influential essay "Visual Pleasure and Narrative Cinema,"[55] we have also become accustomed to the idea that fetishism is a predominant psychosexual structure of cinematic representation. The television image is rarely "beautiful" in the way of a photograph, or a cinematic shot,[56] nor does its evanescent mobility allow the petrification necessary for fetishistic investment. The regressive unconscious defense mechanisms invoked by television, as it funnels suffering and excitation into our box in the world theater, as it pours all the world's broken cities into our *interior*, are different from those invoked by photography and cinema photography. They produce a different space.

For all its "thick-skinned" stupidity, television is also a fragile permeable membrane of near-global extension. Its web of instant mutable satellite links, indiscriminately crossing fixed meridians and old frontiers, has turned global space from a graph paper into a palimpsest. Virilio has remarked that both Benjamin and René Clair compared architecture to cinema, in that both address what Benjamin termed "simultaneous collective reception."[57] What Virilio finds of particular interest in this comparison is the implicit recognition of a historical transition from the representational priority of "surface" to that of "interface." Benjamin notes that Baudelaire described the inhabitant of the modern city as "a *kaleidoscope* equipped with consciousness," and that with the coming of film, "perception in the form of shocks was established as a formal principle."[58] The subsequent arrival of television—also, like architecture, a technique of "simultaneous collective reception"—has massively consolidated this principle. In his essay of 1936, "The Work of Art in the Age of Mechanical Reproduction," Benjamin writes: "Our taverns and our metropolitan streets and offices and furnished rooms, our railroad stations and our factories appeared to have us locked up hopelessly. Then came the film and burst this prison-world asunder by the dynamite of the tenth of a second, so that now, in the midst of its far-flung ruins and debris, we calmly and adventurously go traveling."[59] Today, for more anxious, less adventurous, armchair travelers, the "far-flung ruins and debris" of exploded towns are routinely projected into our living rooms through the aperture of television. Television, "the box," is today's "box in the world theater"—so often a theater of war. For Virilio, it is television that has definitely marked the end of perspectival space, the orderly concatenation of façades. He writes: "The blind alley disappears into the superimposed vision of a . . . television that never turns off, that always gives and receives . . . all surfaces and all the pieces of a tele-topological puzzle."[60] All the surfaces and all the pieces of the body form a complex puzzle we were once required to solve in order to become human. Like the elements of a building, the completed puzzle-picture holds together more or less provisionally: here, cracks may run wild under a calm façade; there, they may shatter a transparent carapace; and other structures may endure only in mute and fearful isolation. Today, the autistic response of total withdrawal, and the schizophrenic anxiety of the body in pieces, belong to our psychocorporeal forms of identification with the teletopological puzzle of the city in pieces.

NOTES

1. Susan Buck-Morss, *The Dialectics of Seeing: Walter Benjamin and the Arcades Project* (Cambridge and London: MIT Press, 1989), 8.

2. Ibid., 11.

3. Benjamin submitted his completed dissertation in 1925 and was "advised to withdraw his petition . . . rather than suffer the embarrassment of rejection." See Buck-Morss, *The Dialectics of Seeing*, 22.

4. In Walter Benjamin, *Reflections*, (New York and London: Harcourt, 1978).

5. It lists seven items of advice—advice that I suspect is still, to this present day, widely offered to graduate students. For example, the first item advises that "the whole composition must be permeated with a protracted and wordy exposition of the initial plan"; the final item urges: "A number of opponents all sharing the same argument should each be refuted individually." See "One Way Street," in Benjamin, *Reflections*, 79.

6. Asja Lacis, *Revolutionär im Beruf: Berichte über proletarisches Theater, über Meyerhold, Brecht, Benjamin und Piscator* (Munich: Regner & Bernhard, 1971) 43–44; quoted in Buck-Morss, *The Dialectics of Seeing*, 15.

7. Walter Benjamin and Asja Lacis, "Naples," in Benjamin, *Reflections*, 165–166.

8. Ibid., 167.

9. Ibid., 171. For example: "If the father of a family dies or the mother wastes away, close or distant relatives are not needed. A neighbour takes a child at her table for a shorter or longer period, and thus families interpenetrate in relationships that can resemble adoption" (172).

10. We may moreover recall that the circle and the square are the diagrams of, respectively, the *orbis terrarum* and the *castrum*—the subject territories of the Roman empire and the Roman military camp.

11. Françoise Choay, "La ville et le domaine bâti comme corps dans les textes des architectes-théoriciens de la première renaissance Italienne," *Nouvelle revue de psychanalyse* 9, (Spring, 1974).

12. Ibid., 248.

13. Ibid., 244.

14. Indeed, the Renaissance idea of the corporeal city included not only the external appearance of a body seen in Vitruvian terms of harmony of proportions, but as the idea of the body as an ensemble of mutually dependent organs; albeit, Choay remarks, no part of the city is seen as equivalent to the genitals.

15. Henri Lefebvre, *The Production of Space* (Oxford and Cambridge, MA: Basil Blackwell, 1991), 271.

16. *De Re Aedificatoria*, written about 1450 and published, after his death, in 1483.

17. Lefebvre, *The Production of Space*, 201.

18. Luce Irigaray, *Ethique de la différence sexuelle*, quoted in Margaret Whitford, *Luce Irigaray: Philosophy in the Feminine* (London and New York: Routledge, 1991), 53.

19. Lefebvre, *The Production of Space*, 25–26.

20. Ibid., 25–26.

21. Walter Benjamin, *Charles Baudelaire: A Lyric Poet in the Era of High Capitalism* (New York and London: New Left Books, 1978), 37. This "essay" is actually part of Benjamin's larger unfinished Paris arcades project. At the time of its completion, in 1938, Benjamin intended that it should form part of a longer book about Baudelaire which he planned to extract from his *Passagen-Werk*.

22. It might be objected that Benjamin would not write about Haussmann until the *Passagen-Werk*, but Benjamin himself reminds us that for historians, as for psychoanalysts, what comes before may be determined by what comes after.

23. Richard Sennett, *The Conscience of the Eye: The Design and Social Life of Cities* (New York: Knopf, 1990), 104.

24. Benjamin saw the Paris arcades as "the mold from which the image of 'the modern' is cast."

25. Walter Benjamin, vol. 5 of *Gesammelte Schriften* (Frankfurt am Main: Suhrkamp Verlag, 1972), 292; quoted in Buck-Morss, *The Dialectics of Seeing*, 303.

26. "How are we to imagine an existence oriented solely toward Boulevard Bonne-Nouvelle, in rooms by Le Corbusier and Oud?" See Benjamin, "Surrealism: The Last Snapshot of the European Intelligentsia," in Benjamin, *Reflections*, 189.

27. Kenneth Frampton, *Modern Architecture: A Critical History* (London: Thames and Hudson, 1987), 155.

28. Lefebvre, *The Production of Space*, 175–176.

29. Benjamin, *Reflections*, 154.

30. Beatriz Colomina, "Intimacy and Spectacle: The Interiors of Adolf Loos," *AA Files* 20 (1990).

31. My thanks to Peter Wollen for suggesting this metaphor.

32. Lefebvre, *The Production of Space*, 93.

33. Jean-François Lyotard, *Économie Libidinale* (Paris: Éditions de Minuit, 1974), 10–11.

34. In the perspectival "prospect," which in the Renaissance became the dominant form of organization of urban space.

35. Lefebvre, *The Production of Space*, 99.

36. Ibid., 184.

37. Paul Schilder, "Psycho-Analysis of Space," *International Journal of Psychoanalysis* 16 (1935).

38. Ibid., 295.

39. Sigmund Freud, vol. 23 of *The Standard Edition of the Complete Psychological Works of Sigmund Freud* (London: Hogarth, 1955–1974) 300.

40. Paul Schilder, *The Image and Appearance of the Human Body* (New York: International Universities Press, 1950).

41. Schilder, "Psycho-Analysis of Space," 295.

42. Schilder, *The Image and Appearance of the Human Body*, 172.

43. Frances Tustin, *Autism and Childhood Psychosis* (London: Science House, 1972), 106.

44. Octave Mannoni, "La part du jeu," *L'ARC* 69 (special issue on D.W. Winnicott—date of review unknown).

45. Paul Thévenin and Jacques Derrida, *Antonin Artaud—Dessins et portraits* (Paris: Gallimard, 1986). My thanks to Lindsay Waters for having brought this essay to my attention.

46. Ibid., 79.

47. Ibid., 63.

48. Ibid., 70.

49. Freud, "Inhibitions, Symptoms, and Anxiety" (1926), in *Standard Edition*, vol. 20, 137. (Since first giving my paper—at a conference, "The Visual Arts in a Technological Age: A Centennial Rereading of Walter Benjamin," Wayne State University, 4 April 1992—I have come across an essay by Patricia Mellencamp in which she makes precisely the same point: see her "TV Time and Catastrophe: of *Beyond the Pleasure Principle* of Television," in Patricia Mellencamp, *Logics of Television* (Bloomington and Indianapolis: University of Indiana Press, 1990).

50. See Didier Anzieu, *The Skin Ego* (New Haven: Yale University Press, 1989).

51. Klaus Theweleit, *Male Fantasies* (Minneapolis: University of Minnesota Press, 1987) vol. 1; (1989) vol. 2.

52. Paul Virilio, *Lost Dimension* (New York: Semiotext(e), 1991) 79.

53. Octave Mannoni, "Je sais bien, mais quand même," in *Clefs pour l'imaginaire ou l'autre scène* (Paris: Seuil, 1969).

54. Victor Burgin, "Photography, Phantasy, Function," in Victor Burgin, ed., *Thinking Photography* (London: Macmillan, 1982), 190–191.

55. Laura Mulvey, "Visual Pleasure and Narrative Cinema," (1975) in *Visual and Other Pleasures* (London: Macmillan, 1989).

56. I am thinking of the type in which a Sternberg frames a Dietrich.

57. Virilio, *Lost Dimension*, 69–70.

58. Benjamin, *Charles Beaudelaire*, 132.

59. Walter Benjamin, "The Work of Art in the Age of Mechanical Reproduction," *Illuminations* (London: Fontana, 1973), 238.

60. Virilio, *Lost Dimension*, 71.

<small>FIG. 1</small> Bust of Adolf Loos

The English and Americans. . . are also true virtuosos of relaxation.

Adolf Loos, "Furniture for Sitting," 1898

People with a more highly developed culture walk faster than those who are still backward. The American walks faster than the Italian.

Adolf Loos, "Footwear," 1898

The fact is, for the man of high culture, linen is uncomfortable.

Adolf Loos, "Underwear," 1898

The modern, intelligent person must have a mask for other people. This mask is the specific form of dress common to all people. Only the mentally deficient have individualized clothing.

Adolf Loos, "On Thriftiness," 1924

Adolf Loos
Ornament and Sentimentality

Harry Francis Mallgrave

It has been rightly observed that in the last several decades historical judgments of Adolf Loos have passed through different stages. The 1960s view of Loos as the avant-garde modernist (the austere Lohengrin magically appearing with swan and sword to slay the deceitful Friedrich of ornamentalism) gave way in the next decade to an appreciation of Loos as the material sensualist, the visual voluptuary basking in the whorls of his Cipolinian marbles or Persian carpets. This view, in turn, was supplanted in the 1980s by regard for Loos as a classicist, a born-again Vitruvian quite willing (like his latter-day historicist admirers) to ransack antiquity for a pleasing Doric column or two.

To these generalizations can be added what is surely the predominant historical view of the 1990s—Loos the psychoanalytical *objet trouvé*, the politically suspect and opinionated architect to be taken to Lacanian task for his witty solipsisms and postmetaphysical slippages.

Architects continue to read Loos, nevertheless. Nearly all profess to like him. A few Italian critics, judging by the volume of that country's literature devoted to him, even love him. And if these changing perspectives have something to say about the intrinsic instability of historical judgments, they at least offer us a range of options by which to evaluate his 1898 essay "Plumbers." Personally, I confess that I have always leaned toward the view of Loos as a sensualist—and not just because this view suits my own salacious appetites and Jacuzzi preferences. In our polite political age of faltering academic standards and fashionably indifferent ideologies, Loos the intellectual dandy and cultural epicure simply becomes more intriguing than before. His words emit a rare and unaffected honesty. His sarcasm brims with a self-acquired privilege and purposeful civility, neither anger nor false modesty.

But Loos the architect (and in this capacity I would argue his works have certainly been overvalued) remains a difficult persona to discern. When he speaks on plumbing, for instance, he is not speaking as an architect. The essay originated as a newspaper article, one of many that were later altered in both style and content and published in 1921 (in France) and 1932 (in Austria) under the title *Ins Leere gesprochen* (Spoken in a Void).[1]

Most of the articles were written for the occasion of the Austrian Jubilee Exhibition of 1898, a six-month fair in which the fruits of Austrian industries were put on national display. Loos's role, as he was only at the start of his architectural practice, was that of a roving correspondent, a journalist paid to review exhibits of leather goods, hats, footwear, clothing, luxury vehicles, and the like. Few exhibits touched on architecture. Loos the journalist thus preceded Loos the practicing architect. He may even have landed this position with the *Neue Frei Presse* in part because of his journalist endeavors in New York city in 1895, when he wrote occasional pieces for the German-American newspaper *New-Yorker Bannerträger*.

Loos's intention in these essays, then, was to be discerning, funny, and provocative. It was here that he developed with his pen his "peculiar power to irritate, or even better, to unsettle the public," as Aldo Rossi aptly described it.[2] And the special gifts of the critic, as we all know, are identical to those of the successful architect. In the original French production of Samuel Beckett's *Waiting for Godot*, Estragon silenced Vladimir in their ever escalating exchanges of grievous insults by summoning the French word *architecte*. In Beckett's English translation of his play, this word is simply rendered as "critic."

Loos in his essay "Plumbers" is concerned with more than simply plumbing. It is a critique of culture, specifically Habsburg culture. To be sure, the plumbing pipe and its receptacles allow the daily bath or shower with its salutary effects on the skin and one's health. But its most beneficial effect, Loos suggests, is not as much medical as psychological. Access to bathing in one's own bathroom possesses a liberating affect on one's capacity to experience life. It invests one with social license: the freedom to chop down a tree, to ride a bicycle, to scale a mountain, "to get down and dirty" as we might say today. The argument in its logic is similar to that employed by Loos a few weeks later in his article on "Ladies' Fashion"—that women's economic and social equality was intricately bound with the cultural right to wear pants (and therefore ride a bicycle or scale a mountain).[3]

As a cultural critique, then, Loos's essay on plumbing should not be considered apart from his other assaults on the feigned "backwardness" of Habsburg culture. Nor should it be considered apart from Loos's own experiences.

His penniless *Wanderjahre* in the United States between 1893 and 1896 certainly provided him with the inspiration to exalt polemically the superiority of American and Anglo-Saxon (also Greek or Western) culture, but so did other aspects of his upbringing. A Moravian by birth (a Czech), he studied architecture in the early 1890s not at the prestigious Vienna Academy of Fine Arts (a prerequisite for higher architectural practice in Habsburg Austria) but rather at the working-class Technical College in Dresden. Thus when Loos chose to relocate to Vienna after his American adventures, he did so specifically as an outsider, albeit as a citizen within a collapsing multicultural empire and later with some astute and talented friends. But he had by virtue of his schooling already surrendered his claim to monumental practice. His early commissions were largely confined to the realm of interior decoration.

This humble status and its ramifications is reflected in Loos's caustic relationships with such better anointed peers as Josef Hoffmann and Joseph Maria Olbrich, both gold-medal winners of the Vienna Academy. It has been said that Loos's animosity toward Hoffmann came about when the latter snubbed him and his request to display work at a Secession exhibition. History, or rather the historical apostates of Loosian satire, have still never forgiven Hoffmann for this breach of etiquette.

And neither did Loos, even if history would come to treat him rather well. He has been lauded for his modernity, for his dapperness, for his appreciation of materials and craftsmanship, for his classicism, and today especially for his social darts. The art of criticism, for him, even escalated into something of an obsession in 1903, when this intentionally sanctimonious architect (a.k.a. Bekettian critic) went so far as to start his own newspaper, *Das Andere: Ein Blatt zur Einführung abendländischer Kultur in Österreich* (The Other: A Paper for the Introduction of Western Culture into Austria).[4]

Prompted by his experience with the poor table manners of a seafaring countryman, Loos in typical satirical form installed here a regular column on etiquette. He promised in the future to address not only such general questions as "how we should live" but also quite specific ones, such as how feasts should be celebrated, the proper protocol for social calls, and the wording of invitations. Thus he may have been the first modern architect to aspire to become the "Miss Manners" of his day. We should laud him for such courage, even emulate him.

Returning to the essay on plumbing, however, one can discern a few aspects of this broader cultural critique. Loos's fervid exaltation of American and English cultural trends, as many critics have already noted, was exaggeration intended for rhetorical effect. Still it should not distract the reader from the more serious side of his argument. The self-sufficiency of the well-dressed English gentleman who brushes, saddles, and mounts his own horse (that is, without the assistance of servants) is in some respects an uncomplacent call to arms inspired by an awareness of social changes taking place. This plea for universal plumbing might then be interpreted as an ode to the individual's promise of freedom in a more democratic and bourgeois society of the twentieth century. It intimates a leveling of class values in the waning days of Habsburg aristocracy.

But Loos was anything but bourgeois in his haberdashery and good manners. He was decidedly antibourgeois in his rhetoric, and in this regard he possessed more of a nineteenth-century outlook than we have previously presumed. He was an elitist, to use a word of dubious connotations today. In reading his diatribes against state support of the arts, for instance, one cannot help but recall Friedrich Nietzsche's disdainful references to bourgeois "good taste," now being institutionalized (in 1873) by a bureaucracy destined to stifle the great deeds of monumental history and art.[5] The polemics of Loos also bring to mind Gottfried Semper's anguished decision in the mid-1850s to surrender his long-standing democratic views because of the restraints that state and judicial bureaucracies impose on superior individuals:

I am coming to the conviction—to be no republican. Or rather, the basic principle of my republic is different than the Swiss or any other existing type. My polity is a community of trust, which grants to him who measures up to its mark full authority in matters of work, giving him free reign in that which he best understands and surrendering to him the full responsibility of his position. Here it is the republic of majority rule, which provides the small fellow with desired security so that he—despite his worthlessness—counts just as much and works just as much as another.[6]

Loos's battle, however, was waged not as much for art as for the inauguration of a culture. And if the plumber for him was the "billeting officer" in this cultural revolution, the unsullied regiment in Loos' command was also to have its quartermaster: the tailor.

Loos carefully selected the uniform of the modern man and woman of culture. The outer jacket was an inconspicuous, fine wool frock coat: exquisitely cut, shaped, and sewn. The shoes were laced patent leather, unstylized and fitted "to the type of feet possessed by the dominant social class."[7] Socks were preferred to leg wrappings, and underwear had to be knitted rather than woven.[8] Hats were to be purchased in, not imported from, the fashionable quarters of London. (The English, he suspected, were exporting hats of lesser quality.)[9] Dickeys and pre-tied ties were forever to be banned (Olbrich and Hoffmann wore them).[10] Women could wear pants. Above all, people were to strive to be "well dressed" rather than "beautifully dressed."[11] The exterior of buildings, incidentally, should be as inconspicuous as the well-tailored dinner jacket.[12]

These tenets were to fall in line, as has been noted, with some of the contemporary analyses of the German philosopher and sociologist Georg Simmel, who incidentally was also drawn in no small way to the thought of Nietzsche.[13] Simmel regarded the inconspicuous frock coat as not only socially polite but also as a well-divined strategy that would assist the urban resident in preserving his or her anonymity and therefore intimacy, amid the psychological pressures and perils of living in the big city.[14]

But what does this strategy say about Loos's architecture? Was it equally as polite and inconspicuous in its modernity? This is only partly the case, for in the last few years we have come to look past the paradigmatic (rear!) façade of the Steiner house (the presumed essence of his

FIGS. 2 & 3 Adolf Loos, Looshaus, Michaelerplatz, Vienna, Austria. Façade, Column.

modernist sensibility) and to gaze upon the true satrapic splendor of some of his interiors. And here we find much that is conspicuous and indeed visually voluptuous: a bevy of variegated and costly materials ranging from brass, bronze, and copper to gold mosaics, colorful floor tiles, painted glass, decorative plaster, classical cornice and frieze work, patterned wall paper and curtains, mahogany wall panels, and above all—a truly Roman array of highly chromatic marble dressings.

Accoutrements were no less exotic. They included Oriental rugs, vivid shades of paint, mirrors placed for illusional effects, deep-pile shag carpets (for the bedroom), Hepplewhite chairs, classical columns, and even his early penchant for feigned rusticity.

When we now view color images of Loos's domestic fantasies (why did it take historians eighty years to become familiar with the sumptuous bath and halls of the Villa Karma?), we must admit that he becomes truly interesting, if not entirely for his architecture. Glancing at this evident glitter, we might even ask if Loos the antiornamental critic and Loos the interior architect were not two entirely different people. Did he secretly sport a tattoo?

Loos was complex but probably not inconsistent. One key to understanding this architect and advocate of universal plumbing is another article that he wrote for the occasion of the Austrian Jubilee. Entitled "The Principle of Dressing" (*Das Prinzip der Bekleidung*), it was his response to a theory put forth by his intellectual mentor Gottfried

Semper.[15] The extent of the latter's influence on Loos has seldom been appreciated and it no doubt goes back to Loos's student days in Dresden.

This is not the place to dwell on Semper's rather complex notion of the "dressing," which was instilled in him through his image of classical architecture as highly polychrome in its finishes and overtly theatrical or masked in its effects.[16] Loos, in any case, subtlety transposes Semper's argument into a new form.

The historical use of the primitive dressing as a spatial enclosure (for Semper, mats and woven walls), later utilized as a protective coating (tapestries placed over solid walls), is considered by Loos under his "law of dressing," which insists that every material employed in the dressing of architecture possesses its own language of form. Hence the architect should never confuse the material "dressed" with its "dressing"—that is, one must never paint wood the color of wood or score stucco to imitate masonry. The violation of this principle is what Loos terms "surrogate art."

Loos also pursues the Semperian notion of the dressing as a theatrical mask, that is, in its artistic or symbolic mode. Following Semper, Loos traces the motive of the dressing to its early industrial origin in weaving or in the making of a cover, leading to the interesting architectural premise (also present in Semper's theory) that the manufacture of the dressing (inherently ornamental in the knotting or interlacing of animal or vegetable fibers) preceded the structural framework later devised to support the dressing. Saying this another way—ornament, for Loos and for Semper, preceded structure.

The implications of the dressing's priority, Loos argues further, is what separates "*some* architects" from "*the* architect" (italics his). Lesser architects design walls, then look around for a covering or dressing they deem appropriate. The better architect, however, designs in the opposite manner. As Loos says:

> . . . the artist, *the architect*, first senses the effect he wishes to produce and then envisions the space he wishes to create. The effect he wishes to bring to bear on the beholder (*Beschauer*)—be it fear or horror in a prison, reverence in a church, respect for the power of the state in a government bureau, piety in a tomb, a sense of homeyness (*Gemütlichkeit*) in a dwelling, gaiety in a tavern—this effect is evoked by the material and the form (italics his).[17]

This passage should be considered in depth, because it speaks volumes about Loos's architectural theory. First and foremost is the preference Loos gives to the "effect" that the architect is seeking, over and above the actual act of space-making or design. It recalls an important distinction Loos made in a later essay, "Architecture" (1910), between art and architecture. Making a work of art, he argued, is necessarily a private affair: autonomous, distracting to the viewer, revolutionary in intention—in a word, provocative. Making a work of architecture, by contrast, is a social and purposeful event, one that is comfortable to the user and conservative in intention. But the purpose of a room, as the above passage makes clear, is not its utilitarian value (although comfortable chairs are certainly a necessity) but rather its "effect." In short, architecture is evocative; the domestic architect should strive first of all to evoke the feeling of comfort.

Another important term in this sentence is the word *Beschauer*, which I have rendered as "beholder." The German word *Beschauer* carries the meaning "to look at," "to view," "to behold," "to contemplate" something. It is to be distinguished from the German word *Zuschauer*, which refers to a "spectator" at a film, play, or sporting event. *Beschauer* implies contemplation or examination, a spiritual connection, or experiencing with a detached yet curious glance.

This distinction is important, because Loos's interiors have already been described—quite correctly I would argue—as contrived "stage sets."[18] But one should also be cautious in making such an appraisal. Loos's theatricality arises in the way he was interpreting the image of the Semperian dressing or theatrical mask. The notion of theatricality should be used in the positive sense of the Greek word *théatron*, which has the meaning "a place to view, to behold."

Loos believed the inhabitants of his domestic interiors should feel or sense the architect's desired effect through the dressings or backdrops that they visually apprehend. The sartorial effect of a room is something that should be beheld by all who enter it. And the most desirable effect for Loos's domestic interiors is that quality of "homeyness," a surprising remark for someone who has always been portrayed as an urbane, dyed-in-the-wool modernist. But this remark is surprising only because the older historical paradigms of Loos really do not fit him—at least not as well as his own haberdashery. Homeyness, that wonderful German word *Gemütlichkeit*, implies a certain sentimentality, a heartfelt pandering to the sentiments of comfort and familiarity. Loos's domestic interiors, it must now be admitted, were designed to be sentimental. He was, at heart, an ornamentalist.

Finally, Loos at the end of the cited passage mentions the means that the architect employs to evoke the sentiment of homeyness. These are the architect's choice of materials and forms—that is, constructed and applied craftsmanship. Such a strategy is, in fact, the other side to Simmel's sociological equation. Individuality can only be preserved in a bourgeois society (which is increasingly repressive in its political and social control of individual behavior) when it hides behind the shell of the inconspicuous frock coat. But once inside the home, one is free to remove the mask and be oneself.

But what does this say about Loos' more general view of architecture? If his exteriors are to be as inconspicuous as a well-dressed gentleman in polite society, his exquisitely detailed polychrome interiors speak to the human individual (ungendered), to the sensual side of human emotions. Loos, it has been said, cut his marble dressings (with the veining patterns at the joints of panels carefully considered) thinner than other architects of his time knew how to cut them. They could have been paper-thin for his purposes, however, for they were preeminently ornamental dressings—smooth, planar, costly pattern-making. Haptic is the word that comes to mind here, for it is another term much bandied about during this period. His surfaces, like the preferred cashmere fabric of his frock coat, longed to be touched.

It is also important, however, to clarify Loos's fundamentally ornamental conception of architecture (for this is what emerges here) and to distinguish it from that of Henry van de Velde, one of his principal antagonists.

When Loos attacked the ornamental designs of van de Velde (or those of Olbrich or Hoffmann) he was also responding in a sense to the contemporary psychological theory of empathy (*Einfühlungstheorie*). The notion of "empathy" (the psychological projection of the beholder's emotions into the objects of contemplation) came down from mid-nineteenth-century aesthetic theory and especially that of Friedrich Theodor Vischer. The last was also the first to associate the yet-to-be-named notion with architecture. Vischer argued that architecture was intrinsically a symbolic art, in which the architect has the task of rhythmically animating form and inserting "buoyant life" into the material through the play of lines and the planar suspension of bodies. Hence, the sensuous masses that the architect fashions and manipulates appear to move, lines rise and fall, and circles flow in space—so much so that it is "as if the ear hears the echoing sounds that reverberate from these movements."[19]

As this approach to architecture developed in nineteenth-century aesthetic discourse, empathy eventually came to be interpreted by architects like August Endell and van de Velde as a powerfully expressive, psychological tool. Endell in 1898 published a chart of similar but different building elevations in which he explored the psychological effects (energy and tension) of certain lines and forms.[20] Van de Velde employed the theory as a means to justify earlier art nouveau tendencies. A line, he argued, was a force, active in a psychological sense. When several lines are brought together in a design, they reinforce or oppose one another, in the same way that forces in physics support or cancel one another. Thus these forces can be orchestrated or composed (say, in the design of a desk) like tones in a musical work. Van de Velde even eventually came to favor abstract ornament over naturalistic motifs in his furniture designs for the reason that the former lent themselves more easily to harmonic or psychological manipulation.[21]

Loos, of course, was van de Velde's greatest critic during the early years of this century, but from the emotional response that he too sought to elicit in his own interiors he was, in fact, not far from the Belgian's position.

Loos famously derided any form of linear ornamentation as an atavistic mode of tattooing that was no longer suited to modern, that is, cultured sensibilities. But this objection dealt exclusively with the decorative tattooing of surfaces and not with the expressive characteristics of the material dressings in themselves, which in fact he always sought to exploit. In his view the pure, non-programmatic music of Beethoven had simply superseded the representational goblets of the Renaissance, and with this passage also came the artistic responsibility to retain or materially objectify this more abstract stage of artistic development. Loos, in sum, viewed van de Velde's empathetic tattooing as a form of maudlin sentimentality (as opposed to theatrical sentimentality), out of step with the evolving direction of Western culture. He also objected, of course, to van de Velde's attempt to impose high art, from above, on the crafts.

But this returns us to Loos's essay on plumbing and his effort to connect a nation's water usage to its economic level of achievement. The plumber, the tailor, and the shoemaker assumed honored positions in Loos's ideal polity, but not because they necessarily bathed frequently or attended Beethoven concerts. The argument was, in fact, the other way around. The nation that had attained a stage where every home or dwelling possessed a private bathtub was precisely that nation that had acquired a cultured middle class capable of sustaining these highly skilled but nevertheless non-artistic craft industries, already well on the way to extinction. In a sense, he was correct in observing the bathroom's liberating effect on one's willingness to perspire, but he was wrong to assume that the nineteenth-century trades could at the same time be preserved for those new sutlers of culture. What he did not see was that the bourgeois economy that could mass produce a sufficient number of bathtubs or laced shoes would soon learn how to do away effectively with the plumber or shoemaker altogether, not to mention the implied civility of their presence.

But these issues are largely irrelevant to Loos's standing as a theorist, or rather as a critic. What is pertinent is how he came to be embraced by architects under so many different ideological mantles. He was by his own admission a mason who had learned Latin, but he was also a scholar of stone and its emotive effects. He was overtly a classicist, but also a forward-thinking modernist (a friend of Arnold Schoenberg, Oscar Kokoschka, and Ludwig Wittgenstein). He could propose a colossal column for downtown Chicago, but he could also disallow the gabled roof for urban townhouses on both functional and economic grounds. The problem with these seemingly conflicting views is that many modern architects and historians (Le Corbusier among them) seized Loos's critique of gabled townhouses as an attack on all gabled forms, including those pedimental temples of Cicero—those roof forms conceived to carry away rainwater but which over time acquired a greater symbolic necessity, "with the consequence that even if one were erecting a citadel in heaven, where no rain could fall, it would be thought to be entirely lacking in dignity without a pediment."[22]

Loos honored dignity; his demeanor and sense of decorum exuded it. I also think that he would have found some amusement in our subsequent historical confusion over his purposely enigmatic *koans*. Still, I doubt if he would have concerned himself too much with it. For this Zen priest of modern (now postmodern) architecture would have probably insisted that

we should read Cicero while taking a bath—this, the most ancient purifica-
tory ritual of classical civilization—in order to think "modern."

NOTES

1. The 1921 edition was published by Georges Crès in Paris after Austrian publishers turned
   down the manuscript. The 1932 edition was published by Brenner Verlag in Austria. It
   would be an interesting task for someone to compare the texts of the two editions with
   the originals and see what changes were made.
2. Aldo Rossi, Introduction to the English translation, Adolf Loos, *Spoken into the Void: Critical Essays 1897–1900*, trans. Jane O. Newman and John H. Smith (Cambridge: MIT Press,
   1982), viii.
3. Ibid., 99–103.
4. The short-lived paper or journal ran only two issues. The German text has recently been
   published in Massimo Cacciari's *Adolf Loos e il suo Angelo: "Das Andere" e altri scritti*
   (Milan: Electa, 1992), 37–53 and 65–80.
5. Friedrich Nietzsche, "The Use and Abuse of History," *Thoughts out of Season*, trans.
   Adrian Collins (New York: Macmillan, 1924), 16–23.
6. Gottfried Semper, letter to Princess Sayn-Wittgenstein, 8 December 1857, Semper
   Archive, ETH-Zurich. Published in Harry Mallgrave, *Gottfried Semper: Architect of the
   Nineteenth Century* (New Haven: Yale University Press, 1996), 234.
7. Adolf Loos, "Shoemakers," in Adolf Loos, *Spoken into the Void: Critical Essays 1897–1900*,
   60.
8. Adolf Loos, "Underclothes," *Spoken into the Void*, 72–74.
9. Adolf Loos, "Men's Hats," *Spoken into the Void*, 52–53.
10. Adolf Loos, "Underclothes," *Spoken into the Void*, 74–75 n2.
11. Adolf Loos, "Men's Fashion," *Spoken into the Void*, 11.
12. Adolf Loos, "Architecture," in *The Architecture of Adolf Loos* (London: Arts Council Exhibi-
    tion, 1985), 107.
13. Georg Simmel, in addition to his voluminous sociological writings, also wrote a book-
    length study *Schopenhauer and Nietzsche*, trans. Helmut Loiskandl, Deena Weinstein, and
    Michael Weinstein (Urbana: University of Illinois Press, 1991).
14. This point was made by Beatriz Colomina, *Privacy and Publicity: Modern Architecture as
    Mass Media* (Cambridge: MIT Press, 1996), 273. See also Georg Simmel, "Fashion" and
    "The Metropolis and Mental Life," *Georg Simmel: On Individuality and Social Forms*
    (Chicago: University of Chicago Press, 1971).
15. Adolf Loos, "The Principle of Cladding," *Spoken into the Void*, 66–69. I have argued on
    several occasions that "cladding" is absolutely the wrong translation for *Bekleidung*. The
    general theory of Adolf Loos, with its direct connection to clothing, is an excellent exam-
    ple of why "cladding" is the wrong translation.
16. For a fuller treatment of Semper's theory of dressing, see my *Gottfried Semper: Architect of
    the Nineteenth Century*, 180–81, 290–302.

17. Adolf Loos, "Der Prinzip der Bekleidung," *Ins Leere gesprochen* (Vienna: Georg Prachner, 1987), 140.

18. See Colomina, *Privacy and Publicity*, 269. See also John Summerson's foreword to *The Architecture of Adolf Loos*, 7.

19. Friedrich Theodor Vischer, *Aesthetik; oder Wissenschaft des Schönen*, ed. Robert Vischer, 2nd ed. (1846–57; Munich, 1920–22), section 561, 237.

20. August Endell, "Formschönheit und dekorative Kunst," *Dekorative Kunst* 2 (1898), 119.

21. Henry van de Velde, *Kunstgewerbliche Laienpredigten* (Leipzig, 1902), 188–195. See also *Die Renaissance im modernen Kuhnstgewerbe* (Berlin, 1901), 97–108.

22. Cicero, *De Oratore*, Book III, 180.

Poché

Donald Kunze

IS THERE A SPACE OF ARCHITECTURAL RECEPTION? THAT IS, IS THERE a place or space "within" the domain of particular buildings, where the realization of an architectural "idea" takes place or, alternatively, an arrangement of spaces that leads to that realization?

This is an obtuse question, if only for the reason that so many of its terms are obscure or unestablished. There may in truth be such a thing as an architectural idea, but there are many "ideas" about what this might be. Also, in architecture, the notion of space or place is unstable. To conflate the various kinds of space involved in the planning, construction, and experience of building would be to ignore the widely recognized principle that architectural space is defined largely by action (virtual or actual) and intent (conscious or subconscious). Each kind of space has its own terms of measure, and the wonder is that, for any given location, human beings, who have the ability to see things from many different points of view, can seem to live in the same space, conceived as a common place; and even more remarkable that the idea of living in a single world is not only thinkable but a sometimes unavoidable necessity.

The third and most severe incongruity lying within the original question has to do with reception. Fifteen years of critical theory have established "reception" as a useful term for designating the various kinds of response of audiences to works of art, mostly literature. In fact, the notion of "response," as in "reader response," has conditioned the view that the work of art is a "stimulus" and that the phenomena surrounding the production and consumption of art might be divided according to something being sent out and that same something being accepted, or at least signed-for. This is a troublesome metaphor to begin with, and particularly problematic for architecture, which is only rarely considered to be anything like a presentation or performance, and which, if it can be said to have an audience in any sense of the term, has nothing like the patrons who pay for a seat in the theater, buy a book, or line up to witness mega-exhibitions organized by major art museums.

This is not to overlook the widespread practice of seeing buildings as such, whether inadvertently (taking in I.M. Pei's glass pyramid on the way to a day at the Louvre) or intentionally (a pilgrimage to Le Corbusier's Villa Savoye). Nor should one omit the audience-show relationship of most touristic environments, where architecture serves as the stage-set for romanticized re-creations of the past. The place of such intentionally consumed architecture is different from the space of work-a-day buildings, but we shouldn't overly rely on the position or thickness of the line that separates them. There is a sense in which all architecture is meant to be received, a sense in which something is always presented and always construable, even if in the background of our thoughts. It is the distribution of these actions that makes them almost impossible to describe, for there is rarely any figure/ground relationship, no permanent temporal or spatial bounds.

Architectural presentation drawings romanticize particular ways of looking at buildings, and because these ways exist more for the drawing than for the real experience of the building, even when computer simulations attempt to recreate a realistic walk-through experience, we can look to representation for a hint of what presentation and reception attempt in real life. Unlike a building, whose spaces are folded, torn, concealed, extruded, and crinkled (to use but a few of the possible metaphors), drawings necessitate a space (in front of the paper) that corresponds to a place where one might stand to see the really informative view. The similarity between the architectural drawing and the painting is not so much the quasi-perspectival manner of representing space but the *place* given to the audience to come to terms with the graphic marks representing some scene.

FIG. 1 Frank Lloyd Wright, Falling
Water, Bull Run, PA

FIG. 2 The main drive, The Biltmore
Estate, Asheville, NC

Therefore, using the space in front of the representation as a model for the space of reception is entirely understandable. Its existence is physical as well as metaphorical in the case of paintings, other flat art, and even sculpture. For most modern architecture, the on-site spaces of reception cannot keep pace with those perpetrated by photography and presentation drawings. A famous case is Frank Lloyd Wright's "Falling Water" home for the Kauffmans, almost always shown from a point down the hill from the house's most dramatic cantilever [Fig. 1]. This is the point from which the idea of the house is received, although it is rarely a point from which it is presently or even possibly viewed. But, once the image of stone extending over water at a heroic angle is fixed in the imagination, the rest of the house's experiences are subordinated to this primal scene. In contrast, the *allée* of the Biltmore Estate in North Carolina, designed by William Morris Hunt, is able to deliver the mansion's façade in full elevation to every visitor who uses the main drive [Fig. 2]. Like the transitional scenes in Peter Greenaway's film *The Draughtsman's Contract*, where drawings are lap-dissolved into real views, the spaces of reception in architecture are idealized by the presentation drawing and, if all goes well, adequately appointed real sites.

Architecture's more common spaces of reception are distributed differently, inserted among the paths of use and maintenance, regulated in some cases by framed spaces, *allées*, courtyards, etc., but more often woven into the building's utility as an invisible thread smuggled into the woof of sack-cloth. Reception, then, is only occasionally located in the romanticized point of view celebrated by architectural drawings and photographs. It is more of a condition, a subjunctive tense of architecture: "if." Following this restriction, there are still some things one might say about the importance of reception. First, like the reception of a work of art, architectural reception is imagined as an event that takes place at the "site" of the viewer, an apotheosis of the inhabitant who unravels the spatial puzzle. The "in front of" that characterizes the space of reception even when it is woven into pockets and folds is matched to an equally potent "behind" that approaches us from the infinite distance or the innermost chamber. We know we have arrived at the prescribed point in art when we meet this equal and opposite force. Reception meets production.

Taken literally, production is a hodgepodge of any and all activities that produce the work of art. There is no space or time that characterizes the invention stage of art. Its physical home is discontinuous, often barren: the desk of the writer or the studio of the artist. Apart from *La Bohème*, with its romanticized garret, there is not much point in showing it. However, this is not what the audience encounters in the process of receiving art. The chief basis for thinking of the production process as a space at all is the symmetry demanded by the audience's reception. In *Sanatorium under the Sign of the Hourglass*, Bruno Schulz compared this symmetry to clandestine contact concealed by furniture: ". . . [A]ny *true* reader—and this story is only addressed to him—will understand me anyway when I look him straight in the eye and try to communicate my meaning. A short sharp look or a light clasp of his hand will stir him into awareness, and he will blink in rapture at the brilliance of The Book. For, under the imaginary table that separates me from my readers, don't we secretly clasp each other's hands?"[1]

The love between reception and production goes beyond holding hands. This is a romance between a Tristan and Isolde, Heloise and Abelard, Paolo and Francesca. After all, the lovers must commit a double suicide. This is enacted through the traditional rule that turns the space of representation and the spaces of reception and production on either side of it metaphorically into a double-pole electrical switch: when one is on the other is off.

ZONE

		PRODUCTION	REPRESENTATION	RECEPTION
TIME	BEFORE/ AFTER PERFORMANCE	*active*	silent	*active*
	DURING PERFORMANCE	silent	*active*	silent

When the stage lights go on and the curtain rises, the stage-hands must remain silent, as silent as the audience. This double-pole switch system brings about the mock death that the philosopher Mikel Dufrenne describes as an alternation between competing zones of reality:

> . . . [T]he witness, without leaving his post in physical space, penetrates into the world of the work. Because he allows himself to be won over and inhabited by the sensuous, he thereby penetrates into the work's signification—we may say that the meaning penetrates him, so close is the reciprocity of the subject and object. In front of a figurative painting. . . [N]o lighting is impossible, because the lighting belongs to the painting. . . . This does not mean that the painting partakes of the unreal. It means that I have derealized myself in order to proclaim the painting's reality and that I have gained a foothold in the new world which it opens to me, a new man myself.[2]

The audience is *abjected* into the required trance-like state. It becomes a collective of individual corpses whose spirits now mingle in the paradisical light of the play. That reception is like death is nothing new in Christian iconology [Fig. 3], where the tomb becomes a gateway. Even, as in the case of Botticini's "The Assumption of the Virgin," heaven is shown as a mirror of the theater. Reception pulls us into what is idealized as an echelon of angels that speed our step-wise progress toward the climax. What we know of art, however, returns us to the alternating current model where reception and production take turns being alive. After Mary reaches heaven, art would have it that the prop men move in and unceremoniously return the suspended rings to properties storage and the angels, leaving

FIG. 3 Botticini, "The Assumption of the Virgin," c. 1474.

their wings with the costume mistress, loiter outside, call their agents to see if their are any scripts to read, or drop in at a local café for a double espresso.

The space of reception can be understood in its full cosmic implications without too much trouble. It is another matter, however, to imagine a complementary space existing, metaphorically, "behind" the representation, hiding while the audience undergoes zombification in the auditorium, restored to ordinary life as soon as the curtain falls. The theater analogy works well as a model for the space of reception, but it falls short of describing an equally potent "space of production." In actuality, reception is an appointment with the idea of the work of art, and this meeting is with someone who is both well-known and a stranger to us.

The model I wish to demonstrate ("de-monster-ate" literally, for there are two parts that refuse to weld together) is that of a spatial sandwich, where two outer spaces, a space of reception and a space of production, compress a space of representation. These might be allowed to exist as mere characterizations, but I would go further, to demonstrate a real presence of these spaces, brought into being because of the mind's representational proclivity. When this proclivity turns instrumental, that is to say, when it attempts to turn representation into a tool to dominate the represented, the spaces of reception and production are not so much destroyed as they are redecorated. They become the isolated tower of the Panopticon, the narrow keyhole of Jean-Paul Sartre's voyeur in *Being and Nothingness*. Instrumental representation substitutes, for the anterior space of production, a location lying at an infinite distance which contains the truth that "lies behind" appearances. In Renaissance paintings, this is almost always shown as a classical round temple, brought forward a bit from distant infinity to display its "nice" detailing. The ideal of this *gradus ad Parnassum* is in fact a mountain, a *mons delectus*, such as described in the image of "Cebes' Table," derived from a polyglot text well known throughout the middle ages [Fig. 4]. The base of the mountain ushers in initiates, the "newly born," who are faced with temptations of every kind as they ascend toward the pinnacle, where clouds conceal a centrally placed temple to which the chosen few are admitted the moment they accede to perfect wisdom. The truth is that truth always recedes in this model. Actual possession of the final moment of truth never occurs because, just as the horizon retreats into the distance as we advance through the landscape, new levels of ignorance replace the old ones we dispel using the cone-of-vision idea of knowledge. The contrast between this epistemology of bad infinities and the spatial sandwich of production and reception lies in the latter's insistence on the need for closure.

This "sandwich" includes the role of the viewer, and of viewing. Instrumental representation cannot unify the viewer and the viewed because, once exiled from the visible, the viewer remains alienated throughout the process. The final "vision of truth" follows the same structural rules that limited the vision of appearances.

FIG. 4 "Cebes' Table," from Otto Vaenius, *Theatro Moral de la Vida Humana*, 1672

With the reciprocities set in motion by the spatial sandwich of production and reception, the *process* comes into play, and the final consideration of any ultimate truths naturally includes self-reflection.

In such comprehensive artistic projects as Marcel Duchamp's, these issues are paramount. The vanishing point of fourth-dimensional space becomes a point of confrontation of the nature of vision itself. I would like to demonstrate not only the efficacy of the production-representation-reception model but also to show that it is somewhat more ancient and—paradoxically—more modern than the instrumental cone-of-vision model. To do this, I return to a set of images that demonstrates the presence of a countergaze, where the countergaze not only deconstructs the cone-of-vision paradigm but introduces new terms for the prospect of "completion" of the artistic unity of idea and reception.

A PROOF "OF THE BODY"

I propose transposing the terms of the above in order to demonstrate an important relationship between architecture as it is conceived and built ("production"), architecture as it is construed or perceived ("reception"), and architecture as it is represented (a space "sandwiched" between reception and production). There are conceivably many ways of unraveling this conundrum: gaze and countergaze, the effect of Enlightenment metrics on representation, case studies of particular architects (as "agents of production") and their fates (woes of failed reception). My approach will be based on a regard of the zone of representation as a model for all architectural encounters, in that this zone best exemplifies the role of *poché*, or hidden spaces, as "lying between" and "lying hidden" within perception and conception of an architectural idea. My view of poché accommodates commonplace uses of the term to apply to the space inside structural elements, mechanical spaces, and other hidden wealth of buildings; but it also applies to the specialization of the poché idea in consciously contrived niches, concealed passageways, cabinets, and the like. Furthermore, I would expand the idea of poché to include spaces *not noticed*, especially where this erasure, suspension, or exhaustion of intention has a political or aesthetic effect: the space of servants or marginalized people; the invisibility of slums; the perverse visuality of ruins.

This is not the place for full-scale expansion of this simple term. I will however concentrate on the translation that makes it possible for us to understand how spaces of representation—"natural pochés" lying between two very literal kinds of space—embody the means by which architecture becomes understandable as an idea, as well as the place where an idea is encountered *as architecture*. This can be done in three steps. The first step is a survey of some visual references to the cross-flow of production and reception, sometimes portrayed as gaze and countergaze. The esoteric nature of some of these image-examples may give the impression that the reception idea involves radical mysticism. It does not. It is rather the case that the resources of poché have been exploited most vigorously by those who have applied it to esoteric matters, and applied it well.

The second step involves an understanding of how the space of reception functions poetically. This is most easily accomplished by reference to a parallel theory of poetry put forward by Michael Riffaterre. In a fortunate example of words that are "permanently poetic," Rifaterre chose the word *soupirail* ("vent"), which in French elicits poetic connections without any further modification. Because the vent is architectural, and because the poetic function of the vent depends on architectural conditions, Riffaterre's example serves our project well. The logic of the vent is, *ceteris parabis*, the logic of poché. The *soupirail*, poché, and the space of representation form a solid triangle that—as much as *venustas, firmitas*, and *utilitas*—might be the basis for a more useful, if darker, architectural theory. It is the reciprocity of the three ideas that contributes to the structural integrity of each and the whole; any one is a synecdoche of the idea that architecture is a relationship between the visible and the invisible (or any one of a number of paraphrases that include the idea of reception). As Paul Virilio put it, architecture is a means of occultation.[3]

The third step refines the notions encountered in the survey of representational images and the critical-poetic analysis of the vent. This involves reviving the "calculus" of a somewhat forgotten mathematician, George Spencer-Brown, who in the 1960s invented a symbolic logic using only one term. Fortunately for architects, this term was a boundary, understood spatially and temporally as both a "cross" and a "call" to cross. Spencer-Brown's calculus was intended for application to complicated spatial problems. Spencer-Brown himself applied it to the problem of connectivity of London's Underground, and one of his most devoted followers has examined mathematical properties of knots. Movement and tangles just about sum up my own interest in poché, architectural reception, representation, and poeticity. Because Spencer-Brown's calculus is in one sense extraordinarily easy to grasp, it is possible to give a representative view of its possible application to these issues.

DEAD/ALIVE

The psychiatrist Jacques Lacan tells a story in *The Four Fundamental Concepts of Psycho-Analysis* that is well known in architectural circles.[4] As a young man, Lacan visited the small fishing villages on the Brittany coast in order to escape city life. Out on a frail boat with a local known as "Petit Jean," Lacan and Jean see a sardine can floating some distance from the boat. Petit Jean asks if Lacan sees the can, and Lacan, who at that moment is hit by a ray of the sun glinting off the can's silvery surface, says "yes." "Well, it doesn't see you," Petit Jean replies, laughing loudly, thinking he has made a great joke at the intellectual's expense. Lacan explains that, by this somewhat idiotic expression, Petit Jean had made the point that Lacan did not belong among the working poor who struggled daily on that hard coast. The can did not look back at Lacan the way it would have looked back at Petit Jean. Lacan's gaze intersected the can-Jean world at an orthogonal angle, an independent and indifferent angle. For the can and

Petit Jean, Lacan was abject, dead. Ironically, Petit Jean would be dead in a few years of tuberculosis, a hazard of his class. Lacan remarks that his gaze, isolated from the ordinary perceptions of the locals, humans and cans alike, met with a mark coming from the can, a glimmer that situated his gaze by triangulating seer, seen, and sun in a single instant.

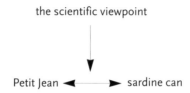

I would like to notate this situation as a matter of vectors. Lacan's gaze sallies forth toward the can, whose indifference could be symbolized as a vector turned sideways (orthogonal) to this gaze. The gleam from the can, which, Lacan remarks, participates in the "ambiguity of the jewel," returns Lacan's gaze from within the anonymous visual depths of the can. Somewhere in the remote expanse of space, the sun that generates this glimmer is at exactly the right place. The glint of sunlight externalizes (= abjects) Lacan from a scene that is totally interior (the world of Petit Jean). The gleam, generated from its remote cosmic source, magnifies this exteriority and alienation, but it also intensifies the interiority of the can.

Who is dead and who is alive in this scene? Stable assignments cannot be made, but what is certain is that the system of glints, gazes, cans, and the drifting psychologist with his local guide fit well within the alternating system established by production/work/reception. It is a matter of 010 or 101, put in binary terms. The glimmer, ambiguous as a jewel, meets Lacan's externalized gaze, between them the sandwiched space containing Petit Jean, his aphorisms, and flotsam.

Before this notation stratagem is allowed to die the death of most arbitrary characterizations, consider a well-known graphic image that, for the most part, duplicates this schema in every detail. This image is Albrecht Dürer's engraving of an artist with his model in the studio, published posthumously in a handbook for artists [Fig. 5]. A brief review of the similarities between this scene and Lacan's boat ride: First, we, the present viewers, come to witness a scene, but instead we witness the viewing of a scene (the artist employing a "lucinda" to draw his model in accurate per-

FIC. 5 Albrecht Dürer, "Artist Sketching a Reclining Nude Woman," woodcut c. 1525

spective), and this viewed viewing takes place at a right angle to our own. By virtue of a ninety-degree rotation, we are exiled from the normal reciprocity that takes place between viewers and representations: the sense that we are looking through a window, with a drawing in a frame substituted for the scene framed by the window. The window in the Dürer has been "moved back," that is to say, the window/frame relationship has been noted but displaced slightly so that we see the window frame framed by the picture's frame, just enough like our eyes to make us think of a possible relation.

Second, as a consequence of juxtaposing both the space of the represented (the model) and the representer (the artist), the engraving is very long. Dürer has suggested, perhaps, a relation between this elongation and our binocular view of it by placing two windows on the studio's wall. Like eyes, they return our gaze. Iconographically, the windows frame two different kinds of subject matter. On the left, we see the sea coast whose contours mimic the model's own voluptuous curves. On the right, the "artist's view," we have a liquid scene dotted with boats.

The third point of coincidence between Lacan's story and Dürer's engraving is in the role of the glimmer off the surface of the can. For us, it is (1) the recognition of the possibility that the windows refer self-referentially to eyes, (2) the comparison of the artist's present activity to our own, and especially the drawing-in-a-drawing, (3) the passing thoughts about how the dead artist, Dürer, fits in this picture, and (4) the iconographical surplus present in the topiary tree, pitcher, and landscape scenes. These are surplus to the didactic role of the engraving, where the image simply instructs the would-be artist in the use of a lucinda. Likewise, Lacan is made into human surplus in the Brittany sea scape. The glimmer fixed him momentarily in a "stable" triangle of eye, can, and sun. The confirmation of this relationship is direct, and unsharable. No two people can see the same reflection. Just as we have been "rotated out" of the scene by Dürer's angle of view, the glimmer isolates ("makes surplus" = externalizes) whoever sees it.

Much of the wealth of the Dürer engraving can be derived from the various meanings of the word poché. Where architects derive this term from the poking style of the pencil that applies fine dots to areas designated as being "inside something," the poke and the pocket (*poche*) come very close. A poke in the eye, a pocket of space. Dürer's artist is almost receiving a poke in the eye from his obelisk-eyepiece, the antipodal mechanism required to steady the eye so that the lucinda registers a constant view. The eye's fixity enables the capture of the model, as if "frozen in time." As a dispersed model of the idea of the camera, the lucinda and eyepiece do not engage the intended faces of nature but, rather, its side views, its unaccustomed and therefore "natural" appearances. Dürer emphasizes this by posing the model to force an extreme foreshortening of the body. Only a misogynist, or philosopher, or both would find optical truth in this "accidental" view. This visual poke is, as the word suggests, rude. But, the point is that pockets and pokes are two sides of the same coin.

Dürer pokes into nature with his drawing device, nearly poking his own eye out. Lacan is poked out of the Brittany sea-side scene by a glint off a sardine can. Both cases involve the intersection of visibility by a vector at a right ("orthogonal") angle, where *ortho* retains the sense of being both independent and authentic. The glimmer, like the landscape, lies beyond the main scene. By connecting with the space of reception in front of the scene, it sandwiches a pocket of representational space in between. This might seem to be only a web of coincidences were it not for other images that capitalize on the versatility of referring to three kinds of space in one scene.

Such a case is Antonello da Messina's *St. Jerome* [Fig. 6], which accomplishes a similar matrix of zones with a more theological undertone.[5] Jerome is shown in his study, an elevated carrel within a cavernous space separated from our view by a *porta coeli*, an archway placed symbolically to represent the gaze of God, and from the rest of the painted world by two windows in back that admit the gaze of civilized mankind (on the left) and wild nature (at right). As in the Lacan story and the Dürer engraving, a spatial cross-flow exists, albeit without the ninety degree shift and with the mortal viewer sharing the divine viewing point, but this time the role of the lucinda is taken up by the lectern, which is posited in the larger form of

Jerome's carrel, which isolates his act of reading within its own special architecture.

Because Jerome translated the vulgate Bible and was an ardent proponent of the view that Mary's virginity was perpetual, the stakes have been raised. We are to understand reception not simply through the allegory of reading but as a matter of conception. As in the Dürer engraving, we are placed in a situation where our own act of looking is implicated in the subject matter of the picture. Moreover, Antonello uses icons within the picture as clues to weave an exceptionally intricate puzzle, one that is only

FIG. 6 Antonello da Messina, *St. Jerome in His Study*, c.1450–55

partly unraveled by discovering that the partridge carries within its Medieval iconology the idea that the divine word impregnates the body of the reader. The symbols on this "page" of painting divide into tiles whose positions replay the impregnation thesis in the eye of the painting's viewer, a visual acrostic that makes word flesh or, recalling Lacan, flash.

The jewel among this treasure is the recurrence of the spatial sandwich, a space within a space that mirrors the image-within-an-image theme of Dürer and the reading-within-a-reading theme of Antonello. Like some interstitial lung, these medial spaces breathe in ordinary meaning and exhale the extraordinary. They are poché spaces in a special sense: they separate two perfectly understandable types of space with a specific form of *invisibility*. Obviously, both images are immanently visible. But, they both mean what they mean by concealing within their visibility another order of relationships. This occultation is best expressed by William Blake's phrase, "darkness shining through the light," a favorite of James Joyce.

The frontispiece of a famous eighteenth-century work, *The New Science of Giambattista Vico* [Fig. 7], shows how useful such a pocket space can be when consciously applied as propaganda. The *dipintura*, as this image is called by scholarly tradition, was most certainly designed and engraved by fellow-Rosicrucians who were aware of the multiple layers of

FIG. 7 "La dipintura," frontispiece, *The New Science of Giambattista Vico*, 1744

secret meanings within their chosen icons. It recapitulates the main points of Vico's "ideal eternal history," a narrative constant lying behind the rise and decline of all cultures. The eye of Divine Providence shines through the clouds onto a jewel pinned to the breast of Metafisica, who in her demeanor is closely related to contemporary images of Justizia. She is depicted surmounting the cosmos, fixed within the divine gaze. Like the *Jerome*, there are spaces fore and aft the main space of representation, but here divinity shines in from the back. Near the stage lights, and nearly serving the same purpose, are emblems representing the main institutions of human culture. Not only is there a front frame and a threshold at the rear that serves the function of a frame—albeit a divine frame—but there is also a direct symbolization of a kind of diastolic and systolic "breath" animated by the divine gaze of Providence that corresponds to Antonello's zig-zag across the "tiles" of icons in the *Jerome*. No less is there here an idea of reading, translated into a puzzle-image. The Jerome of this emblem is Homer, putative author of human institutions, turned into a reader by the "back-flow" principle that Vico used to narrate (= discover) his own new science.[6]

In modern times, direct reference to the idea that representational space is ideologically sandwiched between reception and production has become less obvious but no less complex. In perhaps the most famous image of modern art, Pablo Picasso's "Les Demoiselles d'Avignon" [Fig. 8], two figures stand at the edge of the spatial realms beyond the main image of "prostitutes." The evolution of the figure on the left, which at one time was a medical student holding a skull, has been well documented. Like so many paintings of the eighteenth and nineteenth centuries which construct a double frame by showing the patron or some other figure drawing back a curtain on the "real painting," "Les Demoiselles" personifies the

FIG. 8 Pablo Picasso, "Les
Demoiselles d'Avignon," 1907

FIG. 9 Hans Holbein the younger,
"The French Ambassadors," 1533

Hermetic entrance to the image. Less well understood is the figure shown toward the rear, who peeks through what looks to be a "sky" portrayed in the form of a curtain that can be parted. This voyeur, like the divine eye in Vico's frontispiece, belongs "elsewhere," but it is unclear whether that elsewhere is ours or some other's. In Vico's *New Science*, the answer is clearly connected to the notion that human beings make their own world by conceiving an invisible beyond that is their antipodal double. This division of the psyche for the purpose of making the visible world oracular conceals its own self-nature by making an "other" as remote as possible from the self. "Les Demoiselles" is clearly allegorical, but, apart from the easy identification of the seated figure on the right as a version of the traditional Melancholy, this modern program is not as transparent as that of the *dipintura*.

In many of Picasso's still-lifes, anamorphic representations of skulls may be found that continue the *memento mori* tradition of placing a countergaze to meet the inward gaze of patrons. Hans Holbein's *The French Ambassadors* [Fig. 9] could be regarded as the paradigm-exemplar of this practice, where a stain or smudge is placed so that, in the original placement of the canvas at the top of a stair, the viewer is "incorporated" into the canvas in much the same way sacrificial victims were buried within the poché of walls to secure buildings from danger. If the anamorphic skull concealed and yet found within the bowls of fruit, piles of musical instruments, and the like, are not in some way a reminder of "us" or the artist, this reminder is not a reminder but just a useless new idea on the level of paper placemats found in cheap cafés.

My guess is that the reciprocal silence/speech that governs relationships between zones of production, representation, and reception is in fact a matter of "occultation," of dividing consciousness according to a carefully regulated system of "interests," one of which contains the mysterious antipodal "other" that accompanies our vision with its anti-visual program. What makes this supposition interesting for architecture in particular is that our perception of artificial (constructed) spaces mingles the poché necessitated by perception with the poché spaces inadvertently and intentionally constructed by the architect. Just as the *Jerome*, "Demoiselles," *dipintura* and the Dürer engraving directly symbolized the reciprocity between the visible and invisible *as an architecture*, buildings themselves can even more easily participate in this self-referential process.

THE POETICITY OF VENTS

Architecture's native abilities in opening up the machinations of perception are evident in the way in which other art forms drift towards spatial metaphor when reflecting on their own core functions. Such is the case with Michael Riffaterre's example of "permanently poetic expressions" in literature, phrases or images that are potentially poetic whenever they appear. In Riffaterre's general theory,[7] poetic expressions are those that contain, beneath the surface of mimetic representation (what the expression is "about"), a reference to a "hypogram," a descriptive system characterized by polar oppositions, sometimes a pre-existent text. In comparison to the mimetic function of the text containing the poetic expression, the poetic part is "ungrammatical." That is, it violates the rules of order that demand we read according to language's representational function.

Because a building's poeticity is frequently most intense when ordinary mimetic ("functional") forces give out (the ruin), are disrupted (the courtyard), or do not exist (some monuments), Riffaterre's terms hold considerable promise for architecture theory. Although what might serve as a "hypogram," or poetic antecedent, remains an open question, the notion of ungrammaticality is even more forceful when expressed within the Ruskinian opposition of building as functional and architecture as useless. There is even more cause for interest in Riffaterre's use of an example of "permanently poetic expressions": the *soupirail*, or "cellar vent."

What is startling is that *soupirail* is permanently poetic in literary discourse, that it is perceived as such without regard to context. And even more surprising is that this poetic aura cannot be accounted for by the existence of a literary theme or motif. "Literary" windows serve as settings for contemplation, as symbols of contact between the inner life and the world of sensation. Their glass panes permit visual communication but prevent direct touch, and so they may also be a metaphor for absence, separation, longing, memory, and so forth. *Soupirail*, however, has neither the pane nor the lofty vantage point that makes windows a locus of poetic feelings or meditation. And, finally, *soupirail*'s very specific and inglorious meaning places it among the words most unlikely to fit esthetic norms like those of the French classicism that produced the stock epithet and excluded words representing pedestrian realities.[8]

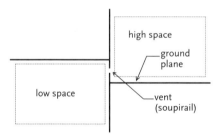

high space

ground plane

low space

vent (soupirail)

FIG. 10 Diagram, the structure of the architectural vent

The hypogram, or "descriptive system," of the vent includes polar oppositions derived from the vent's architectural qualities. The first is between the narrowness of the vent (the body can't squeeze through) and the temptation it offers [Fig. 10]. Such opposition is felt keenly when the resident of one side of the *soupirail* is a prisoner or recluse. The second opposition is that between the wall as material thickness and the vent as an opening. The head, sill, and jambs of the vent directly measure the massiveness of the wall which it penetrates. Although a void, it emphasizes weight and impenetrability. The third polar opposition is between the narrowness of the vent and the immensity of the voids that open on either side of it. This effect works from either point of view. Standing

FIG. 11 Giambattista Piranesi,
Carceri, Plate IX, 1761.

outside, the vent near the pavement suggests an unlimited infernal space beneath a building—unlimited mostly in the sense that one is unable or unwilling to measure it precisely. From the inside perspective, the vent's restriction of view amplifies the immensity of free space beyond. The best example of this perspective is Giambattista Piranesi's strikingly unusual view, Plate IX in the *Carceri* series. Through the opening of this ruined dome we can see, in a rare glimpse, a sky that is made more vast because of the ruin beneath it [Fig. 11].

Riffaterre's *soupirail* brings fresh insight to the function of the middle space of representation. First, a summary is in order. The vent/*soupirail* is clearly and foremost a sign of poché. It refers to the massiveness of the wall in which it sits; it suggests an infinite void when viewed from the exterior; and it expresses directly the theme of "impossible passage"—a place that the imagination may visit without the body intact. But, the most significant feature of the vent is that it leads to a system of polar oppositions that serve as its hypogram. These oppositions are no more and no less than a map of the relationships that bring poché out of general service and into the special applications required of architectural representation. The dynamic dualism of the spaces of production and reception, the simultaneous "thickness" and "thinness" of the work of art between them, and the infinity of the voids suggested on either side of the representation's "surfaces" are key to the physics of the gaze and countergaze within our samples of visual art and suggestive of the more dispersed properties of poché within architecture.

In short, Riffaterre has provided a theoretical perspective from which the relationship of the visible to the invisible within architecture might be productively and philosophically approached. This permits us to advance beyond simple characterization of architectural qualities of poché space (labyrinthine, tomb-like, subterranean, etc.) and toward a notion of the function that such spaces play individually, culturally, and historically. I have argued elsewhere that the connection between ideas about the security of buildings is directly demonstrated by the definitive use of poché in foundation rituals (foundations, cornerstones, walls, etc.). The continuing psychological associations of concealed spaces, utility and marginal spaces, for example, suggest that foundation rites are not limited to archaic cultures but simply displaced into secular forms. It is possible to speculate that, because poché is the spatial counterpart to the suppressed content of consciousness, that it is equally oracular in revealing these suppressed contents. A thesis similar to this lay behind Ben Nicholson's project for the "Appliance House," a large wooden "compartment" constructed to hold the deposited contents of children killed on Cabrini Green in Chicago. Working at the social and individual level, Nicholson's poché displays a mathematical rigor, as if recovering the things whose existence we often deny still requires a magic formula.

"Reception," then, is not a simple matter of passive perception but of a radical inversion of the normal hierarchy that conceals some kind of signification beneath the representational surface images that are normally taken as the intended meanings of works of art. Reception, it would be more accurate to say, is a process of occultation and revelation, of putting in and taking out, abjecting and resurrecting, denying and affirming. Within this no/yes strategy lies the capability for inclusiveness denied to logically consistent systems who make the truth-telling and lying Cretin into the same kind of confidence man. The no/yes, with a considerable theological history behind it, seems to ignore Russell's paradox of sets that proclaims that the knower cannot be included in the known. In fact, the no/yes of poché thinking seems to focus especially on including the knower within a matrix where he/she is temporarily abjected (made invisible, disguised, etc.) and then revealed. Like the anamorphic skulls popped into paintings as *mementi mori*, the recovery of self lies at the "end" of the reception experience. It is the *terminus ad quem* of the life of art, vampirishly revivified by the presence of a temporarily "dead" audience.

I would argue that the yes/no logic of poché is widespread both as an element of literal works of architecture and as a mechanism of our reception of those works. Also it seems clear that poché is primitive in a radical sense. If (and it seems to be the case) the grave precedes the house, historical primacy equals conceptual primacy. *Poché* precedes architecture in an ontological and causative manner.

If this is true, then the semiological relationships between poché space and the apparent forms of architecture should be consistent and well formed in a mathematical sense. This would be impossible to demonstrate with the usual forms of logic, if only for the reason that most logics presume a point of view that is external to the system being described. In the case of poché, as our paintings suggest, the reciprocity of gaze and countergaze include the viewer with the viewed in an act of final assimilation. The reception process is, if anything, a deconstruction of the original point of view that afforded the concealing and successive discovery of a whole system of poetic significations. What follows is an experiment with a calculus that is an exception in that it does not depend upon a point of view. This is the unusual symbolic logic invented by George Spencer-Brown, a logic which has only one symbol, the "cross" (⌐) and only two axioms.[9] Because the cross is interpreted both as a physical movement across a spatial or temporal boundary as well as an instruction to move across such a boundary, the cross is both a cross and a "call." The axioms state that (1) to cross and then cross again is equivalent to not crossing, and (2) that a call and a call again is equivalent to a single call. The axioms are written, respectively, as:

$$\neg\,\neg = \neg$$
$$\overline{\neg}\, =$$

It would be impossible to present more than the bare fundamentals of Spencer-Brown's calculus here, but it is possible to show how the axioms lead to an expression that seems to account for the action of poché in concealing and revealing systems of signification.

Spencer-Brown himself encouraged interpretive applications of his logical system. This is one such application. The cross, for art, is most easily construed as the frame that separates the audience and its quotidian world from the zone in which art suspends some rules and invents others to fashion its own spatial and temporal realm. The boundary between the quotidian and art is conventionally identified with the frame of a painting or the edge of the stage. In our case, it is both a spatio-temporal boundary

and a call to cross that boundary. Expressed in the language of the calculus, the audience 'a' regarding the artwork 'b' could be written as:

$$\overline{b}\,|\,a$$

In the case where the space of representation contains a space "within it" that is also "beyond it" by showing a landscape visible through "binocular" windows (Dürer, Antonello), a theological hole through appearances (Vico), a curtain—which parts or rolls up reality [Fig. 12], or an anamorphic smudge that reminds the viewer that he/she must die by placing a reflection of his/her face within the depths of the image (Holbein, Picasso, *et al.*), the new condition could be represented by placing another frame and a self-referential space within the basic expression:

$$\overline{\overline{a}\,|\,b}\,|\,a$$

In what Spencer-Brown calls the "consequences" of calculus, the axioms and their derivatives are used to show how simple expressions may contain within them more complex unanticipated expressions. In "Consequence 4. Occultation," Spencer-Brown shows that the original term that I have assigned as "simple viewing," presuming that I am referring to the kind of gaze that Lacan discovered on the Brittany coast, yields exactly the expression shown above.

$$\overline{\overline{a}\,|\,b}\,|\,a = a$$

The critical value of paintings within this category has been that they have seemed to do just what Spencer-Brown's consequence suggests: revealing within painting the essence of "looking at painting" itself. Our interest now is in what the calculus may have to say about the role of poché, or the poetic logic of the *soupirail*, in this process of revelation. This may be discovered in the demonstration of the above consequence, which the reader unfamiliar with Spencer-Brown's calculus may follow through my annotations. The first step is to add, to the simple term 'a,' a double-cross that contains duplicate expressions, 'ab' and 'ba.'

$$\overline{\overline{ab|ba}|a}$$

The addition of a double-cross, whose value is zero, could be interpreted symbolically by saying that art, as representation, is a surplus "gratuity," a superfluity. In other words, art is fiction.

According to a rule of transposition, the 'b' can be removed from 'ab,' and the 'a' from 'ba' (the reader interested in a proof of this move is referred to *Laws of Form*).[10]

$$= \overline{\overline{a}|ba}|a = \overline{\overline{a}|b}|a$$

The resulting expression, which is read as "*a cross one, b cross two, a,*" suggests that, in our case, any and every viewpoint involves a transposition of the viewing subject, 'a', to a poché within the representation, expressed or not, and that every frame is in fact a double frame. The space of reception before the work of art presumes a space of production *behind* it, where it encounters some form of identity.

$$\overline{|\ \text{the space of representation}\ |}$$

The formula for "occultation" leaves us with a sense that the process of concealing and revealing, implied by the vent, poché, and their poetic/architectural cousins, operates according to inner rules of the kind that Lacan unearthed in his extensive analysis of the gaze. There are other possible points of tangency: the tourist's search for authenticity amidst the

FIG. 13 Le Petit Hameau,
Versailles, France

degraded souvenirs of travel, the special framing techniques of toy-worlds
such as Marie Antoinette's *Petit Hameau* at Versailles [Fig. 13], the hollow
resonance of ruins, the perfect architecture of fireworks.[11] In these examples, which seem at first to occupy the margins of architecture rather than
the epistemic heart, we find a certain essence that is obscured once "nor-
mative" issues take over.

In a sense, all encounters of architecture are versions of Lacan's
encounter with the sardine can; that is, simultaneously an abjection of
vision and a connection, via some triangulated schema, to a distant glimmer. The important point is that there is other stuff in between: representational stuff that is required by decorum, by anxiety, by use, by custom. This
"stuff" is valuable simply because it is not poetic; because it returns meanings but not significance. The sandwiched space of representational meaning (which includes nearly everything we normally think of as potentially
architectural) is valuable because it can become, through a mere glimmer,
a poché within whose abject flotsam we may retrieve an archaeological past
and prophetic future.

The distribution of such glimmers is not consistent with the publicity of buildings assigned by journals and the profession that identifies
the work of certain architects as "significant." Nor does it correspond sys-
tematically to the examples cited within the volumes of architectural history. It is a product more of the trained eye, which glories in mundane as
well as fashionable spaces. Correspondence between the self-training and
subsequent education of this eye is due to the fact that many architects
have such an eye and have exercised it well, even in the face of the demands
of clients, colleagues, and communities.

FIGS. 14 & 15 Pedro Ravara,
Pharmacy, Lisbon, Portugal.

As a coda, I would include some photographs of a tiny project in Lisbon by Pedro Ravara, a minuscule pharmacy that uses mirrors, glazing, and tilted surfaces to bring about an infinity within the boxes of analgesics and diuretics [Figs. 14 and 15]. Ravara's project is a perfect example of poché: not only is the store a pocket within space but its function is a pocket within time; and, the architect responds by "poking" upwards to make this in-between place workable. The eye is "de-oculated" to consider that, in this case, the moment of meeting between the habitable world on the street and the mysterious remedies promised within the boxes and bottles stored behind the counter is sufficient for the mechanics of occultation as described by Spencer-Brown. Between the marks of the double-cross, an infinity opens up. The transaction between anterior zones of production and reception are negotiated within the taine of the mirror. One is not required to pay attention, however, to this transaction. Like all art, it happens in a background to which we are largely indifferent, as W. H. Auden noted in his comments on Pieter Brueghel's painting of the falling Icarus.

NOTES

1. Bruno Schulz, *Sanatorium Under the Sign of the Hourglass,* trans. Celina Wieniewska (New York: Viking Penguin, Inc., 1987), 1.

2. Mikel Dufrenne, *The Phenomenology of Aesthetic Experience,* trans. Edward S. Casey, Albert A. Anderson, Willis Domingo, and Leon Jacobson (Evanston, IL: Northwestern University Press, 1973), 57.

3. Paul Virilio, *The Lost Dimension,* trans. Daniel Moshenberg (New York: Semiotext[e], 1991), 13.

4. Jacques Lacan, *The Four Fundamental Concepts of Psycho Analysis,* ed. Jacques-Alain Miller, trans. Alan Sheridan (New York: W. W. Norton & Co., 1978).

5. See Penny Howell Jolly, "Antonello da Messina's Saint Jerome in His Study: An Iconographic Analysis," *Art Bulletin* LXV, 2 (1983): 238–253.

6. See Giambattista Vico, *The New Science of Giambattista Vico,* trans. Thomas Goddard Bergin and Max Harold Fisch. (Ithaca: Cornell University Press, 1958).

7. Michael Riffaterre, *Semiotic of Poetry* (Bloomington, IN: Indiana University Press, 1978).

8. Ibid, 43.

9. George Spencer-Brown, *The Laws of Form* (New York: E. P. Dutton, 1972).

10. Ibid., 32.

11. "Yes, just as all the erotic forces contained in your movement have been consumed for nothing, architecture must be conceived, erected, and burned in vain. The greatest architecture of all is the fireworker's: it perfectly shows the gratuitous consumption of pleasure." Bernard Tschumi, as cited in Tschumi, *Architecture and Disjunction* (Cambridge, Mass.: MIT Press, 1994), 262 n 9.

Enter your skiff of Musement, push off into the lake of thought, and leave the breath of heaven to swell your sail. With your eyes open, awake to what is about or within you, and open conversation with yourself; for such is all meditation: It is however not a conversation in words alone, but it is illustrated, like a lecture with diagrams and with experiments.

Charles S. Peirce[1]

The Pneumatic Bathroom

Marco Frascari

I AM INTERESTED IN PROMOTING AN ANGELIC VIEW OF PLUMBING. As everybody can tell by walking through a newly completed building, contemporary architecture has a harmful smell. This curious phenomenon is part of an intellective process that Peirce calls the play of "musement." Progressing into the play, the mephitic properties of contemporary architecture are understandable, but not acceptable. To fight this fetid condition I penned the following essay, which I perhaps should title:

The Spiritual Enigma Of The Origin Of Humanity And The Happiness Of Bathroom Imagination Reflected In My Design For A Dream House That Originated In A Curious Examination Of C. Scarpa's Design Of Bathrooms

This title, which is commensurable with the ones used by Lina Wertmuller in her macaronic movies, is too long. Notwithstanding the fact that I am interested in macaronic language and its influence on creative criticism, I cannot impose it on my wonderful readers. The short title I have selected instead possesses its own arty spirit. This is because the real value of a bathroom for human existence can only be understood through the power of the *ars macaronica*.[2] Ostensibly, at this point, I should summon for help the same powerful must evoked by Giordano Bruno in his *La Cena Delle Ceneri*:

Or qua te voglio dolce Mafelina che sei la musa di Merlin Cocai.

By now I really need thee, sweet Mafelina, who are the muse of Merlinus Cocaius.[3]

I need the euphonious muse of Merlinus Cocaius—Teofilo Folengo's pen-name—the contriver of the macaronic art, to give me the oratorical flair necessary to carry on this "exercise." I need Mafelina's gift to unfold my musing and analogical thoughts on plumbing.

I have graphically elaborated these thoughts on plumbing in a recent conception of the design for the bathrooms of a *Dream Tower*. I am going to use them as pretext for construing architecture as the source of *vita beata*; and to air the idea that the work of the architect is to design a place for "happiness." A beautiful existence, a *vita beata*, is a way of life free from impairment caused by psychic activity.[4] Architecture promotes a beatific life when it increases her inhabitants' potential for investing in psychic ability. Unfolded in a macaronic progression, my thoughts on the bathroom as the pneumatic core of a house for a *vita beata* aim to stimulate someone else's architectural spirit.[5]

Dreaming up buildings is the best way for putting together an architecture conducive to a *vita beata*.[6] Macaronic wondering is always a constructive dream, demonstrating that the architectural discipline is still and will always be sustainable, flexible, and fertile. As I have already noted, this macaronic musing is based on the house-tower I designed for an exhibition at the Contemporary Art Center in Cincinnati called "The Architect's Dream: Houses for the Next Millennium."[7] My notion of the bathroom as the entirety of the house-tower results from oneiromancy. By predictive dreaming, I do not mean Freudian stupor, but rather a creative manner set in the Peirceian mode, of the *lume naturale*. These are images I generated during the wakefulness of slumber, in my daydreaming.[8]

I will work my macaronic way surreptitiously, with the hope that my crusade in favor of bathrooms will help to bring architecture back to its original function.[9] My aim is to restore within the art of building its original scope: the production of numinous rooms[10] where a *vita beata*, a "happy" life, can take place.[11]

Before consulting the oracle of Trophonios at Bolotia visitors used to drink from two fountains which were called the water of Lethes (Forgetfulness) and the water of Mnemosysne (Memory); later they were to set upon a chair called the throne of memory (Thronos Mnemosysne).

Pausanias 9.39.8-13

Under the spell of the modern goddess Hygiene, bathroom design has lost its capacity to become the focus of relaxing psychic activity.[12] Instead, the bathroom has become a place—or better, a metonymic space—a closet of secret constrains.[13] The bathroom is no longer considered a dignifying place where a sacred spring or a mundus is located, but rather a space where water is present and should be swiftly removed with hydraulic efficiency. It is a space that can be determined on the one hand by what the Germans call *existenz minimum*,[14] or on the other by the partial or total refusal of that code, and by construing the space under the mandate of a "de luxe" design lavishness. In other words, a bath can be conceived within Spartan rigor or as tasteless ostentation of material wealth.[15] This ambiguity reveals that our modern attitude toward bathrooms is Manichaean, grounded in what Louis Kahn would have probably called the "volume zero" of the crumbling history of architecture.

My curiosity about the nature and design of bathrooms arose during my professional training, which took place in Verona, a city abundant with Roman hydraulic dreams.[16] In the office of Arrigo Rudi Architetto, during the development of any design, our first task was the meticulous refinement of the plan and sections of the bathrooms and the layout of the ceramic tiles. These bathrooms never employed plan diagrams published in the Italian graphic standards, the *Manual dell Architetto*. Instead they were custom-designed every time, the result of a slow process of refinement that often took the same amount of working time as the remaining part of the design. At the beginning, I was annoyed by this waste of time. However, a few years later, during an after-dinner consideration, while I was eyeing Carlo Scarpa's plans for the Fondazione A. Masieri in Volta di Canal[17] I came to realize the importance and the transcendence of the design of bathrooms. Like Paul on his way to Damascus, it dawned on me that the bathroom was the ideal place for fostering a beatific life. It is the only *metaphysic* place left within the mundane metaphytic house, the last locus of architectural union between *voluptas* and *venustas*, between sacred and profane.[18] The bathroom, in current architecture, is the terminal station of the *pneuma* that leads our lives toward a beatific state, the last domicile of Synesius' *phantasikon* pneuma,[19] of Bruno's *spiritus fantasticus*.[20] This *pneuma* or *spiritus* dwells in the bathrooms as a reminder of when the *pneuma* freely flowed through the totality of the house, making human dwellings always numinous places.

What was it that struck my soul as I looked at Scarpa's design of bathrooms? It was the relationship between the placement of the bathrooms and the plan of the building. In most of the buildings I had collected for my design library, a bathroom was successful if it didn't stick out like a sore thumb in the layout of the plan. It did not matter if they were de-luxe or minimum existence bathrooms. The geometry of the bathroom was subdued; it fit the dominant theme of the plan configuration. Scarpa's bathrooms ignore this convention. In the plan of the Fondazione Masieri, as in many of his other designs, the bathrooms are the dominant architectural theme within the symphony of the plan.

A 1915 advertisement by Trenton Potteries demonstrates exquisitely this understanding of the bathroom pneuma [Fig. 1]. The ad depicts a luminous and ethereal bathroom at the heart of a house shown in silhouette. This bathroom, projected into the house through a clever manipulation of scale and perspective, is not lit by the light that comes from a window or an electric fixture; it is illuminated by the divine radiance of the *spiritus fantasticus*. What this commercial image visually proves is that the bathroom is a numinous place. The numinous manifests itself as a power or a force that is different from the forces of nature.[21] Musical instru-

FIG 1. A 1915 advertisement for Trenton Potteries Company

ments, architectural forms, beasts of burden, vehicles of transportation, and prostheses have been and will always be numinous objects.

The bathroom is a place of numinous objects and it is in itself a numinous place.[22] During the everyday use of the bathroom, hierophanies can take place. A hierophany separates the thing that manifests the sacred from everything else around it. Hierophanies can become symbols that are then translated into symbolic forms. These forms become sacred, because they embody directly the spirit or power of transcended beings. For example, the pearl throughout history serves as a symbol or a numinous object representing a cosmological center that draws together key meanings associated with the moon, women, fertility, and birth. The same can be said about the bathroom and its objects, since they can draw together meanings of initiation, love (both profane and sacred), beauty and ugliness, mutation and transformation, and birth. The bathroom manifests *mundus* (Greek: *kosmos*): we walk in unclean (in Italian, rhetorically: *immondi*) and walk out clean (again, in Italian: *mondi*).[23] The bathroom is the last architectural artifact where an understanding of the cosmos is present as a symbolic expression of a human cosmogony and cosmetic quintessence.

The cardinal role of architecture is to make our life congenial and satisfying, in other words, to make it a *numinous place for a vita beata*. The proper professional should be concerned with the constitution of these numinous places. The numinous place is a particular place dealing with the canonical dimensions of inhabitation—the holy dimension of dwelling. Such a place emits a sense of well-being. A numinous place is a special ambit that stands for a holy place, minus both its moral and rational aspects. It is a non-rational place of well-being. In numinous architecture, buildings are therapeutic, and within them we can have a beatific life.

Andrea Palladio's villas, perfect places for the *vita beata*, are idyllic demonstrations of a numinous architecture. Their numinous rooms are the result of a triple integral of numinous constructions. Their measures, decoration, and proportion concern time, place, and personality. Palladio's rooms—in Italian, his *stanzas*—are therapeutic places where someone can enjoy a respite from the worries of human and environmental negotiation. They are places for the non-rational presence of *otium*, the spiritual *sine qua non* of the *vita beata*.

In these spiritual villas, no one room is labeled "bathroom"; the majority of these rooms were numinous. Consequently, the performance

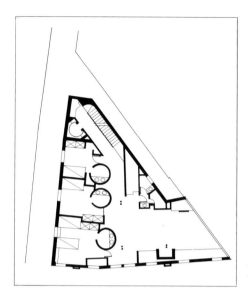

FIG 2. Carlo Scarpa. Plan for the Masieri Foundation in Volta di Canal, Venice, Italy.

of bathing or other bathroom activities could take place in any of the rooms. The virtuously happy owners of a Palladian villa could enjoy beatific ablutions or discharges, in the "room of the muses" or in the "room of Seasons." They could do it looking out in whichever direction was more visually and thermally delightful, or even having the slipper-bath or the commode dragged before an open fire.[24] The beginning of the industrial revolution and the invention of cheap plumbing and bathroom fixtures fixed the location of the bathroom, a necessary space in the back. No longer would the residents of the house lose breath carrying hot water from the kitchen to the portable bathtub; no longer would they have to look for the chamber-pot under the bed or in the night-stand.

In Italian, we say that a building is of a "large breath" (*di largo respiro*). Numinous places are always of large breath, since they are truly expressions of pneumatic architecture. My use of the term pneumatic is clear by now: I do not mean inflatable or merely aerated architecture, but architecture where pneuma or spirit is a living presence. The building or the room then becomes either a deity or a *machina,* a pneumatic machine.

The bathrooms of Scarpa's Fondazione Masieri (1968) are exemplary pneumatic machines [Fig. 2]; they are small rooms but they make the place of large breath. The cylindrical bodies of the bathrooms determine completely the space of the upper floors of this small building. The original program, housing for architectural students, required an environment that could foster architectural creativity. In these bathrooms, necessary fixtures become sacred fonts, the springs where the nymph Egeria displays her phenomenological expressions. Tectonically, these bathrooms are cylinders coated on the outside with a gleaming and wonderfully colored *stucco lucido*, which on the inside resembles a womb. They provide the means of creative egress.[25] In their tectonic power and in their lustrous plaster omnipotence they reveal the lustral power of a font, where water is analogous to the amniotic liquid within which life originated and which facilitates birth. These bathrooms are perfect analogical details for a lunar building consecrated to the training of the mother-architect.[26] In these bathrooms dwell the extraordinary scented spirit of architecture.

Scarpa is an architect who knows how to deal with the affairs of water in a building. Unlike many of his professional peers, he has not forgotten the joy of water, nor he has overcome his fear.[27] For instance, Scarpa's design for the Fondazione Querini-Stampalia in Venice does not prevent the *aqua alta*, the high tide water that constantly floods this maritime city, from entering the building; here he employs neither visible nor invisible waterproof barriers or restraints. His architecture gently allows the water to come in, making it part of a joyful event, then lets it back out of the building when the tide lowers.[28] In the bathroom, this dimension of water becomes sacred. In this inner aedicula, the detailing of the floor is analogous to the detailing of the ground floor of Querini-Stampalia, ready to deal with the *aqua alta* caused by the shower or an overflowing toilet. The bath is a microcosm, a model of the macrocosm of the edifice.

The combination of shower, basin, and toilet within the cylindrical bathrooms of the Fondazione Masieri becomes a *stanza da bagno* (room for bathing). To a superficial eye reading the plan, the circularity for the baths will appear as a presence of monoblocs expressing the smoothness of prefabrication. They are not interstitial spaces that have become overgrown columns. Within the triangular plan of the existing shell they become *stanzas* for and of thought, just like stanzas composing a poem.[29]

This idea of the bath as a *stanza* is revealed clearly in another design of Scarpa, the Villa Ottolenghi (1974-79), in Bardolino near the Lake of Garda. To enter this house it is necessary to descend within

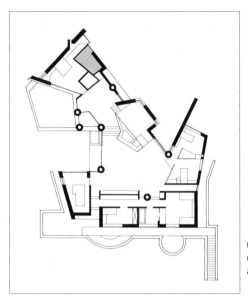

FIG 3. First Solution: bathroom as a closet (shaded area at upper left)

Carlo Scarpa, Plan for Villa Ottolenghi, Bardolino, Verona, near the lake of Garda

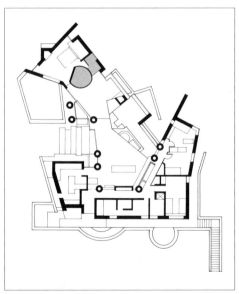

FIG 4. Second Solution: bathroom as an oval (shaded area at upper left)

mother earth. Inside, the "room for bathing" is the stanza of the stanzas making the poem of the house. The Ottolenghi house is a highly therapeutic edifice. It is a chthonic villa, the roof of which is a threshing floor, a cosmological representation under which the dwelling takes place.[30]

Scarpa achieved the solution for the master-bedroom bathroom through a long process of design refinements. First, the bathroom was present as the traditional solution, that of a closet added to the bedroom such that it has no presence or influence within the body of the house [Fig. 3].[31] The bathroom then went through three stages of design during which it evolved from a private space to a numinous place that interacts with the totality of the house [Fig. 4].

Having received our ablutions in memories and disremembering I now turn to memory's odoriferous throne. The nature and location of the "odor of sanctity" has always fascinated me, always caused me to put my macaronic thinking to work, especially since we live in a society that is superciliously proud of being odorless, as the many, obsessive commercials for deodorants on television continually remind us. In this redolent paranoia, hundreds of products that claim to sanitize air and surfaces emit an odor of sanity in order to eliminate the odor of sanctity. Such habits proliferate miasmic buildings, an unwholesome architecture, hard to deplore because it is odorless. In our contemporary culture, scent is good; odor is bad (most deodorants are scented, even unscented ones, which always have some presence of scent). We deodorize our houses the same way we deodorize our bodies.[32]

What kind of smell is the odor of sanctity? When I raised the question with my macaronic grandmother, who supervised my religious education,[33] she answered: the fragrance of roses and incense. However, on the annual visit during *Ognisanti* (Halloween) to many holy corpses kept in the churches of Mantua, my nose told me that the odor of sanctity was not a fragrance, but a musty odor mixed with the stench of old incense and cleansing oils. This strange odor is the odor of the pneumatic beginning of the principle of our humanity. Gianbattista Vico, in his *New Science*, argues it bounds human reason, which he identifies with the burial of the dead and, therewith, the immortality of human soul: "Afterward, the god-fearing giants, those settled in the mountains, must have become sensible of the stench from the corpses of their dead rotting on the ground near by, and must have begun to bury them."[34] For Vico, our being human begins with the act of covering the putrid bodies of the ancestors with *humus*. The smell is their immortal soul, their spirit. For Vico, the pneuma is a sacred odor of memory. Smell, the strongest sense of memory, is the key to the door of the *mundus imaginalis*.[35] From this point of view, bathrooms are the modern locus of the odor of sanctity, an aroma for mental sanity, pneumatic iconostases, the current golden gates to a beatific life.

I have condensed all these concerns for odor and bathroom numinosity in the design of the bathroom for my Tower for the Next Millennium. The pneumatic spaces I have designed for my dream house have ineffable and impersonal aspects, although they have been planned in very particular way and can be used in a specific and individual manner. They are numinous bathrooms and the geometry of their plan is maternal. The materials and the lines of these bathrooms are ruled by the same geomaternal procedures that order the design of the tower.[36]

My design procedure began with a sketch of a bathtub in which an epiphany was taking place. I followed this declaration of intention with a study of details of the different china objects present in bathrooms. Lastly I studied the geometry of the bathroom.

The first sketch [Fig. 5] shows an angelic vision, as the way for entering the pneumatic world of architectural imagining, the *mundus imaginalis*: a world that is ontologically as real as the world of senses and of the intellect. This world requires its own faculty of perception, namely a powerful, imaginative faculty with a cognitive function, a noetic value that is as real as that of sense perception or intellectual intuition. It is a basis for demonstrating the validity of dreams. This world should not to be confused with "fantasy" that is nothing but an outpouring of "imaginings."

Following Scarpa, I refused to treat the bathroom as a closet or an interstitial place. Instead I played the geomater of the tower bathrooms, in one case as an enhancement of the *stanza*, in the other as counterpart of the main column of the structure of the tower. I based the geometry of these two numinous spaces on curved lines that recall anthropomorphic references to organs and skins. In the more detailed drawings, the study of the bathrooms is present only in the study of a detail, the basin and the mirror, selected as emblems of the numinosity of the place [Fig. 6]. In the final drawing, I have studied this detail in parallel with the compass-weathervane set on the roof of the tower [Fig. 7].

FIG. 5 Marco Frascari, "The Dream House for the Next Millenium." Preparatory sketch showing an epiphany taking place in the bathtub

FIG. 6 Marco Frascari, "The Dream House for the Next Millenium." Preparatory sketch of the bathroom basin and mirror

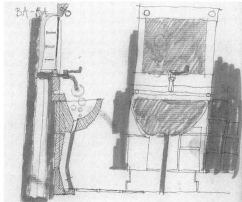

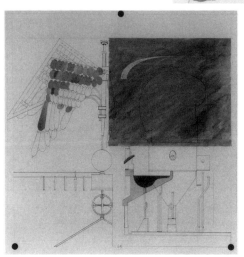

FIG 7. Marco Frascari, "The Dream House for the Next Millenium." Bathroom basin and mirror with compass-weathervane

174

In the bathroom of the master bedroom, the bathtub interacts directly with the main column [Figs. 8 and 9]. It becomes the space of transition between the space of the bed and the elongated niche of the bathroom. Both the spaces are vaulted—finished in *stucco lucido*—only the space above the bathtub is flat, and it is a mirror. I meant to reconnect this configuration to the intention expressed in the first sketch showing the angelic vision the world of the image, the *mundus imaginalis* of architecture. Like the bathroom, the bathtub is a setting that requires its own noetic faculty. This mirror is homologous with the one Filippo Brunelleschi used to conjure up the perspective image of the ancient baptistery, an act he performed three braccia beyond the limina of the cathedral of Florence, thereby inventing *costruzione legittima*. Active imagination is the mirror par excellence, the epiphanic place for images. Lying in the bathtub, *ubi* becomes an *ubique*.

By these bathrooms I aim to promote a beatific existence, a *vita beata*, as a form of being with no detriment induced by psychic trials. The attainment of a *vita beata*, a good spirit, is the goal of human existence. This tower is designed as an ensemble of places for lovers of virtue. Its bathrooms are the loci where the imaginal pneuma or spirit of virtuous happiness dwells. This architecture provokes a beatific life by amplifying her inhabitants' latent talents of investing in psychic efficiency. The body of the dream-tower is odorous again by the angelic plumbing of her bathrooms.

I'm Lost, Lost! Mama! I'M LOST! OH! I AM LOST!
You are not lost NEMO. Go to sleep and Behave! Hear?
Windsor McCay, *Little Nemo in Slumberland*

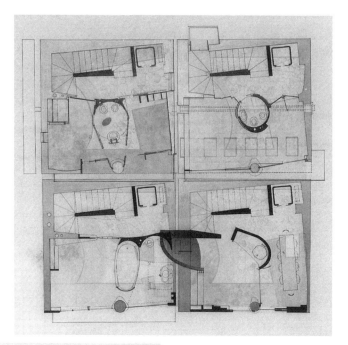

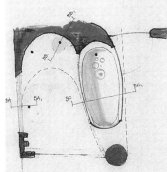

FIG 8. (above) Marco Frascari, plan, "The Dream House for the Next Millennium." Note master bedroom bath in lower left quadrant.

FIG. 9 (at left) Plan of the master bedroom bathtub.

FIG. 10 (below) Preparatory sketch showing the volume of the master bedroom bathroom.

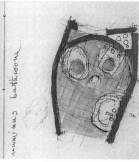

176

NOTES

1. Charles S. Peirce, *Collected papers of Charles Sanders Peirce*, 8 vols. ed. Charles Hartshorne and Paul Weiss (Cambridge: Harvard University Press, 1931–1958), 6.461. The work of Charles Sanders Peirce plays a dominant part in this essay, a "play" which began in odd half-hour increments, but will soon be converted into a 'scientific' study entitled "*Voglia d'architettura*: a musing storytelling for the architects of the next millennium." "Musement" for Peirce is not a solitary meditation, but a pragmatic and poetic habit that can be translated into graphic forms. For an understanding of this playful path of interpretative play, see Peirce, *Collected papers* (6.458 to 6.463); Thomas A. Sebeok *Carnival!* (New York: Mouton, 1984); and Gabriella Fabrichesi, *Sulle tracce del segno* (Florence: La nuova, 1986).

2. Recently I realized I am a macaronic thinker. As any other macaronic person, such as the progenitor Merlinus Cocaius, I am not a revolutionary. My point of view is incompatible with any great program for the recording of the world and my critical thinking is beyond politics, religion, or morals: it is a critique that investigates the basis of our comprehension and representation of the world. The aim of a truly macaronic person is not reevaluation, but demonstration that is a permanent presentation of monstrous evidence. The macaronic art is a special manner of utterance that allows a successful investigation of the unempirical by making analogies resonate in the mind. A macaronic person knows the power of edible expressions that, instead of being simulated or dissimulated, can be assimilated by the reader. Digesting these resonating and analogical utterances, readers are forced to carry out a phenomenological reading. The importance of this phenomenological reading lies in a thorough enlightenment of the awareness of a person wonderstruck by the associations built into the analogical images. A non-reformed friar who lived most of his life in Cipata near Mantua (Italy) under the paternalistic ruling of the Gonzage, Teofilo Folengo, used the name Merlinus Cocaius to sign his macaronic writing. The most famous among them is the *Baldus*. The word "macaronic" was coined by Folengo himself, whose *Macaronic Book (Liber Macaronics)* was published in 1517. He explains that the macaronic art is so called from macaroni, which is "quoddman pulmentum farina, caseo, botiro compagination, grossum, rude, et rusticanum." (2nd ed. 1521)

3. Giordano Bruno, *The Ash Wednesday Supper*, ed and trans. E.A. Goesselin and Lawrence S. Lerner (Toronto: Toronto Press, 1995), 113.

4. *Vita beata* is what the Greek philosophers call *eudaimona*. The attainment of a *vita beata*, a good spirit, was the telos of human existence, an *arete* (virtue). For this understanding of virtuous happiness, see Helen North *From Myth to Icon: Reflection of the Greek Ethical Doctrine in Literature and Art* (Ithaca: Cornell University Press, 1979). The only architect who addressed the topic of virtuous happiness in an explicit manner is Antonio Averino, known as Filarete.

5. The design of this tower-house is a set of manic projections, transforming non-semiotic materials—such as stone, wood, glass, textile, nuglos, conjunctions—into indeces, icons and symbols allowing mental joy and despair. Although I am completely responsible for the house-tower design, Alice Ghum and Claudio Sgarbi contributed labor and thoughts for "The Architect's Dream: Houses for the Next Millenium" exhibition at the Contemporary Arts Center in Cincinnati, November 19, 1993 to January 23, 1994.

6. As Novalis (psuedonym of Friedrich von Hardenberg) has suggested in his *Allemeines Brouillon*, dreams instruct us on the facility of our spirit in penetrating every object and transforming itself in every object. Novalis, *Philosophical Writings* (Albany: State Univer-

sity of New York Press, 1997). Through daydreaming, the reader can enter my dream bathroom. This is the only real way to read drawings of architecture. No other procedure allows us to transmute the composition of lines describing a future building in an assembly of meaningful rooms and details. Dreaming is the critical, necessary procedure for designing and for understanding designs that aim to create an architecture for a *vita beata*. In his *Scientific-Natural Studies of Freiberg*, Novalis has indicated that dreams originated in the peristaltic movement of the brain and defined daydreaming as a beatific circumstance (ed. 1 p. 82). Dreaming is a macaronic art.

7. On the one hand, I strongly believe that real architects should never talk about their own designs to explain the theory and the practice of architecture. On the other hand, I also cogently trust that architects should always present their dreams, as a way to foster the theory and the practice of the discipline. The design presented here has been a dream, therefore I can delight in presenting it. On the topic of my drawing, see Marco Frascari, *Una Pillola per Sognare. . . Una Casa* (Milan: Editrice Progetti, 1995).

8. For the Peircean mode of dreaming, see Vincent Colapietro, "Dreams: Such Stuff as Meanings are Made on," *Versus* 49 (1988): 65–79 and Fabrichesi, *Sulle tracce del segno*, 215–227.

9. In response to an invitation by the magazine *McCall's*, readers commented on their dream house. Most readers preferred a cozy cottage and soft color schemes. Many readers saw the bathroom as a holy refuge and wanted a Jacuzzi. See Andrea Bauman, "How to get your dream house!" *McCall's* (7 October 1994): 122, 144.

10. Numinous rooms are places inhabited by a human or spirit that elicits in most of us the reaction of awe or memory. These places are fabricated instances of material culture. The numinosity of an architectural artifact (i.e., its intangible and invisible significance) operates in association with the artifacts inhabiting the virtual world that architectural users carry within themselves. These associations have always had an emotional weight that can be understood through the telling of a story. The story I have in mind is told by the architectural details of the artifact in question. Stories embodied in details are the interaction of emotions, ideas, and beliefs within a material culture.

11. The first practitioner to point out that the scope of architecture is to foster a *vita beata* was Andrea Palladio. In his *Four Books* (1570:6), he states that architecture helps a person "to achieve those things. . . that make him/her happy (if any happiness can be found down here) [*a conseguir quelle cose, che lo possono render felice (se felicita alcuna si ritrova qua giu)*]." For the relationship between *beata* and "happy," see North, *From Myth to Icon* and Acquaviva, Sabino S., *L'Eclissi del sacro nella civilta industriale* (Milan: Comunità, 1971); see also Acquaviva, *Progettare la felicita* (Rome: Laterza, 1994).

12. See Georges Vigarello, *Le propre et le sale: l'hygiene du corps depuis le Moyen Age* (Paris: Le Seuil, 1985). This is the first monograph that deals directly with the correspondence in the change of body perceptions and social cleanliness. The study focuses on the evolution of bathroom life in France since the Middle Ages. The Middle-Age bath that had served relaxation and pleasure rather than hygiene is perceived as a serious threat for the open-pored baroque body whose interior is in constant flux and upheaval. The work is particularly strong on seventeenth- and eighteenth-century documentation.

13. See Alan Stewart, "The Early Modern Closet Discovered," *Representations* 50 (Spring 1995).

14. Within the discipline of architecture the word *existent* appeared during the Modern Movement and it is generally related to the minimum standards for living. *Existent* is a peculiar

German word that made its way into architectural thinking in the locution *existent minimum*, but it cannot be translated into the English cognate "minimum existence."

15. The idea of "de luxe" design and the problem of ambiguous attitudes toward bathroom-canons can be explained by knowing that the idea of luxury (*lusso*) derives from lechery and lust (*lussuria*).

16. The thought elaborated here originated during my training as a professional in the office of Arrigo Rudi, where I worked for two years after my graduation at the IUAV in Venice. Rudi is the architect who helped Carlo Scarpa during the work of transformation of the Museum of Castelvecchio, in Verona. Among the people working in the office there was the strong belief that this absorption with the bathroom was one of the many "Scarpismi" or "Scarpate" that Rudi had in his bag of design-tricks. Indeed, Scarpa was completely in love with the designing of bathrooms. One of his favorite dinner stories was how wonder-struck he was when he visited the bathroom at the Four Seasons Hotel in New York, during his only trip to the U.S.

17. Angolo Masieri, a young architect from Udine, was a pupil and collaborator of Carlo Scarpa. Masieri died in car crash on his way to perfect his study of architecture with Frank Lloyd Wright, in Arizona, in 1952. After his death, the parents who had commissioned Wright to design their house in Volta di Canal on the Great Canal, in Venice, changed the scope of the design and decided to build a special residence for students in architecture. After Wright's design was refused by a city administration that could not understand the future of Venice nor the importance of architecture for it, the building stood as an empty shell until it reached near collapse. At that point, Valcrianno Pastor, one of the first pupils of Scarpa, was commissioned to design the student facility. After Pastor restored the walls, the commission was given to Carlo Scarpa. Scarpa died before the completion of the building. It was completed by Franca Semi, who had collaborated with Scarpa on the design from the beginning. Today the building serves as a museum and exhibition space, which drastically alter the magic qualities of this edifice for architectural edification.

18 A properly numinous bath belongs to what Alberto Sartoris calls *Architettura della Metafisica*. See Alberto Sartoris, *Metafisica della architettura* (Pamphlet Architecture No. 10). trans Ty. Geltmaker and Diane Ghirardo (New York: Pamphlet Architecture Ltd, 1984); and see also Sartoris, *L'actualité du rationalisme*. Preface by J. Gubler (Paris: Bibliotheque des arts, 1986).

19. Syndesis of Cyrene, a Platonic philosopher-bishop whose acceptance of Christianity was provisional and remained secondary to his commitment to Neoplatonism, wrote an influential work on the phenomenon of dreams. This work embodies a theory of allegory together with a study of the efficacy of dreams for the art of divination. For a historical understanding of Pneuma, see Margaret J. Osler, *Atoms, Pneuma, and Tranquility: Epicurean and Stoic Themes in European Thought* (New York: Cambridge University Press, 1991).

20. In his *De Magia*, Bruno follows Synesius's thesis and relates the pneuma to the subtle body—the *corpo sottile*—of angels. See Robert Klein, *Form and Meaning: Essays on the Renaissance and Modern Art*, trans. Madeline Jay and Leon Wieseltier (New York: Viking Press, 1979), 54–57.

21. Pioneers in formulating ideas about the numinous element are Carl Jung, Lawrence Kuber, Thomas Troward, and Rudolf Otto. Otto, a German scholar of religion, coined the

term "*numinous.*" It derives from the Latin *numen*. By analogy with the word coinage "omin>ominous," Otto coined "numen>numinous." The word *numen*, in Latin, is connected with the concept of the sacred (holy), indicating the sacred dimension of magic.

22. Otto says that the idea of the numinous does not exist in modern religion; per by extension we can say that the idea of numinous space is a category of evaluation that does not exist in modern design. The subjunctive nature of this space is unacknowledged by modern designers.

23. For the opposition between clean and uncleanness, see "Guilt or problems and rites of purification," Proceedings of the XI International Congress of the Association of History of Religion, Sept. 1965, vol. II, Leiden, 1968.

24. This mobile nature of bathing was very comfortable. See Tony Rivers, Dan Cruckshank, et al. *The Name of the Room* (London: BBC Books, 1992), chap. II.

25. *Egeria* and "egress" have a common root, meaning "to carry out"; *Egeria*, from (*egerer*, push out) was the nymph one invoked to ensure a good childbirth.

26. In the beginning of the second book of his treatise, following in Leon Battista Alberti's animalistic footsteps, Filarete suggests that buildings are alive like human beings, and that the architect is the mother, whereas the client is the father. If they don't know each other, it is physically impossible to deliver a design in the constructed world. During the architectural pregnancy, using fantasy (*fantasticare*), the mother-architect grows the baby-building in his-her memory. After nine or seven months the baby-building, a small wooden model is born. This is a monster that will, with proper construction and care, grow into an adult-building. See Filarete, *Trattato di architettura* (1460), 29. For Scarpa's maternal understanding of architecture, see William Braham and Marco Frascari, "The Geomater of Architecture," *Paradosso* 8 (1995): 16–27.

27. For the fear and joy of water, see Gerhard Auer, "Living Wetter, On Consumption of Water in the Townhouse" *Daidalos* 55 (15 March 1995).

28. Scarpa's first expression of this Zen approach to the predicament of high tide water is found in the restoration of the ground floor and the garden of the Fondazione Querini-Stampalia, near Campo Santa Maria Mator Domini in Venice.

29. "And here one must know that this term (stanza) has been chosen for technical reason exclusively, so that what contains the entire art of the canzone should be called stanza, that is a capacious dwelling or receptable for the entire craft. For just as the canzone is the womb (grembo) of the entire thought, so the stanza enfolds it entire technique." Dante, *De Vulgari Eloquentia* II, 9; see also Giorgio Agamben, *Stanzas* (Minneapolis: University of Minnesota Press, 1993).

30. The origin of this roof design is in the threshing floor elaborated for the courtyard of the Villa Al Palazzello in Monselice, near Padua. This Paduan floor, called by Scarpa himself "The Moon And The Sun," becomes in Casa Ottolengthi a fully developed cosmological floor under which all aspects of the house take their configurations.

31. The architecture of the closet and its cultural influence is clearly discussed in Stewart, "The Early Modern Closet Discovered." Closets are places of utter privacy. They promote total withdraw from the public sphere of the house. This condition was forced upon bathrooms from the rigorist position taken by few of the theoreticians of architecture that Joseph Rykwert has labeled "early moderns," and by the German fancy for *existenz minimum.*

32. Contemporary architecture smells bad. It is malodorous; desperately we need to restore a

pleasant odor. Unfortunately, an analysis of this topic is malodorously beyond the scope of this article. For further acquaintance with the question of smell and architecture and a set of considerations on the present-day aromatic paranoia, see Annick Le Guerer, *Scent: The Mysterious and Essential Powers of Smell*, trans. Richard Miller (New York: Turtle Bay Books, 1992).

33. For instance, my grandmother's explanation for the acronym DOM, found on the doors of many churches, was the imperative "Done Omeni Marieve" ("women and men get married"), instead of the official "Domine Omnia Mundi," which for her meant "God cleans all of us."

34. Gianbattista Vico, *Principii di Scienza Nuova* (Naples, 1744), paragraph 529.

35. The theory of the *mundus imaginalis* is closely bound up with a theory of imaginative cognition and of the imaginative function, which is truly a central, mediating function, owing both to the median and mediating positions of the *mundus imaginalis*. The cognitive function of imagination provides the foundation for a rigorous analogical knowledge permitting us to evade the dilemma of current rationalism, which gives us a choice only between the two banal, dualistic terms of either "matter" or "mind." Henry Corbin defines the *mundus imaginalis*, as an *intermondo*, a space where visual imagination establishes true and real thoughts—an imaginative perception and an imaginative knowledge, that is, an imaginative consciousness. Henry Corbin, *Mundus Imaginalis or the Imaginary and the Imaginal* (Ipswich: Golgonooza Press, 1976), 57

36. I have elected to call this tool for the pursuit of the *vita beata* in architecture "Geomater." This term was coined by James Joyce, who combined matrix, *mater* (mother), and meter with geo-(earth) in a pregnant metaphor describing geometry as a discipline of measurement, prediction, and genesis. I am an image-maker who constructs and construes geomaternal figures in and on the world. These maternal figures are the materialistic nature of the "graphplot" (i.e. the full-bodied science of architectural representation). This "graphplot" is structured in three parts according to the nature of the architectural imagination: mantic geometry, projective geometry that makes visible the invisible; body geometry, metric geometry that makes tangible the intagible; and color geometry, topical geometry that makes material the immaterial. These categories have been used to unfold the image-making potential of architecture, historically and didactically. They are not so much divisions of kind as different aspects of the imaginative metaphysics that is Geomater. They overlap in their procedures and share the logic of magic and poetics.

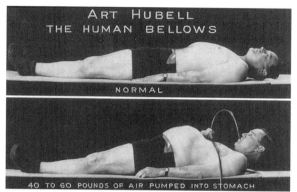

ART HUBELL
THE HUMAN BELLOWS

NORMAL

40 TO 60 POUNDS OF AIR PUMPED INTO STOMACH

FIG. 1

. . . avec cette Acropole au fond de moi, dans le ventre.
. . . with this Acropolis deep within me, in the belly.
> Le Corbusier, as cited in Persico Punto, ed. *Capo per l'architettura*

I am so full of ideas. . . that I am likely to blow up or commit suicide
unless I can let them out on paper.
> F.L. Wright, letter to Hilla Rebay, curator of
> the Solomon R. Guggenheim Foundation, June 1943

I must express what I have inside, otherwise I will explode.
> "Architect" Kirk Douglas speaking to "Surveyor" Kim Novak,
> in Richard Quine's 1960 film *Strangers When We Meet*

What am I saying, O my belly? You are cruel, you separate children from
their fathers. No! I don't love you anymore. Now you're just a full sack, O
my belly smiling at the navel, O my stretchy, bearded, smooth, bombed,
dolorous, round, silky, ennobling belly. Because you do ennoble me, I
had forgotten that, O my belly more beautiful than the sun.
> Guillaume Apollinaire, "The Poet Assassinated," in
> *The Poet Assassinated and Other Stories*

Architects' Bellies: Reflection on the Plumbing of Masculine Conceptions

Claudio Sgarbi

THERE ARE THREE STORIES I LIKE TO TELL TOGETHER. THE FIRST IS an historical account on the representation of architecture as a female body, and the image of the architect as a pregnant woman. The second is my account of the famous movie by Peter Greenaway, *The Belly of an Architect*, in which an architect becomes obsessed with his own cancerous stomach while his wife experiences a happy pregnancy. The third is a version of a popular ballad in which a master mason buries his pregnant wife in the wall in order to be able to complete his building. These stories are quite far away from each other in time and in space, yet they suggest a continuity in human thinking about architecture, architects, and their genders. The meanings of these stories are too deep to be explained. Nevertheless, I enjoy venturing into their various meanders.

To begin, permit me to share a passage from a letter I wrote to a student and dear friend of mine:

> . . . I remember you asked me something I will never be able to answer: Where is your room, your *raum*, in this manscape? I do not know what I will ever be able to understand of the mysterious woman which resides in my fertile emptiness (shall I say my fertile nothingness?), since she is inevitably other than all I will happen, hope, or pretend to be. As I told you, I believe in the huge, immense difference of genders. Too many stu-

pid efforts have been made to flatten this difference. I am not oriented toward the consumption of goods, but toward the fertility of inner space. This inner space and the richness of interhuman relationships it creates is the very aim I tend toward. This implies a deep criticism of the professional (man-made) tools I use as an architect.

Dear L., I have no secrets to tell. Uncertain fathers always die before unveiling a secret they pretend to know. Mothers do not. They breed the secret they are. . .

And L. answered in this beautiful way:

. . . Slowly and surely, each day, I am using my father's tools to make my mother's room. For me the question is no longer "is it male or is it female?" I know I am male and I am female. I am my mother and I am my father, a whole (hole) and complete person. I am still distrustful of what architecture is about today but I have recently remembered the magic of my own forgotten hands. . .[1]

The following essay is simply my attempt to reestablish the ground for this conversation.

PERSONIFICATION AND TRANSSEXUALITY

Martianus Capella[2] was the first to state clearly that all the arts have female bodies. This was not an original idea. Objects and concepts that nowadays occupy neutral space used to be located either in a masculine or in a feminine domain. Their gender was not a grammatical issue, insofar as thinking and doing always established a relationship with someone and not with something.[3] Ontogenesis and philogenesis indicate that our imagination is anthropomorphic.

Music, Mathematics, Astronomy, Poetry—all the classical arts and sciences—have been traditionally represented as women, but prior to the nineteenth century, they were generally practiced by men who celebrated the female nature of conception. To have an idea in one's mind is like housing a baby in one's belly. The fertile womb of a woman, her nurturing breasts, and her domesticated surroundings are the archetypal metaphor for letting something in, nourishing it, presenting it in good shape, and then raising it in a good manner. This is true for all arts and sciences, but for Architecture there is something here deeper than metaphor and analogy. Indeed, the womb is not just an archetype of inner space, and the mother's body not simply a representation of the first house; rather they are inner space and first house in themselves.

The gap between the magic of the belly and the magic of the head was not felt as a problem by men speculating on their own conceptions. Before the modern era men of art and science knew that the power of conceiving was female and they dedicated their work to a female body of knowledge. Their conceptions were just a mimesis of female fecundity.

When Vitruvius wrote about Architecture, leaving us the only extant treatise from the ancient world, he imagined this *scientia* as a female body with ten holes, the *Ten Books on Architecture*.[4] During the Renaissance, the body of she-Architecture was carefully represented; each member, its posture, ornaments, and garments, acquired peculiar meanings. Giovan Battista Caporali showed Architecture like a goddess barely contained inside her temple [Fig. 2]. In the frontispiece of the second edition of Marc-Antoine Laugier's *Essai sur l'architecture*, the representation of Architecture suggests pregnancy [Fig. 3]. Daniele Barbaro and Andrea Palladio centered the composition of their frontispiece of *De architectura* on the swollen belly of a woman standing on a pedestal [Fig. 4]. Berardo Galiani exaggerated this idea even more so in his depiction of Architecture with a very large belly, ready to deliver her baby [Fig. 5].

The first known document comparing the architect to a female who is fecundated by the client was written by Filarete around 1460.[5] In Filarete's universe the architect was meant to keep the "idea" of a building for nine months in his "belly," then deliver it in the form of a little wooden model. Here officially for the first time the gender of architecture was translated improperly in the body of the transsexual architect who has to change his nature in order to be fecundated. This transsexual architect is not like the primordial androgyne,[6] complete in itself and able to self-fecundate. He is male, but needs to shift to the female gender in order to offer his body as a house for another male's fecundating power.

I would like to stress the fact that here not simply Architecture, but the architect, too, is female. The architect and architecture are one thing. Jean-Jacques Lequeu's self-portraits as male, female, prostitute, and hermaphrodite are an ironical bequest of this uncomfortable metaphorical

FIG. 2 Architecture appears as a divinity enthroned in the cell of a temple barely big enough to contain her. She displays her attributes: a compass open to the sky on her head replaces the crown and symbolizes *ratiocinatio*; in her right hand, instead of a scepter, she clasps an instrument of measure; in her left hand, standing on a stool, is a plumb line. Frontispiece, M. Giovan Battista Caporali di Perugia, *Vetruvio in volgar lingua raportato*,1536.

FIG. 3 Frontispiece from Marc-Antoine Laugier's *Essai sur l'architecture*, 1755. Note she-Architecture's well-rounded belly.

FIG. 4 Andrea Palladio and Daniele Barbaro's illustration of she-Architecture. This goddess is looking at the unity of measure she holds in the left hand; she opens the right hand like a compass toward it (or toward her breast). The dress unfolds around her belly in an eye-shaped manner. Indeed, the navel seen through the transparent veil is the focus of the entire composition. Frontispiece, D. Barbaro, *Vitruvio. I dieci libri di architettura*, 1567.

FIG. 5 Architecture is in full bloom, not just a woman with a nice belly. Indeed, she is ready to deliver a baby. Outside the threshold of her temple, she prepares all the other arts for the event. In her left hand she holds a plan, in her body she houses a model ready to be delivered, and with the right hand she addresses the site where the building will be built. In this scene, Architecture herself, not the architect, has the pleasure of conceiving and delivering. Frontispiece, Berardo Galiani, *L'Architettura di M. Vitruvio Pollione*, 1758.

Frontispiece, Vincenzo Scamozzi, *Idea dell'architettura universale*, 1616.

FIG. 6 Representation of Mrs. Architectural Practice. The left hand points a measuring instrument toward the earth and the right hand opens like a compass in the same direction. The right arm also shadows the periphery of a perfect circle drawn by a folding of the dress around a spherical belly.

FIG. 7 Representation of Mrs. Architectural Theory. The right hand points toward the sky and the left holds a book on the belly. The belly is framed by a folding of the vest, creating an eye shape, where the navel is the pupil. The eye, the belly, the book, and the hand are all connected.

FIG. 8 Jean-Jacques Lequeu (1757-1825) portrayed himself as
a nobleman, a lady, a prostitute, and a hermaphrodite.

inheritance [Fig. 8]. This architect, who is also she-Architecture, still needs a client to fecundate him. The intellectual architect, however, can refuse to marry the bad client. With a new vision of intellectual architects and their profession, and finally with the invention of the discipline of architecture in the academy, this architect tends toward the primordial androgyne who is completely autonomous: architect, architecture, and client all in one. This is the moment when the magic of the belly and its secret is eclipsed by the magic of the head. This is the moment when the magic of the head betrays the female nature of its source, the magic of the belly.

In Vignola's frontispiece for his treatise, she-Architecture is substituted by the architect's bust [Fig. 9]. The architect has no belly to show. The architect takes the place of she-Architecture, surrounded by females that simply constitute an iconographical reference.

A little known nineteenth-century representation shows that, even after being manipulated by positivism and the new professionalism, the head and the belly still remain the two poles for she-Architecture [Fig. 10]. But this woman has small breasts and no belly! Her power is even further cooled by that compass, which points directly to her genitals. Her motherness tends to disappear in favor of a flourishing and blooming head, where all her magic power is now to be found.

To imagine architecture as a large, fertile woman is no longer comfortable for the intellectuals who hold themselves as the only reference for every possible idea on building. Architects are no longer dedicating their work to a mother, but rather to themselves. They are eager to self-celebrate, to self-fecundate.

FIG. 9 Jacopo Barrozzi, called Vignola, takes the place of Architecture in the frontispiece of *I cinque ordini dell 'Architettura*, 1635. Two thin female bodies (theory and practice) squeeze between the window frame and the outside perimeter of the triumphal arch.

FIG. 10 She-Architecture has no big breasts or big belly to show. She rests a compass on her genitals, cooling down her nature. She can then turn her rational sight toward the sky, while her head and hair are blooming into Achanthus leaves. The magic of the belly is clearly overthrown by the magic of the head. Umberto Ruini, detail of the fresco "Allegory of Architecture" 1904. From the entry to the Biblioteca Poletti, Modena

L'io solitario che gira intorno a se stesso e si nutre soltanto di se finisce stroz-
zato da un gran pianto o da un gran riso.

The solitary ego who revolves around himself nourished only by himself
ends up strangled either by a great cry or a great laughter.

Stendhal, cited in Federico Fellini's film *8 1/2*

THE POISONED BELLY AND THE FERTILE BELLY

In Peter Greenaway's 1987 film *The Belly of an Architect*, Stourley
Kracklite is an intellectual Chicago architect invited by Italian benefactors to
set up an exhibition in Rome on the visionary architect Etienne-Louis Boullée.[7] Kracklite has nine months in which to deliver his architectural exhibit,
which he considers the greatest achievement of his career. Not unlike Boullée, Kracklite is an architect who failed to materialize his greatest ideas, his
most important realization being an unusual house built for *himself.* In the
very moment his wife realizes she is pregnant, the architect begins to suffer
acute abdominal pains, the first symptoms of stomach cancer.

The story unfolds around two parallel narrations: the wife is very
happily experiencing the growth of life in her belly; Kracklite is constantly
worried about the growth of illness in his. First he fears that he is the vic-
tim of poisoned figs; he suspects and eventually accuses his wife of poisoning him. Rather she is poisoning his mind by exhibiting to the public
signs of a fertility he can only envy.

The relationship between the architect and his wife becomes
impossible. Everything seems to fall apart when he sees photographs of
her pregnant belly. He finds the big belly repulsive, as if it were deformed,
a sort of insult to aesthetic sensibility.

The architect who is not interested in the banality of construction,
but only in exceptional conceptions, finds unbearable the deformation
implied by giving birth to an animated being. But his purity, his chastity,
his sublime sterility, and his simulated renunciation, are undermined by a
deep, poisoning illness growing inside his body. Kracklite palpates,
watches, analyses, and photocopies his flaccid abdomen [Figs 11–15]. He
compares it with another famous poisoned belly, that of Augustus Caesar.

Greenaway's film contains an especially vivid sequence where
Kracklite, waiting in the physician's office, twists a long plastic tube and
compresses it over his swollen belly to imagine what he has inside. In
another sequence, someone shows him an unknown Boullée portrait (the

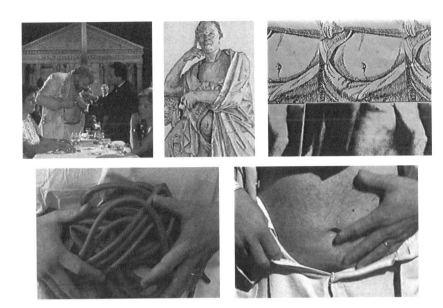

FIGS. 11–15. Film stills from Peter Greenaway's 1987 film *The Belly of An Architect*. The protagonist, Stourley Kracklite, obsessively examines his belly, comparing it to E-L Boullée's.

face however is that of Piranesi). Kracklite is immediately struck by the architect's belly, a sort of swollen, hanging bag which is staring at him with a lonely eye, the navel. Certainly this visionary architect, a hybrid of Boullée and Piranesi, was also sick in his belly.

As the project enters its ninth month, the moment when the exhibit will open and the wife will give birth to the baby, Kracklite feels totally abandoned and isolated. His body has been poisoned by cancer, his marriage by infidelity, and his project by administrative and financial politics. Obsessed by his belly, he commits suicide, jumping from the window of a monument to Vittorio Emmanuel while his wife opens his exhibition on Boullée, and where her water breaks. For Kracklite, the male architect's simulated conceptions become not only futile but sickening, while the woman houses and gives birth to the life in her body.

The end of Greenaway's movie overturns the end of the movie version of Ayn Rand's famous novel *The Fountainhead*, where the enraptured lover of the architect is taken up to the top of his glorious skyscraper. The poisoned belly of the architect can also be seen as a sad revision of the kind-hearted conclusion of Federico Fellini's movie *8 1/2*, where a sterile director finds new meanings in his life after unveiling a public monument to that very sterility.

THE WOMAN IN THE WALL

There is a ballad that people from eastern Europe have been singing to each other in thousands of different ways. Since the 1850s scholars have been writing down, recording, and studying the so-called "Ballad of the Walled-up Wife."[8] Very generally speaking, the story is about a master builder, often named Manole. Manole and his guild are beginning to raise a bridge or castle. Unfortunately, something goes wrong—what the workmen build by day falls down at night. They decide to offer a human sacrifice. The guildsman determine that master builder Manole must bury his wife in the wall in order to prevent the construction from falling apart. Only then will they be able to complete the building.

The variations of this ballad abound. In the Greek version, the impossible construction is a bridge involving forty masters and sixty workmen. An angel announces to the crew that the head of the master masons must sacrifice his wife. Desperately, the master tries to postpone this moment, but the wife is guided to the building site by a treacherous bird. She finds her husband in great sorrow. Asking why, the master builder answers that he has lost his wedding ring in the foundations. When the wife enters the site to search for it, the other masons immolate her. She dies complaining about her fate and that of her sisters, who died in the same tragic way, one under another bridge and the other under the city walls. In another version, we discover that a woman has been buried alive in the foundation of a church, one of her sisters under a monastery, and the other sister under the Danube Bridge.

Such an earth populated with buildings raised by master masons who wall up wives alive reveals too literally the underlying theme of the male's constructional enterprise. Yet, what I find even more curious is a cruel detail that is present in may of the variations: the woman who is to be buried in the wall is pregnant, or must care for a newborn baby. In the second case, she persuades the masons to leave a little window in the wall exposing her breasts, so that she can continue to nurse her baby.[9] It is not just a building sacrifice that these ballads represent. It is the sacrifice of a woman—moreover, a pregnant woman—victimized by professionally impotent master masons. Other versions of the ballad tell stories of masons who bury in the wall boring and nasty wives of whom they are tired, but these conceal the true nature of the art. In the more poignant and tragic versions, the masons are burying in the building the substance and image of what they will never be able to reproduce with artifice: the inner life of a pregnant woman.

Yet all the possible meanings of a popular song are rather insignificant compared to the penetrating simplicity of its oral narrative, which I have tried to capture in the following adaptation:

> . . . Manole kisses her beauty, he holds her in his arms,
> Gets up on the scaffolding and places her inside the wall.
> And jokingly he says:
> "Stand still my beauty, don't worry my beloved,
> If we wall you up a bit, it's because we play with you."
> Anna trusts him.
> She laughs gaily, but Manole sighs sadly.
> And he begins to wall the wall, fulfilling the dream.
> The wall gets up, walling her up,
> Up to her ankle, up to her calf.
> She, poor, laughs no more.
> She says over and over again:
> "Manole, oh Manole, Master Manole
> Stop this joke, because I like it no more.
> The wall is clutching me, breaking my little body."
> But Manole keeps silent, and always is walling.
> The wall is raised, and she is enclosed
> Up to her ankle, up to her calf,
> Up to her tender ribs, up to her breasts.
> Oh poor little woman!
> Always is crying and always is saying,
> "Manole, oh Manole, Master Manole
> The wall is clutching me tightly
> My breasts are crying, my baby is dying."
> Manole is affected, and always is working,
> The wall is raised, and she is enclosed,
> Up to her sweet ribs, up to her lovely breasts,
> Up to her tender lips, up to her wet eyes,

And she, poor, cannot be seen any more.
Yet you can hear her voice, saying form inside the wall:
"Manole, oh Manole, Master Manole
The wall is clutching me tightly, my life is fading slowly."

The end of this story is as sad as the end of Kracklite in *The Belly of an Architect*. The client of Manole's guild realizes that the master masons now know how to build another building which may be better than his own. Jealous, he decides to imprison the masons on the roof of the building he built, like Daedalus in the Labyrinth.

. . . The lord orders:
"Let's destroy the scaffolding, let's remove the ladders,
Let's strand those masons, those great ten masons
Let's strand them along, to rot on the beams, up on the roof."
The master masons think, and this is what they do.
Light flying wings, with thin wooden strings.
And then the wings are spread, flapping the masons in the air.
Sudden are the mason's falls
And where they fall, their bodies cleave.
But poor Manole, Master Manole
Now he tries to take wing,
Now he listens, from inside the wall
A voice dimmed down, a voice to long for.
And she says over and over again:
"Manole, oh Manole, Master Manole
The wall is clutching me tightly,
My breasts are crying, my baby is dying,
My life is fading slowly."
As soon as he hears her, Manole goes astray.
His eyes become misty.
The world overthrows him, the clouds whirl around.
From up above the beams, from up above the roof,
He, poor, now falls down dead.
And right where he falls, what do you see?
A light springing meager water,
Salty, tear-soaked water.

This is not the shining sun melting Icarus's wings. Manole is attracted to the earth next to the wall where he has buried the earth's motherness. Manole, like Kracklite, is a Daedalus with no Icarus to blame. Kracklite is a lonely hero; Manole sacrifices all his family. These solitary intellectual egos, far removed from the collective enterprise, fail tragically in their attempt to fly.

It is interesting to compare the different destinies of Anna (Master Manole's wife) and Dominique, who is Howard Roark's lover in *The Fountainhead*. Both Anna and Dominique reach their husbands on their building sites. The popular ballad couples collective suffering and despair with human making; the popular novel celebrates "Howard Roark, Architect," taking Dominique's future for granted. In both cases, men who build diminish or suppress the natural reproductive power of the feminine.

Mr. Architect

It is well known that architecture has been one of the many professions organized by males. Males have been arguing, agreeing with each other, and awarding each other with gold medals for centuries. They have created their own stories and we have had to cope with them. Females have been kept in the houses built by males for centuries. One says that they were protected there, the other that they were imprisoned. We all have the history we deserve.

On one hand it can be said that males have been envious of the female power to conceive. As Gregory Zilboorg put it, "woman-envy" on the part of men is "psychogenetically older and therefore more fundamental" than Freudian "penis-envy" on the part of woman.[10] As everyone knows, envy is bad whether you are a man or a woman. These stories show directly or indirectly the consequences of a kind of envy particular to men. On the other hand, it can be said that men celebrate the mothers they cannot be, dedicating their work to maternal power. In this context I see powerfully big ladies and their bellies. I picture them like the Venus of Willendorf described by Camille Paglia,[11] a bit like *Hon* by Niki de Saint Phalle, Jean Tinguely, and Per Olaf Ultvedt [Figs. 16 and 17], and a bit like that Greek goddess barely contained inside her temple [Fig. 2].

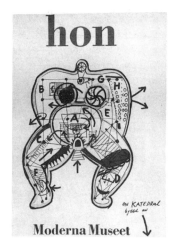

Figs. 16 & 17 Poster and installation view, "Hon," Niki de Saint Phalle, Jean Tinguely, and Per Olaf Ultvedt.

My three short accounts of these stories are obviously partial and restrictive. Indeed my effort is that of finding out if it makes any sense at all to discuss the gender of architecture and architects. Do we have to dedicate our work to abstract entities or populistic and demiurgic ideas, or do we have to look for someone and not something to work for? Do we have to make the effort to occupy a neutral domain, or do we have to understand the difference that exists between the he- and she-architect?

Not long ago, I was discussing this problem with a female friend. She told me that once she heard a famous contemporary architect (who must remain nameless) say that women cannot be "great" architects because they cannot reach beyond a certain level of hypocrisy. By "hypocrisy," my friend concluded, this architect apparently meant that a woman might have a hard time simulating conceptions, since she has the ability to experience a real one.

Indeed, Filarete's transsexual architect, Kracklite's poisoned belly, and Manole's cruel sacrifice imply simulation, envy, and deception for the sake of self-celebration. Nowadays the level of hypocrisy among intellectual architects has reached an apex. This hypocrisy is the inheritance of the sick plumbing of masculine conceptions. In older, traditional societies, master masons could build without knowing whether or not they were building "Architecture." After the middle ages, male intellectual architects

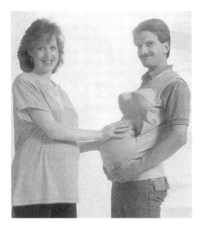 

FIG. 18 (above, left) "The Empathy Belly" is a sort of bust for men simulating pregnancy. The device weighs more than twenty pounds and contains water and other weights.

FIG. 19 (above, right) The Medusa-like character of this woman's head combines the polarity of belly-magic and head-magic. Advertisement for maternity products for Prenatal.

began to worship an image: she-Architecture. Today's male intellectual architects think they *are* Architecture. Some even speak about the buildings they design as "My Architecture."

The contemporary male architect's architecture is the miscarriage of *couvade*, man's simulated motherness.[12] Hubris and envy have displaced the celebration of the otherness of human making, natural motherness, the fertility of Gaia.

Our professional and intellectual tools are masculine and the stories I tell here are man-made. To hide behind a fake equality between the sexes is misleading. We have lost any possible personification for Architecture and architect; now architecture is just a neutral thing resulting from a neutral, consumerized professionalism. I look for a new gender of architects, or maybe an older gender of Architecture. Architects should not perpetuate the mistakes of Mr. Architect. She-Architecture can teach us to forget about self-celebration, about overstressed apotropaic emulations of an original conception, and celebrate instead the fertile voids that house our private and public life and the beauty of their inner space.

NOTES

1. Correspondence with Lisa Yau, February and March, 1993. For broad examination of these topics, see Beatriz Colomina, *Sexuality & Space* (New York: Princeton Architectural Press, 1992).

2. Martianus Capella wrote his treatise in the fifth century C.E. The treatise was famous in the Middle Ages; it was printed in Venice in the 1499 with the title *De Nuptiis et Philologiae* and remained the main source concerning the origin and the classical interpretation of the liberal arts.

3. Concerning the argument see Ivan Illich, *Gender* (New York, Pantheon Books, 1982).

4. See Claudio Sgarbi, "Rereading Vitruvius," *Space & Society* 55 (December 1990): 68–75.

5. For a different reading of this passage from Filarete's treatise see Diana Agrest, "Architecture from Without," in *Sign and Symbols in Architecture* (Cambridge, MA: The MIT Press, 1991), 173–195.

6. See Elemire Zolla, *The Androgyne, Reconciliation of Male and Female* (London: Thames and Hudson, 1991).

7. The exhibit on Boullée took place in Rome in the 1960s and was designed by Constantino Dardi.

8. See Lajos Vargyas, "The Origin of the 'Walled-Up Wife,'" chap. 3 in *Researches into the Medieval History of Folk Ballad* (Budapest: Akadémiai Kiadó, 1967), 173–233; also see Mircea Eliade, "Master Manole and the Monastery of Argeş,"chap. 5 in *Zalmoxis The Vanishing God: Comparative Studies in the Religions and Folklore of Dacia and Eastern Europe,* trans. Willard R. Trask (Chicago: The University of Chicago Press, 1972), 164–190. For an alternative reading of the legend of Master Manole—and a critical discussion of the "builder's sacrifice"—see Manuela Antoniu, "The Walled-up Bride: An Architecture of Eternal Return," in *Architecture and Feminism*, ed. Debra Coleman, Elizabeth Danze, and Carol Henderson (New York: Princeton Architectural Press, 1996), 107–129.

9. This variant was rendered into fiction by Marguerite Yourcenar, "The Milk of Death," in *Oriental Tales*, trans. Alberto Manguel (New York : Farrar Straus Giroux, 1985).

10. Gregory Zilboorg, "Masculine and Feminine: Some Biological and Cultural Aspects," *Psychiatry* 7 (1944): 289. About attempts to dissolve the bodily nature of the misery of conception, see Barbara Duden, *Disembodying Women: Perspectives on Pregnancy and the Unborn*, trans. Lee Hoinacki (Cambridge, MA: Harvard University Press, 1993).

11. Camille Paglia, *Sexual Personae: Art and Decadence from Nefertiti to Emily Dickinson* (New York: Vintage Books, 1990).

12. This definition emerged during a discussion with Ivan Illich in 1991. On *couvade*, see Zilboorg.

FIG. 1 Siegfried Giedion prepar-
ing dummies for publication

The problem of the bathroom has never been clearly stated. . .
With one exception, every room in the American home of today has a his-
tory that stretches back to feudal times. The exception is the bathroom.
This room is modern—it is American.

Standard Sanitary Company[1]

Siegfried Giedion and the Fascination of the Tub

William W. Braham

WHILE IT IS TRUE THAT THE BATHROOM—THE ROOM OF MODERN fixtures—has little real history, the activities which it houses certainly do. In the final chapter of *Mechanization Takes Command,*[2] Siegfried Giedion traces the modern bathtub back to the "regenerative" bathing habits of the ancient world, locating the shift to mere cleansing in the political and corporeal anxieties of the early modern period. My aim is to reconsider this moist intertwining of habits, habitats, and inhabitants, not to tell the history again, but to understand the architectural implications of a mass-produced artifact like the tub. By using Giedion's own historical method, the anonymous history, this paper seeks to connect his ambivalence toward mechanization with the hygienic and visual ethic of modern construction. We continue to build rooms with tubs virtually identical to those of the three-fixture configuration that was standardized around 1920, and from that perspective we remain thoroughly modern and thoroughly American.[3] In other words, our own reconciliation with the modern will not be complete until we have understood the compulsion to sustain that particularly efficient and secretive configuration.

Giedion made extensive use of illustrations in his book, precisely pairing images to "convey the broad outline independently of and simultaneously with the text."[4] He coupled paintings by Paul Klee, Wassily Kandinsky, and Joan Miró with time-motion studies by Eadweard Muybridge, Frank Gilbreth, and E.J. Marey, while using Max Ernsts's surrealist collages to reveal the psychic distress embedded in ornamented objects and interiors. These are didactic, even dialectical, comparisons that seek to explain the logic of individual artifacts and their historical implications. He intended the images to make the story comprehensible to the "hasty reader," that busy architect for whom cleanliness is as much a visual as a technical or therapeutic concern. Those concerns intersect in the splendid artifact with which Giedion concludes the book and his argument about mechanization.

> The concise line of this white bathtub will perhaps bear witness to later periods for the outlook of ours as much as the amphora for the outlook of fifth-century Greece. It is a luxury article, which the combinations of refined metallurgical and technical skills transformed into a democratic utensil. In its own way, this double-shell tub, which on the other side of the Atlantic still smacks of luxury, numbers among the symbols of our time.[5]

Giedion hoped that a recovery of regenerative bathing might redeem industrialized culture, even as he recognized that the comforts and democratic dreams of the smooth, white tub were not sufficient to guarantee that redemption. The concluding paragraph of the chapter on bathing explains this contradiction using the terms of the postwar debate about work and leisure.[6]

> A culture that rejects life in stunted form voices a natural demand for the restoring of the bodily equilibrium of its members through institutions open to all. Whether as Roman marble halls or as Siberian log-cabin is unimportant. Neither, as so often claimed, is finance the decisive factor. Financial considerations are often no more than pretexts.
> A period like ours, which has allowed itself to become dominated by production, finds no time in its rhythms for institutions of this kind. That is why the nineteenth century failed in its efforts to revive the regeneration of former ages or to devise new types shaped to our specific needs. Such institutions stood in contradiction to the period. Regeneration is something that cannot arise in isolation. It is part of a broader concept: leisure. Jacob Burckhardt found in the word ἀρετή [arete] the key to Greek con-

duct. Leisure, in this sense, means a concern with things beyond the merely useful. Leisure means to have time. Time to live. Life can be tasted to the full only when activity and contemplation, doing and not doing, form complementary poles, like those of a magnet. None of the great cultures has failed to support this concept.[7]

In the postwar discourse on work, leisure is neither a release from work nor a form of recreation, but a condition in which "activity is performed for its own sake."[8] Neither cleanliness nor physical comfort contribute directly to this elusive state. This argument is the source of Giedion's deepest ambivalence, unresolved even in his concluding call for the dynamic equilibrium of "Equipoise," and extends the popular suspicions of mechanization to the point of crisis. The dreams of the smooth white tub are based as much on fear—of germs, time, nudity, and mortality—as on any positive achievements of production. Giedion himself would be intrigued by the fact that over thirty per cent of the new tubs installed in homes today include mechanical Jacuzzi features meant to transform the tub and the bathroom into sites of relaxation, but ultimately, the regenerative leisure he described cannot be mechanized. Thinking about the mass-produced tub is an encounter with the limitations of hygiene and the persistently redemptive aspirations for water.

In 1948, the *Journal of the A.I.A.* published a terse review of *Mechanization Takes Command* that illustrated the difficulty its argument presented to his contemporaries: "If you need Dr. Giedion's painstaking research and oratory to convince you that we are living in a machine age, here they are."[9] The following month the *Journal* printed a letter from John Burchard by way of apology. He called the piece "a snippy little review, like a *New Yorker* remark about a second-rate theatrical performance,"[10] arguing that it was essential for professionals themselves to better understand the machine age within which they were operating. Compared to Giedion's earlier blockbuster, *Space, Time and Architecture,* the book on mechanization must have seemed like little more than a detailed sequel. From the perspective of a practicing American architect, it lacked the immediate relevance and, certainly, the polemical thrust of the previous work.

When Nikolaus Pevsner reviewed *Mechanization Takes Command*, he called it "the most thrilling book on matters of design I have ever read," and suggested that the difference in the two works was one of historiography.[11] In *Space, Time and Architecture*, Giedion had written as an authoritative apologist for the modern movement, seeking to explain its particular historical momentum. He identified the use of iron, glass, and concrete as the "constituent facts" of nineteenth-century architecture, and, as a consequence, relegated all other developments to the category of "transitory facts." The book was an extension of his role as secretary of CIAM and he quite explicitly called his historical method "dynamic."[12] Pevsner objected to any method which would consign Karl Friedrich Schinkel, William Butterfield, Charles Garnier, C.F.A. Voysey, and Charles Mackintosh to such a secondary status:

> Surely, Dr. Giedion is trying here to replace what is constituent in the sense of essential for an understanding of the style of the nineteenth century by what is constituent in the sense of essential for an understanding of the genesis of the twentieth century. Dr. Giedion enthrones one set of values—and very important values they are—at the expense of all other values, because they happen to be of the greatest interest to the present and future of architecture. This changeover from telling historical truth—the whole truth—to blasting a trumpet, be it ever so rousing a trumpet, is a sin in a historian.[13]

Historian or prophet? The A.I.A. reviewer certainly wanted to hear the prophet. Giedion had continued to blow the prophet's horn as *Space, Time and Architecture* went into multiple printings, contributing repeatedly to the unfolding debate over monumentality and mass culture in the mid-1940s. In contrast, *Mechanization Takes Command* is a work of history.[14] And it is to the historian's sin of which Pevsner accused him, and the artifacts of mass culture, that Giedion directed his first paragraph:

> History is a magical mirror. Who peers into it sees his own image in the shape of events and developments. It is never stilled. It is ever in movement, like the generation observing it. Its totality cannot be embraced: History bares itself only in facets, which fluctuate with the vantage point of the observer.[15]

In this description, Giedion drew a simple visual analogy between the mirror and historical writing as two kinds of reflection. His device underscored the visual logic at work and also resonated with a number of other topics. The first was the multiple nature of perception, so central to the issue of space-time. He denied the existence of a single historical truth, and although he was not making the case for radical relativity, he proposed the presence of a shifting historical subject. He described that subject as the relation between historical facts, which by analogy with astronomy would be a "constellation" or, by analogy with biology, "a moving process of life." His essential proposition was that these historical relationships could be more easily read in the "humble things," in tools and artifacts of use like the bathtub, whose appearances are not the subject of sustained aesthetic reflection.

Giedion's development of anonymous history makes the book profoundly important for design studies, but though he is credited with the invention of industrial archeology,[16] he was certainly not the first to investigate a history without heroes. Attention to the works of engineers and unknown builders had been integral to his previous work, as it had to other canonical modern works, such as Le Corbusier's *Vers une Architecture* (1923) and Erich Mendelsohn's *Amerika* (1926), though both works primarily address the logic of building construction. Closer to the anonymous history of mechanization are Le Corbusier's essays in *L'Art décoratif d'aujourd'hui* (1925) and especially those Adolf Loos wrote at the turn of the century on topics like furniture, footwear, and, of course, plumbing. Both Le Corbusier's and Loos' writings follow from Gottfried Semper's general proposal that dressing (*bekleidung*) was a primary motive in architecture, a proposition that bound its development as a discipline to that of the minor arts and challenged the idealist separation of high and low art. Each of these works raised questions about the connection of style and visual appearance to historical dynamics, but Giedion's investigation of mechanization and bathing pushed the discussion about style to its limit, even as his search for the "inner nature" of our period stayed well within the Swiss art-historical tradition of Heinrich Wölfflin and Jacob Burckhardt.[17]

The scope of his activity was nearly as broad as that of the *Annalistes*—Marc Bloch, Lucien Febvre, et. al.—who were beginning their own radical critique of narrative history in the same moment.[18] Unlike the

Annalistes' search for wholly objective historical material in the lists and data of a given period, Giedion's initial image of the mirror reminds readers that they are always inspecting their own images in historic accounts, an act which necessarily involves questions concerning motive and judgment. His vast and meticulous research into bathing habits seems to form a direct answer to the program which Friedrich Nietzsche called "Something for the Industrious" and which demanded inquiry into "the reason, passion, and superstition" of "men's experiences of living together," establishing the pursuit of "moral climates" as the task of the historian.[19]

The first question of such laborious research as Giedion's is the nature of the materials to be interpreted—annals, chronicles, histories, artifacts—and their relation to the intentions of their authors or producers. Architectural writers work largely with artifacts or their visual representations, but in accordance with the disciplinary model of textual history, they must determine the intentions of any artifact from corollary texts, or from the political, economic, and sociological trends of the time. Is it possible to interpret an artifact like the tub directly? Within the textual model, such interpretations are suspect as a kind of secondary conjecture.[20] Yet even though such readings are necessarily provisional, they are fundamental to anonymous history. Furthermore, Giedion's image constructions, which pair visual examples with their instructional contraries, offer demonstrations not available through his textual pairings.

The interpretive aspect of Giedion's approach is closest, perhaps, to Sigmund Freud's use of inadvertent details to reveal the repressed memories and desires of his patients. This mode of interpretation is a heuristic and intuitive reading of clues which, as Carlo Ginzburg has shown, forms part of a much larger evidential paradigm exemplified, for example, by Sherlock Holmes, and traceable to the art-historical propositions made by the Italian physician, Giovanni Morelli, in the 1870s. Under the pseudonym Ivan Lermolieff, he published a series of articles describing a new method for the attribution of old master works, which concentrated on the minor details of paintings, such as earlobes, fingernails, and so on, rather than on their overall stylistic features. His attributions provoked immediate controversy and his method was called mechanical, but Arthur Conan Doyle, Sigmund Freud, and others were impressed and inspired by Morelli's approach. It certainly influenced art historians and Burckhardt, in particular, read his work and even met Morelli to discuss his methods.[21]

Giedion proudly located himself in the Swiss historical tradition that Burckhardt had initiated with *The Civilization of the Renaissance in Italy* (1878) as an explicit response to the "romantic historiography stimulated by the teachings of Hegel."[22] Burckhardt's search for the inner logic of style in every dimension of human production used exactly this mode of inquiry. Giedion, too, quite explicitly sought to discover the "inner coherence" that united the specialized details of styles, inventions, or artifacts with broad economic and sociological patterns.[23] He had previously relied on space-time as the organizing principle of modern work, but the concepts of mechanization offered a more direct explanatory link between the particular features of artifacts and the inner nature of the period. It was a link made visible in both the concept and representations of movement, by scientists, artists, and engineers alike. The deeper concept of style required more than simple causal connections; therein lay the promise of an anonymous history of the tub. It sought to discern the motives and desires—the moral climate—of hygiene as it shapes modern life and its artifacts. The economy of desire knows no limits and has no direct indices; it is inscribed directly in artifacts like the tub whose image Giedion attempted to evoke in his magical mirror.[24]

In his introduction to *The Living Eye*, Jean Starobinski outlined the ethics of historical reflection in the dialectic between particular and general views:

> Perhaps the most comprehensive criticism is that which aims at neither totality (the panoramic view) nor intimacy (intuitive identification). It is the product of a gaze that can be panoramic or intimate by turns, by knowing that truth lies in neither one nor the other but in ceaseless movement between the two. Neither the vertigo of distance nor that of proximity is to be rejected. One must aim for that double excess in which the gaze is always close to losing is power entirely.[25]

Martin Jay used this paragraph to conclude the introduction to his own exhaustive inquiry into the changing status and constitution of the gaze in twentieth-century French thought.[26] The subsequent paragraph by Starobinski suggests, in addition, the self-reflection which is always lurking in the mirror of history and the risk it entails to the equipoise of any inquiry.

Yet criticism is wrong perhaps, to seek to discipline its gaze in this way. Often it is better to forget oneself and make room for surprise. We may then be rewarded by the feeling that the work is developing a gaze of its own, directed toward us, a gaze that is not only a reflection of our interrogation. An alien consciousness, radically other, seeks us out, fixes us, summons us to respond. We feel exposed by its probing. The work interrogates us. Before speaking for ourselves, we must lend our voice to the strange power that queries us, yet docile as we may be, there is always the risk that we will prefer comforting tunes of our own invention. It is not easy to keep our eyes open, to welcome the gaze that seeks us out. But surely for criticism, as for the whole enterprise of understanding, we must say: "Look so that you may be looked at in return."[27]

Thus the historian encounters himself written into the facts and artifacts he has selected for the investigation.

The risk that anonymous history shares with other forms of critical analysis, whether psychological, ideological, or even technological, is not only that researchers read their own dreams in the artifacts they examine, but that they become fascinated with them, like Narcissus before his pool. Pevsner noted this tendency, and concluded that Giedion had tempered his prophet's voice precisely out of sympathy for mechanization. Pevsner's observation suggests that the image of the tub that appears in the magical mirror is more than a simple artifact of mechanization, particularly when read through the tale of Narcissus.

For the newly developed gaze of cleanliness, the target of observation was the microscopic germ. The modern body depended upon hygienic intervention for defense against those germs. This was a passive intervention and constitutes the moment of fascination for bathing. There is no better illustration of that transfixed and reflected gaze than the surrealist collage that Giedion used to illustrate his own confrontation with the nineteenth-century interior. Figure 230 in *Mechanization Takes Command* is a plate from Max Ernst's collage novel, *La femme 100 têtes* (1929), which shows a gentleman looking into his bookcase from which looms one of the "hundred headless women," while an ornamental lion on the armchair has changed into a leering ape.[28] [Fig. 2] In his discussion of the image, Giedion concludes that the objects of mechanization had "proved stronger

FIG. 2 Max Ernst, *La Femme 100 Têtes* (1929)

FIG. 3 Stanley William Hayden,
Narcissus (1952)

than judgment" and "these plates of Max Ernst show how a mechanized environment has affected our subconscious." He doesn't elaborate on his specific reading of this image, but the reader will observe that the gaze returned by the gentleman's furniture is the gaze of a woman and an animal, the repressed others of European man. Mechanization is thus construed as an outside force, responsible for the novel woes that plague mankind, and yet it is constructed in our image.

The mythic confusion of self for other is both an everyday metaphor for self-love and a foundational concept in psychoanalysis. Many theorists have noted that the displacement of the mirror is also a device of primitive magic and have raised the question of how and why it persists in modern thought.[29] Tobin Siebers has pointed out that Narcissus did not simply discover some inner weakness for self-love, but was actively cursed by an injured admirer.[30] The phrase in Ovid's version of the poem reads: "till one spurned youth, with raised hands, prayed, 'So may he love—and never win his love!'"[31] Here Ovid's terms suggest the closely-related Evil Eye, a form of visually transmitted magic which occurs spontaneously, without training or ritual, in a person in the grip of passion, such as a rejected lover. This mythical force is a consequence of frustration and violent desires, not on the part of Narcissus, but rather of those he had ignored.

Siebers has used the tale of Narcissus to explain the amulets that ward off the Evil Eye; the amulet's eye is the reflection and duplication of the gaze that curses. The threat and the mechanisms of prevention share a common identity, between gaze and counter-gaze. Hygienic tales have likewise been used to explain the powers of the clean, white tub; the absence of color and texture equals the absence of germs. The surface of the modern tub is frozen in glass, resisting change or inhabitation. As James Frazer and Marcel Mauss have shown, metaphor (similarity) and metonymy (contagion) are the common mechanism of poetry and primitive magic.[32] The mechanism of the tub is metonymical rather than metaphorical; it is established by a physical property and its extension rather than a visual duplication. The modern tub is both a technical artifact and a talisman.

The persistence of the tale of Narcissus alerts us to the distinction between individual and group psychologies. Their persistence does not necessarily reflect a primitive state of mind, but rather a form of symbolic logic that is neither personal nor merely instrumental.[33] It is the domain of the public gaze for which artifacts are shaped. Narcissus, the nineteenth-century interior, and the modern bathroom not only represent, they demonstrate. "Thus man is born to the admirable destiny that he has invented for himself," Starobinski writes: "he offers himself triumphant to the world's gaze. His greatest happiness lies neither in the act of seeing (*voir*) nor in the energy of doing (*faire*) but in the complex act of demonstrating (*faire voir*)."[34] Cleanliness is a construct that must be made visible to be effective.

From the image in the mirror and its potential for fascination, I hope to develop the background necessary to read Giedion's illustrations of bathing in their own right. The placement of pictures in books can serve many purposes. They may simply illustrate the subject of the writing, in which case different images or versions can be chosen while their placement is dictated by convenience to the text and its composition. They may also constitute the subject of investigation in the text, in which case there may be choices between versions or reproductions, but they nevertheless constitute an integral aspect of the writing. Finally, images such as Giedion's may form an independent text, telling another story through their content or positioning, which may support, parallel, or even contradict the written text. I am referring largely to purposeful choices, although readings that exceed the author's intentions only deepen the distinctions of the latter form.

The demonstrative use of pictures (*faire voire*) seems to have propelled Giedion's books since *Bauen in Frankreich, Eisen, Eisenbeton*[35] of 1928, prepared under the supervision of László Moholy-Nagy.[36] While the graphic comparisons of *Space, Time and Architecture* largely explain the stylistic features of the historical avant garde, *Mechanization Takes Command* refined those techniques for more subtle demonstrations. In the sections of the latter work that discuss the social or political consequences of mechanization, Giedion struggled to maintain the a-historical content of avant-garde imagery. Instead, the close, aesthetic view leads to a fascination with mechanization, a compulsion to investigate its every nuance, even if such investigation undermines the formal and historical claims of the avant garde. Giedion acknowledged this tension, attributing it to the inherent difference between the horizontal, stylistic histories of a period and the vertical, typological approaches that reveal "organic changes" through time.[37] Lewis Mumford, too, noted Giedion's preference for the close view, conceding that he himself suffered from an excess of the long, philosophical view.[38]

The criteria for both approaches belongs to the hygienic ethos by which the avant garde was shaped and for which "fascination" indicated a fixation with "clean" images and artifacts. That fascination is also legible in Giedion's graphic comparisons. On one hand, his aesthetic and political criticisms neatly coincide in the images he uses in the section on "Ruling Taste," where he shows that ornamental excesses derive from the "Devaluation of Symbols" engendered by Napoleon and the new mobile classes after the revolution; illustrations also coincide with social critique in his use of the famous eye-cutting scene from Luis Buñel's film, *Le Chien Andalou* (1929), testifying to the numbing effect of mechanized slaughterhouses and the atrocities of the recent war. On the other hand, in the chapter on bathing, Giedion's use of images is contradictory. Here he confronts the social transformations and collective effects that occur in the history of bathing, resisting both the valorization of simple forms for their own sake and fascination with mechanization.

Giedion's treatment of bathing constitutes a methodological inversion from that which prevails in the rest of the book, presenting the technical advances of bathing almost wholly as details in an epic struggle between ablution and regeneration, between private, even fearful, acts of cleansing and communal acts of restoration. He traces the ethic of modern cleanliness to "The Atmospheric Bath" developed by Arnold Rikli in the 1860s and the subsequent advances of germ theory through the work of

FIG. 4 "Garments for the Atmospheric Cure," Dr. Rikli, c. 1870

FIG. 5 Richard Neutra, The Demonstration Health House, 1930

Louis Pasteur, Robert Koch, and Lord Joseph Lister. According to Giedion, the simple clothing of Rikli's alpine walkers [Fig. 4.] anticipates the functional fashions of fifty years later, though the therapeutic reforms were not so much a product of technical advance as a reaction to mechanized life. That simplicity answers more to the nineteenth century's growing preoccupation with hygiene than to requirements of factory equipment. By the early years of the twentieth century, the economics of mass production led to the meanness of the compact bathroom and the smooth white, five-foot tub, disencumbered of ornament and widely available. Contradictions between fashion and function are integral to the public gaze by which styles are defined.

The chapter on the bath represents only a small fraction of the decades of research that Giedion conducted on the culture and developments of the nineteenth century and parallels Walter Benjamin's inquiry into the dreamscape of the industrial metropolis through its covered arcades, the *Passagen*.[39] Giedion and Benjamin both sought redemption from the errors of the nineteenth century. Though the focus here is on Giedion and the bath, it is instructive to read the two works together, because while Giedion only suggests the redemptive aspirations of his work in the conclusion, "Man in Equipoise," Benjamin explicitly develops a theory of the awakening his study was meant to evoke, which he entitles "Profane Illumination."[40] Benjamin struggled to reconcile a political understanding of mass culture with the psychological insights of surrealism, recognizing that dream worlds and the factual world of mechanization were equally valid cultural indices.

It is on this point that the comparison of Giedion's anonymous history with the surrealist project and Benjamin's theory is most useful. Benjamin initially conceived his *Passagen-Werk* as a montage of photographs and quotations from the nineteenth century, which by the construction of "dialectical images" could awaken the reader to historical truth. He attributed similar tactics to the surrealists, indicating that they were the first to recognize the oneiric energies present in outmoded artifacts, but he worried that they had been lulled by the dreams to which they attended. Like Narcissus, any awakening or redemption presupposes the recognition that images of fascination are collectively drawn. Giedion used Max Ernst's surrealist novels to illustrate precisely those points at which he undertakes the social or political implications of mechanization.[41]

Giedion paired images to negotiate the difference between the progressive, evolutionary history of the style shaped by the clean eyes of modernism, and the disillusionment born of the war and "the end of progress." Significantly, the epic loss recounted in the final chapter about the ascension of cleanliness over regenerative bathing habits is unaccompanied by corollary images by twentieth-century artists. For a final reading of the loss of regenerative bathing, consider the point of view of Giedion's "hasty reader," who only reads those images. He is, in effect, the "model, modern architect," struggling to reconcile the hygienic achievements of the clean, white tub with the fears and desires of industrial civilization.[42]

The choice that Giedion offers in the chapter on bathing is absolute, "External Ablution or Total Regeneration," and it is made legible in the close interaction between people and their tubs. The illustrations in the first half of the chapter describe the rise and fall of public bathing from the Greek gymnasium, to the Roman thermae, to the vapor bath and its several variations in Russia, Finland, and Spain. He uses Albrecht Dürer's engraving of "The Women's Bath" (1496) to show a last European occurrence of the public bath, attributing the demise of such bathing to the effects of the Counter-Reformation, during which nakedness and intimate, potentially political, gatherings became suspect. Eighteenth- and nineteenth-century paintings of men, women and children lolling naked together in a Russian bath illustrate the early modern connection between bathing and lasciviousness. He notes a critical development in the transformation of public bathing in the late Middle Ages: the Islamic masseuse was being replaced by the "barber-surgeon." As the social institution died out, the medical connotation of bathing gathered strength.

Giedion attributes the European rediscovery of bathing in the eighteenth century, illustrated by the rediscovery of swimming and the reinvention of acrobatic and gymnastic exercise, to the development of scientific medical practices and the influence of naturalism. The somewhat more detailed review of nineteenth-century bathing offers a number of intertwined themes: the return to nature, medical hydrotherapy, and the Orientalist fascination with Turkish or Moorish baths. The medical and scientific advances of the century—germ theory, infra-red and ultra-violet radiation—each contributed to the construction of what was soon to be called personal hygiene. There is, however, a critical difference between medical theory and the cultural practices which can be read in the images Giedion deployed, such as in the comparison between the *Venus de Milo* corset from the London Hygienic Exhibition of 1883 and the image of Dr. Rikli in the walking outfit prescribed in his book *Let There be Light or the Atmospheric Cure*. Giedion used these images to mark the dawning of the sun-and-air ethic of the architectural avant garde of the twenties, which had developed in the therapeutic struggle with the great contagious diseases of the late nineteenth- and early twentieth-century industrial metropolis: cholera, typhoid, and tuberculosis.[43] [Fig. 5] The introduction of running water and piped sewage, the legislation concerning light and air in tenement structures, the elimination of sleeping enclosures, and the propagation of open sleeping porches each constituted realizations and demonstrations of the hygienic view of the building environment.[44]

These concerns and practices developed independently of the actual mechanization of the bath. Public health reforms responded to the crises that followed from industrialization; medical and municipal authorities only subsequently mechanized, mass produced, and incorporated therapeutic recommendations into building regulations. Reforms like the widespread introduction of running water and sewer systems in turn caused problems whose solution lay in better and more tightly regulated supplies.[45] The story of hygiene is not simply one of the achievements and setbacks in public works. The regular and abundant presence of water within the household demanded new habits of use and new configurations for its accommodation. The avant garde, whose pre-history Giedion was recounting, found significant power in its alliance with broad changes in

FIG. 6 Knud Lönberg-
Holm, *1910-1930*

anonymous cultural habits involving the most intimate aspects of everyday life. The whiteness and openness of early modern buildings gave a visible face to the fears and remedies of the reformed industrial city. In America that movement resonates with the great sanitoriums and health retreats, like Dr. John Harvey Kellogg's White City in Battle Creek, as well as in writings and prescriptions by the remarkable authors of household and housing reform, from Catherine Beecher (1869), Edith Wharton (1897), and Emily Post (1930), to Mumford's ally, Catherine Bauer (1934). [46]

Both the therapeutic and household reform movements sought to clean out the nineteenth-century interior: take up the carpets, remove the layers of curtains, and eliminate the upholstery. Catherine Beecher lectured on the moral benefits of oxygen and the evils of carbolic acid, while Edith Wharton and Emily Post appealed to the relative simplicity of the neoclassic styles, especially the Georgian. They linked cleanliness and free movement to a new logic of dressing, illustrated by Giedion with the drawing of Dr. Rikli on his alpine walk. In a 1930 article on weekend houses in *The Architectural Record,* Knud Lönberg-Holm assumed that connection between health, clothing, and free movement as commonplace among avant-garde authors. [Fig. 6] Using a pictorial method identical to Giedion's, he amplified his story with a didactic comparison, pairing a couple in formal dress from 1910 with a contemporary woman in white tennis shorts.[47] Progress and its achievements are evident in clothing, stance and expression.[48]

In contrast to the reformers, and in resistance to the Narcissistic fascination with mechanization, Giedion concludes his book with a plea for balance, for "Equipoise" in its application. He describes the widespread

FIG. 7 (near right).
Rain Bath for Medical
Purposes, France, 1870

FIG. 8 (far right).
Dr. Rollier, "Old Doctor
Sun," atmospheric treat-
ment for Tuberculosis

disillusionment with progress after the Second World War as "The Ending of Mechanistic Conceptions." Those concepts fail to explain the complex conditions required for either physical or mental health, and so he argues for active regeneration based on systems theory and Gestalt psychology. The flux he first described in the mirror of history, Giedion now finds in the endless human struggle to maintain health and achieve the "feeling of delight" that accompanies it.[49] The images he published of therapeutic showers show both the passivity of the recipient and the active hand of the doctor and his device. [Fig. 7] Giedion cites in the text, but does not illustrate, the alpine treatment of tubercular, urban youth by Dr. Rollier, which was inspired by Rikli's earlier work. The picture of a darkly tanned boy skiing on the white snow, clad only in a white loincloth, captures precisely the active approach to health.[50] [Fig. 8] Medical ablutions, however vigorously applied, belong to the passive view, while regeneration requires action, initiative, and participation.

To the hygienic dilemma posed by Giedion's examination of the bathtub, I would append the following proposition by Walter Benjamin: "A philosophy that does not include the possibility of soothsaying from coffee grounds and cannot explicate it cannot be a true philosophy."[51] Giedion's anonymous history may not aspire to true philosophy, nor even to common prophecy. The connection between coffee grounds and "truth-telling" is perhaps best understood in the demonstrative sense, like fascination, by which not only pictures in books but objects of everyday life show who we are and act as talismans for the life we want to live.

Bathing is one of our most important social codes. Giedion observed that modern bathing, which reduces to superficial cleansing, "has as its symbol the bathtub," specifically, the clean, double-shelled enameled tub developed around 1920. The appearance of the modern surface—smooth, white, shiny, sanitized—offers sufficient guarantee of protection from disease. An architectural soothsayer, or even a concerned homeowner, can point to a clean tub as evidence of a healthy future. The mechanistic explanations of germ theory sustain the visibility of hygiene. The designer Paul Frankl noted that the modern bathroom "makes personal things impersonal and gives the most impersonal an air of the personal."[52] Activities which can not be discussed are given a place in the home that neutralizes their dangerous content by the visible elimination of moist dirts—grease, sweat, spit, and excrement.

Rules for cleanliness were previously the province of religious doctrine.[53] They are now a medical issue, but they are still exercised in symbolic terms at the level of household activities, expressing and enforcing the social order. In her remarkable study of pollution taboos, Mary Douglas explains that uncleanliness derives from a concept of dirt for which no more precise definition can be achieved than "matter out of place."[54] Shoes which are perfectly clean on the floor are dirty when placed on the table. Unfinished food on a plate is still edible, while the same food placed, however briefly, on a garbage pile is contaminated. These are remarkably rigid definitions, based partly on practical experience, but deriving firmness from their arbitrary and social nature. As Douglas argues: "in chasing dirt, in papering, decorating, tidying, we are not governed by anxiety to escape disease, but are positively re-ordering our environment, making it conform to an idea."[55] The urgencies of modern hygiene are a particular distortion of the general idea of dirt. Understanding the social and ethical dimension of the tub frees Giedion to inquire not only about the shape and material of the bath, but about its modern purposes and location as well.

Throughout the chapter on bathing Giedion traces the historic migration of the tub from public facilities to various rooms within the house to its "final" form as an entirely private and specialized room bound to the bedroom. Two conditions explain this location: the concealment of nudity, and the material demands of moisture and running water. Certainly the exigencies of construction (cost and plumbing configurations) contribute to bathroom size, but it is the concern for privacy that requires one tub for every bedroom. By 1930, Emily Post could state this as a matter

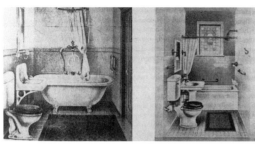
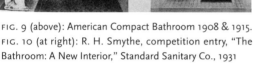
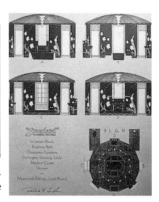

FIG. 9 (above): American Compact Bathroom 1908 & 1915.
FIG. 10 (at right): R. H. Smythe, competition entry, "The Bathroom: A New Interior," Standard Sanitary Co., 1931

of course: "The one essential of comfort in a bathroom is that we may each have one to ourselves. Size and decoration are very secondary requirements." The requirements for plumbing and moisture typify two uniquely modern rooms, the bathroom and kitchen, the mechanical fixtures of which embody domestic habits that seek to control the proportion between work and comfort. The model kitchen is like a factory or a workshop, while the bathroom, as Giedion explains in great detail, is divided between the concept of cleansing as a kind of work and bathing as an occasion for leisure and regeneration. In the case of simple ablution, modern bathing is a form of public service, contributing to the greater good through the management of body odors and the visible removal of dirt. When bathing is undertaken as a form of leisure, a highly suspect pursuit in a culture dedicated to productivity, the dilemma of comfort reappears. Again, Emily Post captures the common-sense quality of the modern judgment against moist leisure. "If there is one place in which you are not likely to want to stay, it is in a room that is misty with steam from a hot bath. A sofa in a dressing-room is another matter; but in this case the plumbing fixtures belong elsewhere."

Giedion's central theme—the conflict between hygiene and regeneration—is still in play today. Certainly the persistence of the canonical, three-fixture bathroom attached to the bedroom, represents a powerful confluence of interests and fears, even as it is challenged or modified in new buildings everywhere. Other equally radical transformations have occurred in the contemporary household, such as the enlargement of the kitchen and the disappearance of the dining room. Even at the moment of triumph for the compact bathroom, entries received by the Standard Sanitary Company competition, "The Bathroom: A New Interior, 1931," were dominated by plans that recalled ancient baths and provided generous space for sun bathing and exercise equipment. [Figs. 9 & 10] Those proposals resemble nothing so much as the private Jacuzzis and luxury bathrooms celebrated in today's shelter magazines. Giedion dismissed them as exceptions which proved the rule of hygiene; they are conceived within the logic of work and function.

The rule of hygiene is not a rule about comfort, but about the very presence of water. Bathroom finishes must resist the accelerated tendency of matter to change state under the influence of water, slipping out of the forms into which it has been worked. Keeping dirt and water in their place and removing any trace of their presence is a strategy for preserving the artifacts conceived by the architectural imagination. The glazed surface of the tub and of the tiled walls in the standardized room of fixtures is unchanging, or nearly so, requiring little of the regenerative maintenance demanded by other materials. These are the material qualities by which the hygienic order is understood and exercised in everyday constructions like the tub.

In summary, I would propose a final pair of images with which to complete Giedion's critique of modern bathing for the model, modern architect. The only "designer" tubs he included in his anonymous history were those developed by Buckminster Fuller for his Dymaxion houses. Giedion takes Fuller to task for missing the point of the bath: "From clean, hygienic enamel, the material is changed to thin metal sheeting, so that the machine may complete its work at one blow. In terms of comfort, this means the jettison of half a century's effort."[56] He chose the earlier patent drawings of the bathroom to illustrate his remarks, even though Phelps-Dodge had manufactured prototypes in copper ten years earlier.[57] [Fig. 11] For Giedion, the problem of comfort turns on the question of material properties and following the general method of the chapter could be illustrated by a comparison between Fuller's copper bathroom and the hygienic enamel tub or even the rejected copper tubs from the nineteenth century. But even as he presented the heroic tale of the enamel tub, he resisted the simple equivalence between comfort and cleanliness.

Ultimately he sought redemption as much from the hygienic logic that shaped the modern tub as from its decorative predecessors. It is a

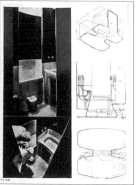

FIG. 11 (near right) Buckminster Fuller, "Dymax-
ion Bathroom," 1937

FIG. 12 (far right) Max
Ernst, *Une Semaine
de Bonté*, 1928

"weak" redemption, the kind that is achieved with everyday constructions and their material maintenance. The image of such a redemption originates with the presence of water and could be drawn from any of
the collages in the second book of Max Ernst's alchemical novel, *Une
Semaine de Bonté* (1934).[58] That book illustrates the second stage of the
alchemical process, the white phase of ablution and purification, which
precedes the red phase of conjunction and the final yellow or gold phase of
birth and rebirth.[59] The symbolic element of the second phase is both
water and philosophical mercury, which represent the principle of corro-
sion and change that all hygienic constructions resist. Regeneration
requires reconciliation with those forces that are characterized as change-
able, corrosive, and feminine.

Architects of the 1940s rejected Fuller's cleansing module,
demonstrating at least one limit to the logic of hygiene. Model, modern
architects of the 1990s must still contend with its authority, although the
collective images of health and well-being have shifted dramatically since
Giedion wrote his book. Systems theory, ecology, and immune-system diseases like AIDS and lupus have encouraged a more active and complex
view of human health.[60] The image which I would now contrast with the
stamped copper tub is an Ernst collage of a woman afloat and dreaming.
[Fig. 12] The pair suggests a tub conceived as both an enduring, hygienic
artifact and as the site of transformations that it cannot guarantee, but
which it dreams of accommodating.

NOTES

1. *The Bathroom: A New Interior* (New York: Standard Sanitary Manufacturing Company [now American Standard], 1931).

2. Siegfried Giedion, *Mechanization Takes Command: A Contribution to Anonymous History* (New York: W.W. Norton & Company, 1948), 628. Hereafter *MTC*.

3. That is, we remain as modern and American as Adolf Loos would have liked the Austrians to become when he wrote the article on plumbers in 1898

4. *MTC*, vii.

5. *MTC*, 701.

6. Josef Pieper, *Leisure, the Basis of Culture*, Introduction by T.S. Eliot, (New York: Pantheon Books, 1952). Originally given as lectures in Bonn, 1947 and published in German as *Musse und Kult* (Kösel-Verlag).

7. *MTC*, 712.

8. Sebastian de Grazia, *Of Time, Work, and Leisure* (New York: The Twentieth Century Fund, 1962), 15.

9. "Books and Bulletins, Review of 'Mechanization Takes Command,' by Siegfried Giedion," *Journal of The A.I.A.* (July, 1948): 42.

10. John E. Burchard, "Review of 'Mechanization Takes Command,' by Siegfried Giedion," *Journal of The A.I.A.* (August, 1948): 89.

11. Nikolaus Pevsner, "Judges VI, 34, Review of 'Mechanization Takes Command,' by Siegfried Giedion," *The Architectural Review* 106 (August, 1949): 78.

12. Eduard F. Sekler, "Siegfried Giedion at Harvard University," *The Architectural Historian in America*. Studies in the History of Art 35 (1990): 266.

13. The title of Pevsner's review refers to the biblical passage from Judges: "But the spirit of the Lord came upon Giedeon and he blew a trumpet."

14. José Luis Sert, Fernand Léger, and Siegfried Giedion, "Nine Points on Monumentality (1943)," *Architecture Culture 1943-1968: A Documentary Anthology* (New York: Columbia Books of Architecture and Rizzoli, 1993). George R. Collins and Christiane C. Collins, "Monumentality: A Critical Matter in Modern Architecture," *Harvard Architecture Review* 4 (1984). Siegfried Giedion, "The Need for a New Monumentality," *New Architecture and City Planning*, Ed. Paul Zucker (New York: Philosophical Library, 1944).

15. *MTC*, 2.

16. Douglas Tallack, "Siegfried Giedion: Modernism and American Material Culture," *Journal of American Studies* 28 (August, 1994): 149-67.

17. Joseph Rykwert, "Siegfried Giedion and the Notion of Style," *The Burlington Magazine*, XCVI (April, 1954): 123-24.

18. Jean-Pierre V. M. Herubel, *Annales Historiography and Theory: A selective and annotated bibliography* (Westport: Greenwood Press, 1994). The unfamiliarity of these methods confused some reviewers. Paul Zucker complained that "the tremendous scope of enterprise makes it difficult for the author to follow the historic, the technical, the sociological, or the aesthetic approach." "Review of 'Mechanization Takes Command,' by Siegfried Giedion," *Journal of Aesthetics and Art Criticism* 7 (1948).

19. Frederich Nietzsche, *The Gay Science, With a Prelude in Rhymes and an Appendix of Songs* (1887) (New York: Vintage Books, 1974).

20. Anthony Cutler, "Stalking the Beast: Art History as Asymptotic Exercise," *Word & Image* 7 (July-September 1991): 223-38.

21. "Old Jacob Burckhardt, whom I visited last night, was extremely kind to me. He is a very original man, both in his behavior and in his thinking; . . . He talked about Lermolieff's book, as if he knew it by heart, and used to ask me a lot of questions—which flattered me a great deal. This morning I am going to meet him again." Letter from Giovanni Morelli, Basel, 22 June 1882. Carlo Ginzburg, "Clues: Morelli, Freud, and Sherlock Holmes." In *Dupin, Holmes, Pierce: The Sign of Three*, ed. Umberto Eco and Thomas A. Sebeok (Bloomington: Indiana University Press, 1983), 111. An expanded version of the article was published in Carlo Ginzburg, *Clues, Myths and the Historical Method*. Trans. John and Anne C. Tedeschi (Baltimore and London: Johns Hopkins University Press, 1989).

22. Rykwert, "Siegfried Giedion and the Notion of Style," 123.

23. Ignasi de Solà-Morales, "La construcció de l'història de l'arquitectura: utillatge mental en la obra de Sigfried Giedion," *Quaderns d'Arquitectura i Urbanisme* 181 (1989): 192-207.

24. The term "economy of desire" is a common but somewhat misleading expression, since the concept of economy is based on a principle of scarcity or limits, while the energies of desire can multiply endlessly.

25. Jean Starobinski, *The Living Eye* (1961) (The Harvard University Press, 1989), 13.

26. Martin Jay, *Downcast Eyes: The Denigration of Vision in Twentieth-Century French Thought* (Berkeley and Los Angeles: University of California Press, 1993).

27. Starobinski, *The Living Eye*, 13.

28. Max Ernst, *The Hundred Headless Woman (La femme 100 têtes)* (New York: George Braziller, 1981).

29. Daniel Lawrence O'Keefe, *Stolen Lightening: The Social Theory of Magic* (New York: Continuum, 1982).

30. Tobin Siebers, *The Mirror of Medusa* (Berkeley: University of California Press, 1983).

31. Ovid, *Metamorphoses,* translated by A.D. Melville (Oxford University Press, 1986), III. 405.

32. Sir James George Frazer, *The New Golden Bough* (New York: New American Library, 1959). Marcel Mauss, *A General Theory of Magic* (1950).

33. "Instrumental efficacy is not the only kind of efficacy to be derived from their symbolic action. The other kind is achieved in the action itself, in the assertions it makes and the experience which bears imprinting." Mary Douglas, *Purity and Danger: An Analysis of Concepts of Pollution and Taboo* (New York: Frederick Praeger, 1966), chap. 4.

34. Starobinski, *The Living Eye*, 7.

35. Siegfried Giedion, *Bauen in Frankreich, Bauen in Eisen, Bauen in Eisenbeton* (Leipzig: Klinkhardt & Biermann, 1928).

36. The importance of Giedion's illustrations was discussed by Stanislaus von Moos, "Le Macchine Impaginate/Nota su Mumford e Giedion." *Parametro,* 22 (July-Aug, 1991), 58-69. In the recent translation of *Bauen in Frankreich*, Sokratis Georgiadis corrected his earlier oversight of those illustrations, publishing a number of the design boards for page layouts marked up in Giedion's hand and describing the relation between text and photograph as a *Gesamtkunstwerk*. Siegfried Giedion, *Building in France, Building in Iron, Building in Ferro-Concrete*, Introduction by Sokratis Georgiadis. (Santa Monica: Getty Center for Art and Humanities, 1995), Appendix: The book as *Gesamtkunstwerk*.

37. *MTC*, 10.

38. "I have always been conscious of our parallel interests and objectives: our divergencies are like the differences between two eyes in binocular vision, or sometimes between 'near' and 'distance' lenses in bifocal glasses." Letter from Mumford to Giedion in 1963, cited

in von Moos, "Le Macchine Impaginate," 67.

39. Susan Buck-Morss, *Dialectics of Seeing: Walter Benjamin and the Arcades Project* (Cambridge: MIT Press, 1989). Sokratis Georgiadis, *Siegfried Giedion: An Intellectual Biography* (Edinburgh: Edinburgh University Press, 1993).

40. That term is developed explicitly in "Surrealism: The Last Snapshot of the Intelligentsia." Walter Benjamin, *Reflections: Essays, Aphorisms, Autobiographical Writings* (New York: Schocken Books, 1978), 177-192. Its role in the formulation of the Passagen-Werk is discussed in Buck-Morss, *Dialectics of Seeing* and in Margaret Cohen, *Profane Illumination: Walter Benjamin and the Paris of Surrealist Revolution* (University of California Press, 1993).

41. Giedion places the Ernst collages according to a precise formal similarity with their adjacent images: the lion in figs. 189 & 190, the decorative drapery in figs. 197, 198 & 199, the plaster statue in figs. 207 & 208, a fauteuil and reclining nude in figs. 221, 222 & 223, and a draped and decorated interior in figs. 230 & 231. *MTC.*

42. The concept of the model reader is discussed in Umberto Eco, *Interpretation and Overinterpretation* (Cambridge: Cambridge University Press, 1992).

43. Erwin H. Ackerneckt, *Therapeutics: From the Primitives to the Twentieth Century, with an Appendix: History of Dietetics* (New York: Hafner Press, 1973). Mark Caldwell, *The Last Crusade: The War on Consumption, 1862-1954* (New York: Atheneum, 1988).

44. Jean-Pierre Goubert, *The Conquest of Water: The Advent of Health in the Industrial Age* (Princeton: Princeton University Press, 1989).

45. Ivan Illich, *H2O and the Waters of Forgetfulness: Reflections on the Historicity of "Stuff"* (Berkeley: Heyday Books, 1985).

46. Catherine E. Beecher and Harriet Beecher Stowe, *The American Woman's Home: Or Principles of Domestic Science; Being a Guide to Formation and Maintenance of Economical, Healthful, Beautiful and Christian Homes* (New York: J. B. Ford and Company, 1869). Edith Wharton, *The Decoration of Houses* (New York: C. Scribner's Sons, 1897). Emily Post (Mrs. Price Post), *The Personality of a House: The Blue Book of Home Design and Decoration* (New York: Funk & Wagnalls Co., 1930). Catherine Bauer, *Modern Housing* (Boston and New York: Houghton Mifflin Company, 1934).

47. Knud Lönberg-Holm, "The Weekend House," *The Architectural Record* 68 (August, 1930), 175-187.

48. Knud Lönberg-Holm, "Architecture in the Industrial Age," *Arts and Architecture* 84 (April, 1967), 22.

49. *MTC*, 720.

50. "Old Doctor Sun," in Paul De Kruif, *Men Against Death* (New York: Harcourt, Brace & World, 1932).

51. Buck-Morss, *Dialectics of Seeing*, 13.

52. Paul Frankl, *New Dimensions: The Decorative Arts of Today in Words and Pictures* (1928) (New York: Da Capo Press, 1975), 50.

53. All of the older religions involved rules for everyday habits as does Islam.

54. Mary Douglas, *Purity and Danger: An Analysis of Concepts of Pollution and Taboo* (New York: Frederick Praeger, 1966).

55. Ibid., 2

56. *MTC*, 709.

57. "Dymaxion Bathroom," *The Architectural Record* (January, 1937), 40.

58. Max Ernst, *Une Semaine de Bonté: A Surrealistic Novel in Collage* (1934) (New York: Dover Publications, 1976).

59. M. E. Warlick, "Max Ernst's Alchemical Novel: 'Une Semaine de bonté'," *Art Journal* 46 (Spring 1987): 61-73.

60. Emily Martin, *Flexible Bodies: Tracking Immunity in American Culture—From the Days of Polio to the Age of Aids* (Boston: Beacon Press, 1994).

CONTRIBUTORS

WILLIAM W. BRAHAM is Assistant Professor of Architecture at the University of Pennsylvania.

VICTOR BURGIN is Professor of Art History at the University of California, Santa Cruz. He is the author of *In/different Spaces: Place and Memory in Visual Culture* (1996), and *The End of Art Theory: Criticism and Postmodernity* (1986), among other books.

XAVIER COSTA is Director of the Architecture Department at the Museum of Contemporary Art in Barcelona, Spain. He is the author of a scholarly edition of John Ruskin's *The Seven Lamps of Architecture* (1990) and the editor of the exhibition catalogue *Kahn's Libraries* (1989).

MARCO FRASCARI is Professor and Director of the Ph.D. Program in Architecture at the University of Pennsylvania. He is the author of *Monsters of Architecture: Anthropomorphism in Architectural Theory* (1991).

DANIEL S. FRIEDMAN is Associate Professor of Architecture at the University of Cincinnati.

DONALD KUNZE is Associate Professor of Architecture and Integrative Arts at the Pennsylvania State University. He is author of *Thought and Place: the Architecture of Eternal Place in the Philosophy of Giambattista Vico* (1987).

NADIR LAHIJI is an architect, theorist and educator.

HARRY FRANCIS MALLGRAVE is Editor of Architecture and Aesthetics for the Texts and Documents Series at the Getty Center for the History of Art and the Humanities. He is the author of *Gottfried Semper: Architect of the Nineteenth Century* (1996).

IGNASI DE SOLÀ-MORALES is professor of history and theory at the Barcelona School of Architecture. He is the author of *Differences: Topographies of Contemporary Architecture* (1996).

HELEN MOLESWORTH is currently completing her dissertation at Cornell University. She is also an editor of *Documents, a Magazine of Contemporary Visual Culture*.

MARGARET MORGAN is an artist and teaches at the California Institute of the Arts, Los Angeles.

CLAUDIO SGARBI is an architect living in Modena, Italy.

ILLUSTRATION CREDITS

INTRODUCTION: **1**. Courtesy of the artist and Metro pictures.

OZENFANT & JEANNERET | THE RIGHT ANGLE: All illustrations taken from "The Right Angle," courtesy La Fondation Le Corbusier, Paris.

LAHIJI & FRIEDMAN | AT THE SINK: **1**. Courtesy of the artist and Metro pictures; **2, 3, 6**. Courtesy La Fondation Le Corbusier, Paris; **4**. Panayotis Tournikiotis, *Adolf Loos* (New York: Princeton Architectural Press, 1994); **5**. Photograph by Alfred Stieglitz, courtesy Philadelphia Museum of Art; **7–12**. Peter Greenaway, *The Belly of An Architect*, 1987; **13**. From Richard Moore, "Academic *Dessin* Theory in France after the Reorganization of 1863," *Journal of the Society of Architectural Historians* 36 (October 1977); **14**. Le Corbusier, *Le Poème de l'angle droit* (Paris: La Fondation Le Corbusier and Editions Connivences, 1989).

MORGAN | TOO MUCH LEVERAGE IS DANGEROUS: All artwork courtesy Margaret Morgan.

MOLESWORTH | CLEANING HOUSE WITH DUCHAMP: **1**. Courtesy Philadelphia Museum of Art.

COSTA | GROUND LEVEL: **1**. Courtesy Galleria Nazionale d'Arte Antica, Rome; **2, 3**. Claude Perrault, *Abrégé des dix livres d'architecture de Vitruve* (Paris, 1674) bk. 8, ch, 6, p. 164; **4, 5**. Andrea Palladio, *I quattro libri d'architettura* (Venice, 1570); **6**. Antoni Gaudí, from Isidre Puig Boada, *L'església de la colonia Güell* (Barcelona: Lumen, 1976), pl. 25; **7–9**. Alfred Hitchcock, *Vertigo* (1959).

MALLGRAVE | LOOS: ORNAMENT AND SENTIMENTALITY: All images courtesy Harry Mallgrave.

KUNZE | POCHÉ: **1, 2, 10, 13**. Donald Kunze; **3, 6, 9**. Courtesy Trustees, The National Gallery, London; **4**. From Otto Vaenius, *Theatro Moral de la Vida Humana* (Brussels: Fr. Foppens, 1672); **5**. From *Underweysung der Messung mit dem Zirkel und Richtscheyt*, 2d ed. (Nuremburg: Hieronymus Andreae, 1538); **7**. Frontispiece from *The New Science of Giambattista Vico* (1744); **8**. Courtesy the Museum of Modern Art, New York; **11**. G. Piranesi, *Carceri d'invenzione* (Rome, 1761); **12**. Courtesy Rizzoli Publishers, Inc., New York; **14, 15**. Courtesy Pedro Ravara.

FRASCARI | THE PNEUMATIC BATHROOM: **1**. From Ellen Lupton and J. Abbott Miller, *The Bathroom, the Kitchen, and the Aesthetics of Waste* (New York: Princeton Architectural Press, 1992); **2–4**. Drawings by Kiel Moe; **5–10**. Marco Frascari.

SGARBI | ARCHITECT'S BELLIES: **1**. ©1987 Quantity Postcards, San Francisco, CA; **2**. Frontispiece from M. Giovan Battista Caporali di Perugia, *Vetruvio in volgar lingua raportato* (1536); **3**. Frontispiece from Marc-Antoine Laugier, *Essai sur l'architecture* (1755); **4**. Frontispiece from D. Barbaro, *Vitruvio. I dieci libri di architettura* (1567); **5**. Frontispiece from B. Galiani, *L'Architettura di M. Vitruvio Pollione* (1758); **6, 7**. Frontispiece from Vincenzo Scamozzi, *Idea dell'architettura universale* (1616); **8**. From P. Duboy, *Lequeu. An Architectural Enigma* (Cambridge, MA: MIT Press, 1987); **9**. Vignola, *I cinque ordini dell'architettura* (Ed. Bernardo Oppi, 1635). **10**. Umberto Ruini, detail of fresco "Allegory of Architecture," entry to the Biblioteca Poletti, Modena, Italy; **11–15**. Peter Greenaway, *The Belly of An Architect* (1987); **16, 17**. Moderna Museet, Stockholm; **18**. Advertisement from Italian magazine. **19**. Photograph by Oliviero Toscani.

BRAHAM | GIEDION AND THE FASCINATION OF THE TUB: **1**. *Rassenga* 25/1 (March 1986); **2, 4, 7, 9**. From S. Giedion, *Mechanization Takes Command: A Contribution to Anonymous History* (New York: W. W. Norton & Co., 1948); **3**. From *In the Age of the Fable* (New York: Heritage Press, 1952); **5, 11**. Courtesy University of Pennsylvania School of Architecture; **6**. *The Architectural Record*, 1930; **8**. Paul De Kruif, *Men Against Death*, (New York: Harcourt, Brace, 1932); **10**. Standard Sanitary Co., 1931; **12**. Dover Publications, Inc., 1976.

INDEX

Adcock, Craig, 80
advertising, 77, 85
Alberti, Leon Battista, 105, 106
American Society of Independent Artists
    exhibition, New York, 1917, 79
analytical cubism, 107
anamorphosis, 157; in Holbein's *Ambas-
    sadors*, 151–52
Annalistes, 205
aplomb, 46, 47
art nouveau, 44–45, 132
Artuad, Antonin, 115
Auden, W.H., 160
Augustus (Gaius Octavianus Ceasar),
    190
avant garde, 75–76

Bachelard, Gaston, 94
"Ballad of the Walled Up Wife," 192–95
Barbaro, Daniele, 185
Barthes, Roland, 115
Bataille, Georges, 50, 54–55; "Dust," 54–55
bathing,17–19, 35–36, 125, 168, 201–20;
    "The Atmospheric Bath," 211
bathroom, bathroom fixtures (see also
    sink), 17–19, 34, 38–40, 77–84, 125,
    201–20; designs of Carlo Scarpa,
    165–66, 168–71; as a numinous
    place, 163–75; public bathing, 213;
    stanza da bagno, 169
Baths of Caracalla, 18
Bauer, Catherine, 215
Bauhaus, 107
Beckett, Samuel, (*Waiting for Godot*), 124
becoming, 87–88
Beecher, Catherine, 215

Beethoven, 132
Bekleidung, 134, 205
Bellmer, Hans, 112
Benjamin, Walter, 10, 103–104, 107–08,
    110, 116, 118, 216; "One Way
    Street," 10, 103, 108; *The Origin of
    German Tragic Drama*, 103;
    Passagen-Werk, 104, 212–13;
    and Siegfried Giedion, 212–13
Bentham, Jeremy, 8, 52
Berlin Wall, 117
Blake, William, 149
body, 7–8, 10, 11, 23, 36–43, 78, 79,
    82–84, 104–105, 111–12, 114, 154,
    174; of architecture, 183; and city,
    105; deodorization of, 173; female
    (as Architecture), 183–88; and
    machine, 82–84, 86–89; male (of
    the architect), 190–91; modern, 208
bodily waste, 35, 36, 39, 44, 81–84, 110
Bois, Yve-Alain, 55
Botticini, *The Assumption of the Virgin*, 141
Boullée, Etienne-Louis, 43, 190
Braque, Georges, 75
Brueghel, Pieter, 160
Brunelleschi, Filippo, 174
Bruno, Giordano, *La Cena Delle Ceneri*,
    163–64; *spiritus fantasticus*, 166
Buck-Morss, Susan, 103, 104
Buñel, Louis, *Un Chien Andalou*, 211
Burchard, John, 203
Burckhardt, Jacob, 10, 205, 206

Caporali, Giovan Battista, 185
Caravaggio, 94
Cézanne, Paul, 31
Choay, Françoise, 105
CIAM (International Congress of Mod-
    ern Architects), 206
Cicero, 134
Clair, René, 118

Gaia, 197
Galiani, Berardo, 185
Garden of Eden, 105
Gaudí, Antoni, 9, 98
gaze, 37–38, 52, 144, 145–46, 157–58,
    210; divine gaze, 150; and coun-
    tergaze, 143, 144, 156, 209, 210
Gestalt psychology, 48
gender: in representations of architec-
    ture, 183–88; of architecture and
    architects, 195–97
geometry, 23–25, 31
germs, 81–82, 203, 208, 210; germ the-
    ory, 211, 214
Giedion, Siegfried, 8, 10, 201–20; *Bauen
    in Frankreich, Eisen, Eisenbeton*, 210;
    Mechanization Takes Command, 75,
    201–20; Nicholas Pevsner's review
    of, 203–5; anonymous history,
    205–7; *Space, Time and Architecture*,
    203–4, 211
Ginzburg, Carlo, 206
glass, 100, 108, 111, 112
Greenaway, Peter, 38; *The Belly of an
    Architect*, 38, 43, 183, 190–91, 194;
    The Draughtsman's Contract, 139
Gropius, Walter, 108–09, 112

Haussmann, Baron George-Eugene, 108
hieratism, 26
Hitchcock, Alfred, 9, 99;
    Vertigo, 99–100
Hoffman, Josef, 125, 127
Holbein, Hans, *The French Ambassadors*,
    151, 157
Hollier, Denis, 50, 55
horizontal, horizontality, 28, 39–41,
    43–44, 93
House and Garden, 80
housework, 76, 78, 84–85
household and housing reform, 215

hygiene, 7, 37, 40, 52–53, 55, 81, 83, 165,
    201–20; London Hygienic Exhibi-
    tion, 1883, 214
hygienic superego, 11, 40, 53

Icarus, 160, 195
impressionism, 29, 31
informe, 43
Irigaray, Luce, 106

Jay, Martin, 8, 51, 207
jazz, 107
Jeanneret, Charles-Edouard, see Le Cor-
    busier
Jennings, George, 80
Joyce, James, 149

Kahn, Louis I., "volume zero," 165
Kant, Immanuel, 113
kitchen, 76–78, 81, 84, 218
Kodak, 29
Kokoschka, Oscar, 133
Krauss, Rosalind E., 37–38, 51–52, 82–83
Kristeva, Julia, 41

La Bohème, 140
Lacan, Jacques, 9, 34, 42, 45, 47, 48, 113,
    114, 149, 157; "Discourse Analysis
    and Ego Analysis," 42; *The Four
    Fundamental Concepts of Psycho-
    Analysis*, 145; "The Mirror Stage,"
    42, 45, 113, 114; and sardine can,
    145–48, 159; and the surrealists, 45
Lacis, Asja, 10, 103–4, 107–8
Laocoon, 95
Ladies Home Journal, 84
Le Corbusier (Charles-Edouard Jean-
    neret), 8, 10, 40–41, 46–54, 109,